REPORT OF THE COMMISSION TO STUDY THE PUBLIC'S EXPECTATIONS OF AUDITS

June 1988

TO THE BOARD OF GOVERNORS OF THE CANADIAN INSTITUTE OF CHARTERED ACCOUNTANTS

We are pleased to submit the accompanying Report of our Commission, which was established by you in February, 1986 with the following mandate:

The Commission is charged to study the public's expectations of audits. Where a gap exists between what the public expects or needs and what auditors can and should reasonably expect to accomplish, the Commission is charged to develop conclusions and recommendations to determine how the disparity should be resolved.

We have sought to give the fullest possible effect to the charge to the Commission within the limits of available time and information and given its volunteer makeup.

The Commission was originally established with nine members. The majority of the members named were not chartered accountants. Of the four who were, only two were partners in public accounting firms. By limiting the number of Commissioners who were CAs, and especially the number of those who were members of firms conducting audits, you wished to ensure that the Commission's deliberations would be free from any pre-dispositions that might have existed if all or most members had a common background as auditors. We believe we have been able to meet this test.

To accomplish our task we have first had to identify expectation gaps and then consider how best to deal with them. Our identification of expectation gaps stems from research, described more fully in Chapter 1, into the opinions of the public at large and of specific groups within the public who have more direct involvement with audits or exposure to audited financial information. We have concluded that some expectation gaps exist based on a comparison of opinions expressed by the public concerning auditors and audited financial information with what we have learned about what auditors actually do. In addition, in the course of our inquiry we have been open to all expressions of individual opinions concerning perceived shortcomings in audited financial information or the work of auditors.

Having identified the existence of some expectation gaps, we have considered the problems these create or, untended, are likely to create for the profession. Our aim has been to provide practical advice that can pass a cost/benefit test concerning measures the profession can take to minimize expectation gaps. If such minimization can be achieved, we shall have served the interests of all parties concerned with financial reporting by strengthening the credibility of an independent public accounting profession and thereby maintaining the value of audits.

Our recommendations point out the general direction in which the profession should move. Suggestions for changes in or amplification of auditing standards flow directly from our mandate. It was not part of our mandate to make a critical examination of accounting standards or disputed legal issues, and we have performed no detailed original research in either of these respects. We have, however, considered the implications of existing accounting standards to public expectations of auditors, and some recommendations have resulted from that consideration.

Our Report as a whole can best be perceived as seeking to develop a contemporary strategy for the profession in Canada in one of the central areas of its concern. This is the need for the profession to retain public confidence by keeping any disparity between reasonable public expectations and actual audit performance to a minimum. The Report is thus intended to be action-oriented to that end. Each individual recommendation is designed to respond to one or more existing or potential expectation gaps in a practical manner that is consistent with the basic philosophy of the Commission. That philosophy, the linkage between the recommendations and the perceived gaps or potential gaps, and the anticipated effects of adopting the recommendations are described in the Report. This should enable the profession and the public to assess for themselves whether the philosophy expressed is convincing and whether the recommendations appear likely to be responsive in a practical and workable manner to what is required.

The Commission gave serious consideration to the need for some basic restructuring to help the profession minimize expectation gaps. We have considered the present corporate disclosure system with its legal requirements for financial statements and auditors' reports and the separate but related responsibilities for financial disclosure assigned to different parties, including auditors, under that system. We have looked at the existing organization of the accounting profession and its arrangements for setting standards and regulating performance by auditors. We have also considered the kinds of businesses engaged in by public accounting firms and their significance to audit performance. Our final conclusion is that the available evidence does not clearly require basic change in any of these structures. Nonetheless, we wish to make it clear that this conclusion could change in the future if the profession does not recognize and respond to the present and potential expectation gap problems which we see as a result of our study.

The profession must not be complacent. Serious concerns about auditor independence and professionalism exist both inside and outside the profession. Commercial pressures, competitive career alternatives elsewhere, and growing exposure to high levels of legal liability pose very real challenges to the profession and its ability to attract and retain the best people and do the best job. These challenges could put at risk the professional competence that is one of the pillars of the profession's standing and reputation. In addition, at the level of the Institute there is a need to revamp methods of standard setting to prevent accounting standards established by the profession falling unacceptably behind the pace of changing events.

The future of the profession will be determined mainly in two places. The first is in the marketplace of users, which depends on user perceptions of cost-effective value added by audits. The second is in the regulatory bodies, governments, legislatures, and courts, where the standards of the profession will be applied and ultimately established and the scope and continued independence of the profession determined. In both places, unswerving independence and impartiality in the face of a difficult structure of relationships and strong commercial pressures is the pearl beyond price and the indispensable shield for the profession. This view pervades each of our recommendations.

In this Report we have described real challenges that require swift and tough actions. There is, nonetheless, every reason for the profession to be confident about the future. Its varied services are in strong demand. It is widely recognized as competent, and audits are widely recognized as adding real, even indispensable, value to financial statements. Both institutionally and as individual practitioners, the profession has already accommodated enormous change during the past 25 years. A defensive attitude is unsuited to a profession that has demonstrated it is capable of such a dynamic performance.

The main messages of the Report are addressed to the Canadian Institute of Chartered Accountants, which commissioned the Report, and to the provincial institutes of chartered accountants whose cooperation is necessary to its implementation. However, there are also messages for individual auditors and auditing firms, including the senior partners and leaders of the major firms; the management of business firms, including chief executive officers; directors; audit committees; regulators; and legislators.

The Commission could not have done its work without the strong support and direction of its Director of Research, Alastair Skinner, FCA, of Pannell Kerr MacGillivray who proposed the research programs and ensured that they were carried out; and of Hollis R.S. Brent, CA, LLB, of McMillan, Binch, who acted as Counsel to the Commission but whose efforts went far beyond matters normally regarded as within the compass of a legal adviser. Donald E. Jeffreys, CA, the Assistant Director, Auditing Standards, was seconded by the Institute to act as Secretary of the Commission. No one was more indispensable or more consistently thorough and reliably on top of all things at all times since the very start of the Commission's work.

Heavy research responsibilities were assumed by Karen L. Hooks, PhD, CPA, and Philip H. Cowperthwaite, CA, among others. In February 1987 the Commission was also fortunate in enlisting the assistance of Ross M. Skinner, FCA. His knowledge, energy, and judgment were indispensable, first in assisting with needed research and, in the final stretch, acting as coordinator of the writing and editing of the Report.

Finally, the Institute itself responded without stint to the requirements of the Commission, without intrusion in any way into its proceedings. At all times support staff were made available when necessary to back up the Commission, not an easy sacrifice given the many competing demands on Institute staff and resources.

The Commission would be remiss if all this vital assistance was not fully and warmly acknowledged and publicly appreciated. The Commission also thanks all those who troubled to write and/or be present in person to give the members of the Commission the benefit of their views and experiences. This particularly includes members of the profession in New York and London, England, who generously assisted Commissioners who were able to visit those two cities. A list of submissions and presentations to the Commission is found in Appendix E.

In March, 1987, one of the Commission's original members, Dr. Wendy K. Dobson, became an Associate Deputy Minister of Finance in Ottawa and felt it necessary to resign because of the heavy demands of her new position. Her contribution while a member was highly valued, and her presence was missed during the final deliberations.

The Commission members are each agreed that from their respective standpoints the opportunity to serve on the Commission was stimulating and challenging, and well worth while. The only initial predisposition of all members of the Commission was that an independent and credible public accounting profession was vital to the effective functioning of the free enterprise system. The work of the Commission has reinforced that basic viewpoint. The Commission will be well rewarded for its work if the Report leads to improvements that strengthen the fundamental independence and credibility of the profession by leading to a closer identity between public expectations of audits and auditor performance.

Toronto
June, 1988

COMMISSION TO STUDY THE PUBLIC'S EXPECTATIONS OF AUDITS

William A. Macdonald, Chairman   Gilles Mercure
J. Peter Gordon   Michael H. Rayner
Richard F. Haskayne   Robert M. Rennie
David L. Johnston   T. Robert Turnbull

Table of Contents

CHAPTER 4 — STRENGTHENING THE AUDIT ENVIRONMENT

CHAPTER 5 — FINANCIAL REPORTING: CONTENT, COMMUNICATION, AND AUDIT CONTRIBUTION

CHAPTER 6 — PROFESSIONALISM

CHAPTER 7 — FRAUD; ILLEGAL ACTS; CHANGE OF AUDITOR

CHAPTER 8 — REGULATED FINANCIAL INSTITUTIONS

CHAPTER 9 — SUMMARY OF CONCLUSIONS

APPENDICES

INDEX

Terms and Abbreviations

Accounting Standards Committee. A committee of the CICA, composed of volunteers, responsible for the study and creation of accounting standards which are published in the *CICA Handbook*.

Adams Committee. The Special Committee to Examine the Role of the Auditor was established by the CICA Board of Governors and published its report in April 1978. Its chairman was John W. Adams, FCA.

AICPA. The American Institute of Certified Public Accountants is the national organization open to membership by all certified public accountants in the United States. Its responsibilities include setting auditing standards in the United States.

Alternative accounting treatments. Accounting methods that represent acceptable alternatives in accounting for a given transaction. Alternatives exist for two reasons: a governing standard may be stated broadly and several methods of implementing it may be adopted; and alternative approaches have gained substantial support in practice and standard setters have been unable or have not attempted to develop a consensus in favour of one approach.

Annual reports. These documents are issued by a company after the financial year end and typically include financial statements and the related audit report as well as other information.

Audit opinions. An "unqualified" or "clean" opinion is one in which the auditor states that the financial statements are fairly presented in accordance with a defined standard. An auditor expresses a qualified opinion, adverse opinion, or denial of opinion (col-

lectively referred to as reservations of opinion) when he or she is not satisfied with the financial statements or is unable to obtain necessary audit evidence. In this Report, for convenience, a reference to a qualification or qualified opinion embraces all types of reservation of opinion.

Audit report. This document contains the expression of an auditor's professional opinion on the fairness of the presentation of financial statements.

Auditing Standards Committee. A committee of the CICA, composed of volunteers, responsible for the study and creation of auditing standards which are published in the *CICA Handbook*.

CA. Chartered Accountant. See **CICA**.

CICA. The Canadian Institute of Chartered Accountants, also referred to as "the Institute," is the national association for chartered accountants in Canada. All CAs become members of the CICA by virtue of their membership in the various provincial institutes of chartered accountants. The CICA's responsibilities include setting accounting and auditing standards in Canada.

CICA Handbook and **"the *Handbook*."** This two-volume publication contains the accounting and auditing standards set by the CICA Accounting and Auditing Standards Committees.

Cohen Commission. The Commission on Auditor's Responsibilities was established as an independent commission by the AICPA and published its report in 1978. Its chairman was Manuel F. Cohen.

Decima survey. A survey of the Canadian public performed by Decima Research Limited for this Commission in order to assess the public's expectations. It focuses primarily on members of the public who have at least limited knowledge of audits, financial statements, and the services of chartered accountants.

FASB. The Financial Accounting Standards Board is the private-sector group responsible for setting accounting standards in the United States.

Financial community. Those members of the public expected to have a greater familiarity with financial reporting and auditing than most of the respondents to the Decima survey. This group includes bankers, financial analysts, public accountants, corporate executives, regulators, and financial journalists.

Financial reporting. Financial statements, annual reports, and other types of financial information released to the public regardless of the medium used.

GAAP. Generally accepted accounting principles is a widely used term referring to the whole body of rules of practice governing the content and presentation of financial statements. The term "accounting standards" is also commonly used and is appropriate since the rules of practice are usually established now by recognized standard-setting bodies rather than by general acceptance alone.

GAAS. Generally accepted auditing standards comprise standards for the personal qualifications required of an auditor, the evidence that must be obtained to support an audit opinion on financial statements, and the form and content of the auditor's report.

Going concern. The assumption underlying the preparation of most financial statements that the company will continue in business for the foreseeable future. When the going concern assumption is questionable, the company must disclose the risks and ramifications associated with that fact.

Independent public accounting profession. The public accounting firms which collectively make up what is also referred to as "the profession" provide a variety of services, normally including audit, tax, and consulting. These firms offer their services to the public on a contract basis and thus are said to be "in public practice."

Internal control. The system of checks and balances instituted by management to safeguard assets and ensure that reliable financial information is produced.

Management discussion and analysis or **MD & A**. Certain additional analytical and interpretive information prepared by management and included in a company's annual report.

Materiality. The threshold beyond which an item of information is believed to be important to the user of information. Whether something is material is usually based on quantitative criteria, such as the dollar amount involved, but may in some circumstances depend on qualitative factors.

Professional code of conduct. A written statement of desirable behaviour that is adopted by a professional association to guide its members in their relations with fellow members and the public. A chartered accountant in violation of the professional code of conduct will be subject to disciplinary action by the relevant provincial institute.

Reasonable assurance. The level of confidence an audit gives regarding the fair presentation of financial statements. Because absolute confidence is impossible to achieve, this level is less than a guarantee.

Stand-back assessment. The auditor's final review of the financial statements resulting after incorporation of individual decisions with respect to accounting policies, accounting estimates and the extent of disclosure. The stand-back assessment is intended to see that the statements are not misleading in their overall effect.

Treadway Commission. The National Commission on Fraudulent Financial Reporting was established in the United States and published its report in October 1987. It was jointly sponsored by the AICPA, the American Accounting Association, the Financial Executives Institute, the Institute of Internal Auditors, and the National Association of Accountants. Its chairman was James C. Treadway, Jr.

1

Introduction

1.1   The Commission has received a threefold mandate. It is first to study the public's expectations of audits. Once this is done, it is to determine whether there is a gap between what the public expects or needs from auditors and what auditors can reasonably expect to accomplish. Then, to the extent there is an identifiable gap, the Commission is asked to make suggestions as to how the gap might be narrowed.

1.2   This Report is addressed to the CICA Board of Governors. However, because its focus is on public expectations, its subject matter is clearly of general public interest. We therefore propose to assume no knowledge of accounting or financial reporting on the part of the reader of this Report beyond that which would normally be possessed by someone who has had some exposure to financial statements in company annual reports or prospectuses. To help the lay reader we shall define and explain certain accounting and auditing terms, concepts, and procedures, even though such explanation is unnecessary for chartered accountants.

CONTEXT OF THE STUDY

1.3   We begin with the fundamental context of this Report—the concepts of accountability and audit. The need for accountability arises when one party entrusts responsibility for property or for the performance of certain duties to another party. It is simply common sense to require the party accepting the responsibility to make an accounting or report on the way the responsibility has been discharged. The concept of accountability has been recognized in a wide

variety of forms from ancient times up to today. With the greater division of functions within a modern society, and the separation of ownership and management typical of modern industry and finance, financial and performance accountability becomes of considerable public importance. When a transfer of responsibility is accompanied by the advance of debt or equity capital to the person accountable, the receipt of that financing and the discharge of the responsibility can be accounted for largely in monetary terms. Much of that accounting is provided today in what we know as financial statements, but, to an increasing extent in recent years, some financial disclosure is provided outside the traditional financial statements. We use the broader term "financial reporting" to cover all disclosure that is primarily in financial or monetary terms, whether it is contained inside or outside the conventional financial statements.

1.4   An audit by a party independent of the person rendering the accounting is a safeguard introduced to ensure, or at least enhance, the integrity of the accounting. The so-called external auditor is appointed primarily in the interests of the parties who have entrusted responsibility to others and who are not in a position to conduct their own audit. The primary function of the external audit is to see that the accounting and reporting are accurate or fair. The value added by an audit is the increase in credibility of the financial report that results from the auditor's work. That increase in credibility depends partly on the competence and reputation of the auditor. It depends also, to a major degree, upon the perception that the auditor is not under the influence of the party rendering the accounting. In ancient and simpler times the auditor was commonly an employee or servant of the party to whom the accounting was due. Today, accountability is owed to many people—such as shareholders, lenders, and depositors. Auditors engaged to report to such wider constituencies are usually independent professionals without a direct relationship with the shareholders and other parties who rely on the audit. Because of this, the precise specification of price and services to be supplied that is customary in marketplace contracting is much less evident in today's external audit arrangements.

1.5   Our inquiry is concerned with the financial accountability of business enterprises, and especially companies with a wide public ownership. Achieving effective financial accountability for a modern corporation is not a simple task. A large corporation must invest in a wide variety of assets and employ a large number of people in order to carry on business. Each month it engages in thousands of transactions, and at all times it is subject to numerous commitments and obligations. To account for all its disparate possessions, transactions, and obligations in an understandable manner and without overwhelming the recipient of the financial report with too much detail is no easy task. That task is not made easier by the fact that most business is continuous. As a result, the financial consequences of many investments and activities at any particular moment will not be complete or capable of being fully known. No change in accounting or auditing standards or performance can alter this reality.

1.6   The auditor's responsibility to form an opinion concerning whether the accounting is fair is likewise difficult. The auditor must not only verify the underlying factual basis of the report—the assets held, the liabilities owed, and the description of the nature of the transactions and obligations. He or she must also judge whether the dollar measurements attributed to assets, liabilities, revenues, expenses, gains, and losses are fairly stated and whether the facts and measurements are communicated in the report so as to portray them fairly and understandably. All this must be achieved economically so that the cost of the audit does not exceed its value to the recipients of the audited information. Moreover, much of the audit is necessarily performed some time after the transactions and events accounted for have taken place. Absolute verification, in these circumstances, is usu-

ally impossible. Because of this, as well as the cost/benefit constraint, an audit cannot give a guarantee of the fairness and accuracy of a company's financial report; it can merely provide a reasonable measure of assurance.[1] Such reasonable assurance is all the public is entitled to expect. It is, however, entitled to expect that the audit function will be performed impartially and efficiently.

ACCOUNTING AND AUDITING STANDARDS

1.7   Because fair reporting of the financial affairs of a sizeable enterprise can raise so many difficult questions, a high degree of judgment is required from those preparing the financial statements. Similarly, a high degree of judgment is required in planning and performing an audit to provide reasonable (but not absolute) assurance with respect to the financial statements. When so much judgment is required, opinions on individual issues, even among highly skilled and experienced individuals, will often differ. When a financial-reporting obligation was laid upon companies by English corporations legislation in the nineteenth century, there was little theory to provide answers or guidance to the questions that could arise in financial reporting and in the conduct of an audit. Over a long period of time some theory developed as to appropriate "principles" of accounting and auditing. But unresolved issues and continuing diversity in practice led to efforts by the accounting profession, sometimes prodded by securities commissions or other regulatory agencies, to develop more formal standards for good practice. As a result, there exists today a very substantial body of accounting and auditing standards.

1.8   The 1978 report of the Commission on Auditors' Responsibilities (the Cohen Commission) said, "There is often a tendency to confuse auditing standards with accounting principles...."[2] To lessen the possibility of such confusion, especially for the non-accountant reader, we offer the following definitions:

Accounting standards are rules of practice governing the content and presentation of financial statements. These rules cover, among other things, the items that may or must be described as assets and liabilities in the financial statements, the bases of measurement of such assets and liabilities appropriate to varying circumstances, the general set-up or format of the financial statements, and the supplementary disclosures required. At one time such rules developed in a relatively unorganized fashion through a process of acceptance. In that period the rules were usually described as "accounting principles," and the whole body of accounting standards came to be known as "generally accepted accounting principles" (GAAP). The phrase GAAP is still very widely used and in Canada is embodied in several statutes governing the contents of financial statements to be presented to shareholders or included in prospectuses. The term "accounting standards," however, is coming into more common use and appears to be more appropriate since the rules of practice are usually established today by recognized standard-setting bodies, rather than by general acceptance. In Canada, accounting standards are very largely established and modified as required by the Accounting Standards Committee of the CICA.

Auditing standards, customarily referred to as "Generally Accepted Auditing Standards" (GAAS), give guidance to the auditor as to three matters: (1) the qualifications and professional attitude of the auditor, (2) the evidence that must be obtained to support a professional audit opinion on the financial information presented, and (3) the form and content of the auditor's report. In Canada, auditing standards are set by the Auditing Standards Committee of the CICA, a committee that is entirely separate from the Accounting Standards Committee.

In effect, albeit simplistically, *accounting standards* determine what companies should tell in their financial statements and how they should tell it. By contrast, *auditing standards* suggest the audit evidence required to provide reasonable assurance that the statement information is true, either precisely or within a reasonable range in cases where estimates and the use of judgment are unavoidable.

1.9 In Canada, regulations under many corporations and securities statutes require that financial statements be prepared in accordance with the standards set out in the *CICA Handbook*. The effect of this is that CICA accounting standards enjoy a special legal status. Contrary to a possible public impression, however, the fact that the CICA is largely responsible for accounting standards does not mean that auditors as such control accounting standards. Adoption of an accounting standard requires approval of two thirds of the membership of the Accounting Standards Committee. In recent years CAs in public practice (that is, members of firms that provide accounting and auditing services to the public) typically constitute about one half of the committee's twenty-one members. Other committee members, usually including a few non-CAs, are drawn largely from industry, commerce, finance, and academe. Up to six of these members are appointed by other organizations such as the Canadian Council of Financial Analysts, the Financial Executives Institute Canada, and the Society of Management Accountants of Canada. It is generally acknowledged that, to be effective, accounting standards must receive broad acceptance by those affected by them, especially those responsible for preparing financial statements.

1.10 Since accounting standards are intended to facilitate the communication of information to readers of financial statements, it is necessary to have some idea of their needs for information and their capacity to understand it. The Commission's view of the nature of financial disclosure desirable for general public distribution is well summed up in a statement of the U.S. Financial Accounting Standards Board: "Financial reporting should provide information that is useful to present and potential investors and creditors and other users in making rational investment, credit, and similar decisions. The information should be comprehensible to those who have a reasonable understanding of business and economic activities and are willing to study the information with reasonable diligence."[3] Consistent with this, we believe general-purpose financial reports should strive to meet the expectations of reasonably informed and intelligent users of financial information, but that it is not necessary to include all information in such reports that might be useful to sophisticated analysts. We do not mean by this that such detailed information should not be made available by other means. There may well be a case for the provision of information in special reports that are not part of general-purpose financial disclosure.

ACCOUNTABILITY AND THE CHALLENGE OF CHANGE

1.11 Accounting and auditing standards require continual revision and development to meet the challenges of a changing world. In recent decades, accounting standards have had to deal with numerous problems, including:

- Turmoil in the economic environment—for example, rapid changes in commodity prices both up and down, general inflation, and great instability in the foreign exchange and financial markets.

- Increasing complexity in taxation and other legislation.

- Greater complexity in business operations and transactions, including innovative financing techniques, transactions departing from the model of the simple purchase and sale, numerous mergers and acquisitions, increased pension and other long-term commitments, and so on.

1.12 Auditors have had to keep abreast of shifts in accounting standards as well as devise audit procedures to cope with such developments as the relative increase in importance of intangible assets compared with physical assets and the greater difficulty of tracking and controlling transactions and events in an electronic world. In addition, auditors have had to cope with increasing pressures in their own economic environment—such as more severe competitive pressures within the profession, a more critical external environment with expanding professional liability, more frequent and larger lawsuits brought against auditors and, recently, increasing difficulty in obtaining liability insurance coverage even at much higher premiums. The rapid and volatile changes in the economic and financial environment compound the difficulty of meeting public needs and expectations from audited financial statements.

1.13 The auditing profession in Canada and internationally has not stood still in the face of these challenges. Much effort has been expended by individual auditors and audit firms to improve personal education and skills. Professional associations have also studied how to adapt their institutions so as to fend off challenges and grasp new opportunities.

- In Canada, CICA studies issued include the 1978 report of the Special Committee to Examine the Role of the Auditor (the Adams Committee), the 1980 report of the Special Committee on Standard Setting, the research study *Corporate Reporting: Its Future Evolution* (1980), and the 1986 report of the Long-Range Strategic Planning Committee entitled *Meeting the Challenge of Change*. Other Canadian professional accounting associations have also conducted important studies.

- Published studies in the United States in the last decade include the report of the Commission on Auditors' Responsibilities (the Cohen Commission) in 1978; the 1986 report of a special committee of the American Institute of Certified Public Accountants (AICPA) entitled *Restructuring Professional Standards to Achieve Professional Excellence in a Changing Environment*; and the 1987 report by the National Commission on Fraudulent Financial Reporting (the Treadway Commission). In early 1988 the AICPA approved nine new Statements on Auditing Standards which will produce significant changes in, and extensions of, standards for audit performance and auditor communication with the public. Similarly, in the United Kingdom there have been many reports by committees and working parties of the several professional accounting associations.

The Commission's thinking has benefited from these previous studies.

LIMITS TO THE COMMISSION'S STUDY

1.14 Although the context of this Report is accountability and audit, there are limits to our inquiry. We have not been asked to assess whether financial disclosure is satisfactory in general or what the future role of the auditor may or should become. However, since our focus is on public expectations of the auditor, we have not ignored these matters completely.

- To the extent that the public believes the auditor to be responsible for determining what is disclosed or expects the auditor to make up for any perceived deficiencies in financial disclosure, it is necessary to consider whether the present financial disclosure system meets public expectations.

- Moreover, to the extent we conclude that expansion of financial disclosure is required to meet present or reasonably predictable future public expectations, we need to evaluate the responsibility that will be attributed to the auditor in relation to such additional disclosure.

- Finally, we have to consider the quality of accounting standards because their adequacy or inadequacy can strengthen or weaken the position of the auditor in those instances when a client is reluctant to provide the most desirable financial disclosure.

1.15 Other limits to our study can be stated more simply. In our recommendations we have confined our attention to public expectations of the auditors of private sector business enterprises. This was a pragmatic decision. The great bulk of the presentations to us dealt only with the audits of profit-oriented enterprises. It was clear to us that we would have had to extend our research and inquiries considerably to be able to draw any legitimate conclusions concerning the audits of governments or other non-business entities. Moreover, at least in the field of governmental auditing, other studies have reduced the need for independent consideration by us.[4] Our attention has also been confined principally to expectations of the auditors of public companies. Again, this was a pragmatic decision. Many smaller business enterprises do not have audits, and their relationship with an independent accountant (if any) is a matter for contract between the owner(s) of the business and the accountant, in which the public at large has little interest. In contrast, audits of public companies are required by law, and the typical separation of the functions of ownership and management makes these audits much more a matter of obvious public interest.

EMPHASIS ON PUBLIC EXPECTATIONS

1.16 The charge to the Commission focuses on public expectations of audits. Our primary efforts were therefore directed at ascertaining the nature of these expectations. We felt that such knowledge was a prerequisite to an assessment whether the expectations are being met or are reasonable and well founded.

Our inquiries were designed to elicit opinions both from the public at large and from segments of the public that have more direct and continuous involvement with audits or exposure to the results of audits.

1.17 Early in our study we commissioned a major public opinion survey from Decima Research Limited under the direction of its chairman, Mr. Allan Gregg. The executive summary of this study is included as Appendix B to this Report. This survey was conducted through telephone interviews. Individuals whose opinions were surveyed were selected by random sampling techniques. Persons interviewed were subdivided for purposes of the study between those who had little knowledge of financial reports and those who could be expected to be more familiar with financial reporting. Additional individuals were interviewed to increase the number of people surveyed who were relatively more knowledgeable about financial reports. The questions asked of knowledgeable respondents were much more extensive than those asked of other members of the public. The answers provided through these more extensive interviews form the principal evidence for statements made by the Commission about the views of the public. That is to say, most of the time when we refer to the opinions or expectations of the public, we are basing our statements on the views of persons with at least a minimum acquaintance with financial reporting. This group is described by Decima as the "reader/investor public."

1.18 In addition to this opinion survey, the Commission adopted various means to ensure that it received a cross-section of opinion from members of the public who might be expected to have an even stronger interest in financial reporting and auditing. These included bankers, financial analysts, public accountants, corporate executives, regulators, financial journalists, and others. We refer to this group collectively as "the financial community." Obviously this group is diverse and, as would be expected, its views vary from one segment to another and among individuals. Information was collected from this financial community principally through written submissions, oral presentations at both public and private hearings, and focus groups and structured personal interviews organized by Decima. Impressions of public opinion have also been obtained by monitoring comments in the media. As well, there have been numerous studies, both in Canada and elsewhere, in which public expectations have formed an element, and these have generally confirmed the impressions we have received from our other inquiries. Some of these studies were referred to in paragraph 1.13 above.

1.19 Our efforts to learn and understand the views of the public, both the public at large and the financial community, have constituted the Commission's principal research thrust, substituting for the conventional literature-search research approach. The intent was and is that our study and conclusions be based primarily on the best assessment of public expectations and not on essentially subjective impressions of the Commissioners or others.

NATURE OF THE EXPECTATION GAP

1.20 To assist the reader's understanding of possible reasons for the existence of an expectation gap, we have prepared a diagram to illustrate its components. In the diagram, the hatched horizontal line represents the full possible gap between the highest public expectations from audits (point A on the extreme left) to public perceptions of what is actually obtained from audits (point E on the extreme right). Point C represents what is called for by present auditing and accounting standards by way of auditor performance and quality of financial information reported. The segment to the left of that point (line segment A to C) represents possible public expectations that go beyond what is called for by existing standards governing auditor performance and the content and quality of financial reporting. This segment is labeled the "Standards Gap." The segment to the right of point C (line segment C to E) represents possible public perceptions that auditor performance or audited financial information fall short of what is called for by the profession's existing standards. This segment is labeled the "Performance Gap."

1.21 The emphasis in this diagram is on public expectations and public perceptions. Those expectations may or may not be reasonable, and those perceptions may or may not be realistic. An unrealistic expectation that is disappointed, or an erroneous perception of performance, can be just as damaging to the public's trust in auditors and audited information as real

COMPONENTS OF THE EXPECTATION GAP

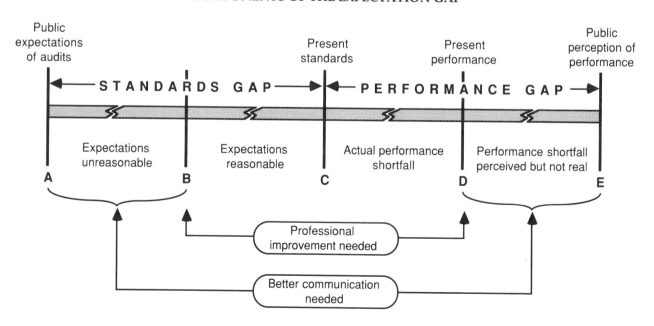

shortcomings in auditing and accounting standards or performance. It is, nevertheless, important to appraise the realism of public expectations and perceptions when the profession seeks remedies to the expectation gap. If the public has reasonable expectations not met by existing professional standards (line segment B to C) or the profession's performance falls short of its standards (line segment C to D), then it can and should act to improve standards or improve performance. On the other hand, if the problem is that the public's expectations are unreasonable (line segment A to B) or its perceptions of performance are mistaken (line segment D to E), then the logical course is to attempt to improve public understanding. Should that not be feasible, the profession must be prepared to cope with the consequences.

1.22 This diagram does not illustrate separately expectation gaps related to the quality of work the auditor does, which is the subject of auditing standards, and gaps related to the quality of financial information with which the auditor is associated, which is the subject of accounting standards. It is necessary, however, to consider each of these separately to cover the full possible spectrum of expectation gaps. Thus, this Report is concerned in total with:

- Possible gaps relating to the work of the auditor attributable to:

  - Auditing standards inadequacies.

  - Auditor performance shortcomings.

  - Public misunderstanding as to (1) what is reasonable to expect and (2) the actual quality of auditor performance.

- Possible gaps relating to financial information with which the auditor is associated attributable to:

  - Failures of accounting standards to require relevant financial information that is appropriate for inclusion in audited financial statements, and the absence of any standards for financial information that is best furnished outside financial statements.

  - Failures of financial reports to comply with accounting standards.

  - Public misunderstanding as to (1) what information can reasonably be provided and (2) the actual quality of information provided.

FOUNDATIONS OF THE COMMISSION'S RECOMMENDATIONS

1.23 This Commission holds certain views that underlie its recommendations and help explain why it supports some proposals and rejects others.

- The Commission believes the public interest is best served by a free and independent public accounting profession that is committed to standards established in a professional setting, independent of the wishes of any particular individual practitioner or client, and free from direct government interference.

- At the same time, it must be recognized that, if it is to survive, public accounting must justify itself in the marketplace as well as having social value. Audit services must be seen to be worth their cost, and audit firms must be sufficiently profitable to attract and retain competent professionals.

- This dual dimension of public accounting can create strong tensions in the short term. The commercial motivation of the marketplace may seem to be at war with the maintenance of professional standards. From a longer-term viewpoint the conflict disappears since the commercial value of an audit ultimately rests upon professionalism; but, in the short term, the tensions are there.

- There is no magic wand to make these tensions disappear. Rather, the Commission sees the need for a series of adjustments—in the legal environment of financial reporting, in the roles of different parties who have responsibilities for financial reporting, and in the standards and conduct of the profession—so that reasonable public expectations from audits can be met and the public interest in a free and independent profession can be supported.

1.24 The Commission also recognizes that complex issues must be faced in deciding how best to help fulfil the public's expectations. Corporations and securities laws provide a context for financial reporting that cannot be changed easily or quickly. Accounting and auditing standards may be set by the CICA but are influenced (quite legitimately) by the opinions of other parties interested in financial reporting, including regulators and people responsible for the preparation of financial reports. Even within the CICA there may be differences of opinion between individual members or segments of the membership. In addition, changes affecting auditors' responsibilities and performance will often require cooperation by the CICA and provincial institutes because of their divided responsibility. For example, accounting and auditing standards are set by committees established by the CICA, but the closely related functions of education and professional discipline are the responsibility of the provincial institutes. Finally, it must be recognized that all accounting or auditing standards are always subject to interpretations established in court decisions.

THE COMMISSION'S PRINCIPAL CONCLUSIONS

1.25 The Commission's inquiries have led it to three principal conclusions:

- First, there is a need to increase the auditor's leverage vis-à-vis the management of client enterprises. We do not intend to suggest that such increased leverage is often needed. In the majority of cases any differences of opinion between auditors and management are well within the range to be expected in view of the degree of judgment required in financial reporting. However, in those cases in which this is not true some strengthening of the auditor's position seems both desirable and feasible.

- Second, there is a need to buttress the professionalism of auditors—largely through their own efforts, but also assisted by actions of their professional associations.

- Third, to meet public expectations as well as strengthen the hand of the auditor, there is a need to improve the quality of present financial dis-

closure and, over time, to extend financial and financially related disclosure.

As things stand now, these conclusions do not require radical restructuring of the profession or the standard-setting process. They do, however, require a considerable number of specific and important changes to keep any public expectation gap to a tolerable minimum, now and in the foreseeable future.

1.26 Our specific recommendations flow largely from these conclusions. We have attempted to interpret each conclusion in terms of specific goals to be achieved. Then we have framed action recommendations to achieve those goals. For example, we believe the auditor's independence and leverage can be strengthened by several means. One way is to emphasize the personal accountability of all parties involved in financial reporting and encourage them to manage their relationships so as to be mutually supportive. Recognition of the desirability of this goal leads naturally to recommendations for the adoption of the audit committee as a focal point in managing relationships involving the auditor and other responsible parties, and to recommendations that will help raise the general standard of effectiveness of the audit committee.

ORGANIZATION OF REPORT

1.27 The remainder of this Report is organized as follows:

- In Chapter 2 we outline the major public expectations from audits as a basis for our identification of gaps between expectations and perceived performance.

- In Chapter 3 we explore the financial disclosure system with particular reference to the legal background. Some weaknesses in the auditor's position are inherent in this established structure for financial reporting. We consider whether these weaknesses can be overcome by a significant change in that structure. We conclude that significant change would be unworkable. This fundamental conclusion means that our recommendations for change in succeeding chapters are all intended to fit within the present established structure of responsibility for financial reporting.

- In Chapter 4 we put forward two principal suggestions for strengthening the audit environment. The first is to nurture and reinforce the auditor's relationships with other parties responsible for financial reporting so as to stress their interdependence and encourage mutual assistance in meeting their responsibilities. The second is to improve accounting standards. Since accounting standards have a strong influence on information reported in financial statements, they are a significant factor in the public's satisfaction or otherwise with audited information.

- Chapter 5 seeks to answer three questions. How can public expectations for financial disclosure best be met? How can public expectations for the auditor's responsibility be met? To the extent expectations are not met completely, how can the resulting expectation gap best be explained and its adverse consequences minimized?

- Chapter 6 explores the attributes of professionalism with special reference to the auditor's position. We make a number of suggestions for dealing with threats to auditors' professionalism.

- Chapters 7 and 8 are devoted to more specialized questions. Chapter 7 addresses questions concerning the auditor's responsibilities in relation to fraud and to illegal acts generally. It also speaks to the need, in certain circumstances, for public disclosure of the reasons for a change in auditors of a company. Chapter 8 considers whether the special character of regulated financial institutions should lead to any modification of the function and responsibilities that fall to the auditor in a normal commercial or industrial company.

- Chapter 9 sums up our conclusions and recommendations, assesses the intended and likely effects of the implementation of these recommendations, and contains suggestions on how the recommendations can be addressed and implemented in a timely and forceful manner.

References

1.   See discussion in *CICA Handbook*, Section 5000, "Audit of Financial Statements—an Introduction" (Toronto: CICA), par. 04.

2.   The Commission On Auditors' Responsibilities, *Report, Conclusions, and Recommendations* (New York: AICPA, 1978), p. 128.

3.   FASB, *Objectives of Financial Reporting by Business Enterprises*, Statement of Financial Accounting Concepts No. 1 (Stamford: FASB, 1978), par. 34.

4.   Within the past ten years the CICA has established the Public Sector Accounting and Auditing Committee, charged with making recommendations applicable to that sector. In addition, the Canadian Comprehensive Auditing Foundation was created to help strengthen management, accountability, and audit in the public sector. The Foundation has recently published the study *Effectiveness Reporting and Auditing in the Public Sector* (Ottawa: CCAF, 1987).

2

Public Expectations from Audits

2.1 This Commission's study would not have been initiated if it were not felt that expectation gaps do exist. It is the goal of this chapter to identify the principal expectations of the public and possible reasons for the standards or performance gaps that are perceived to exist by a substantial body of public opinion, even if not by majority opinion.

2.2 When we refer to public expectations from the audit we are referring, in effect, to public expectations for audited financial information or, even more broadly, for any financial information with which the auditor is associated. The Decima survey and other inquiries made it clear to us that the public at large and even some quite sophisticated members of the financial community have only a vague understanding of the responsibilities undertaken and work done by the auditor. To the public it is the end result, the financial disclosure, that is important. The auditor is quite likely to be the first to be blamed for errors or inadequacies in financial disclosure almost without regard to his or her actual responsibility.

DIVERSITY IN PUBLIC EXPECTATIONS

2.3 It required little investigation to convince us that a homogeneous public with homogeneous expectations does not exist. The Decima survey showed that only a minority of the population has any direct personal interest in financial reporting. Even within the financial community we can discern different segments whose views are likely to differ depending on their depth of knowledge about financial reporting and their particular experience with it—for example, as preparers, users, or auditors of financial reports, or as regulators who rely on such reports in

the performance of their function. Different segments of the public also have uneven amounts of knowledge concerning who is responsible for different aspects of financial reports, what auditors do to enable them to report on financial statements, and the limits of what an audit report conveys. For example, the public at large is much more likely to believe that the auditor actually prepares the financial statements than are members of the financial community. Because of this diversity in public expectations and public understanding, the Commission has had to exercise some judgment in concluding which expectations, or whose expectations, it is important to fulfil.

2.4 In general, our research showed that the majority of the public had little dissatisfaction with auditors or audited information. There have been, however, some significant business failures in the almost two years since completion of the Decima survey. These occurrences may have altered public perceptions to some degree. We are satisfied, nevertheless, that our inquiries were sufficient to establish the existence of any developing expectation gaps. We did find cases where a significant percentage of the knowledgeable public felt expectations were not being completely fulfilled. This was even more true when we looked at the opinions of identifiable segments of the public. We have taken the position that the existence of a substantial minority of the public, or of a significant segment of the public, such as regulators, who feel that some of their expectations are not being met, should be a matter of concern for the auditing profession. We have considered that such expectation gaps should be addressed, even though majority opinion may not yet perceive a problem.

MAJOR PUBLIC EXPECTATIONS

2.5   Today's standard audit report states, in part, that in the auditor's opinion the financial statements examined present fairly the financial position of the company at a specific date and the results of its operations and the changes in its financial position for the year then ended in accordance with generally accepted accounting principles. Based on our inquiries we believe the following simple interpretation of these words would sum up the public's expectations:

> *The public expects that an unqualified audit opinion means that the auditor is satisfied, so far as reasonably possible, that the financial statements convey the financial information about the company that an ordinary shareholder, or person with equivalent interest, should know and can reasonably expect to receive.*

In the above interpretation and throughout this Report we use the terms "qualification" and "qualified audit report" for convenience in the way they are usually used by the public. That is to say, we use them to cover all modifications of the audit report that reflect an auditor's disagreement with, or inability to obtain satisfaction about, information in the financial statements. Technical auditing literature is more precise. An auditor may express a "qualified opinion," an "adverse opinion," or a "denial of opinion," the latter two being more serious or more sweeping than a qualified opinion. Collectively, these departures from a clean audit report are described as "reservations of opinion."

2.6   The ordinary member of the public is unlikely to have thought more deeply than this about his or her expectations from an audit. However, by means of questions such as those in the Decima survey, it is possible to elicit expectations in a more detailed form. Members of the financial community who have particular interests in financial reporting will also have individual expectations that are shaped in part by their interests and by their experience in preparing or using financial information. We set out below our conclusions as to the principal expectations of the public, including members of the financial community, and identify factors that may result in a perception that these expectations are not being fully met. We have classified these expectations between those that pertain directly to the auditor's work and those that pertain to the financial information with which the auditor is associated.

PUBLIC EXPECTATIONS OF THE AUDITOR

The Auditor's Opinion Is Expected to be Impartial

2.7   An auditor's report appears most often accompanying financial statements in annual reports to shareholders or in prospectuses or similar documents. The purposes of these annual reports or other documents are to convey information in fulfilment of the accountability obligation of the directors and management to shareholders, and to assist readers in investment, credit, or other decisions. The reasons for having an auditor are only common sense, and the public is as likely to understand them as is any expert. First, since the auditor has not been involved in the management of the company, he or she should be able to form a dispassionate, unbiased view of the financial results of the company's activities. Second, the independent verification procedures performed by the auditor add to the assurance that the financial information reported is as accurate as it can be, given the uncertainties in all business activities. In spite of widespread public confusion concerning the auditor's role and responsibility, the public is perfectly clear (and correct) that a very important reason for having a person external to the company involved in its financial reporting is the added assurance provided by that person's independent viewpoint.

2.8   The auditor, then, is expected to be independent and impartial in opinion. Certain conditions exist, however, that could be perceived to detract from the auditor's ability to be impartial.

- Audited financial statements are a means of communication to shareholders and other interested parties external to the company. Especially in larger companies, these external parties are the primary beneficiaries of the auditor's work. However, the audit appointment, although nominally made by the shareholders, is heavily influenced by management of the company, and it is usually management that negotiates the audit fee. Some members of the public perceive that this arrangement can put pressure on the auditor's independence. Approximately 30 percent of those questioned in the Decima survey expressed moderate to strong agreement with the statement that because auditors are paid by management they bend the rules to make sure the statements will have an unqualified audit opinion. Forty-five percent expressed moderate to strong disagreement with the proposition.[1]

- In recent decades public accounting firms have diversified by providing a wide variety of consulting services, which make up an increasing percentage of their revenues.[2] Fears have been expressed that the desire to sell such services to the management of its audit clients could weaken an audit firm's willingness to argue for accounting treatments or disclosure in the financial statements that are different from those proposed by management. Fifty percent of the public surveyed indicated moderate to strong agreement with the belief that there is a serious potential for auditors to lose their objectivity when the audit firm provides services such as management consulting or tax advice to an audit client.[3] Members of the financial community also recognize the potential for loss of objectivity but do not have a strong belief that such losses in objectivity are actually occurring.

- An increased competitiveness in efforts to obtain audit engagements in recent years is perceived by some to contain threats to the auditor's independence as well as to the quality of work performed. When it was suggested to respondents to the Decima survey that accounting firms could be charging less than they should for an audit in order to get the business, 35 percent of the respondents felt that this would have a negative effect on the quality of the audit.[4] Some members of the financial community also expressed concern about the potential negative effect of unrestricted price competition.

- Several public accounting firms made reference to the potential harmful effect on auditor independence of the practice of "opinion shopping." The term refers to the action of a management in seeking opinions from accounting firms other than its auditor on matters that are in dispute with the auditor. The pejorative expression "opinion shopping" is intended to suggest that management's objective may sometimes be to put pressure on its auditor to modify his or her opinion, or even to ascertain whether other auditors, if appointed, would accept management's position on the issue in question.

2.9 The foregoing discussion suggests the existence of threats to the auditor's independence. It does not provide firm evidence that these threats are actually affecting auditor performance or that the public generally perceives them to be doing so. In fact, the perceptions of the majority of the public are to the contrary. Our evidence is that members of the public have a significant degree of confidence in audited financial statements and that knowledgeable members of the financial community retain a belief in the profession's high standards. Nevertheless, some members of the public perceive that these threats to auditor independence are having some effect. Moreover, it is probably fair to say that there is danger of an increase in the public concerns given the more skeptical attitude prevailing today with respect to all professions and institutions, and given the fact that the public trust in auditors is based on such limited actual knowledge of their work.

The Auditor Is Expected to Attain and Maintain the Level of Skill Necessary to Fulfil His or Her Obligations

2.10 Professionals hold themselves out to the public as being possessors of special skills and a high level of competence. The public is entitled to expect, and does expect, that these attributes will be exhibited— by auditors as by other professionals.

2.11 The Commission has heard relatively few criticisms of the competence of auditors. According to the Decima survey, 91 percent of the public surveyed was somewhat confident or very confident of the auditor's report and 88 percent had a great deal or some confidence in audited financial statements.[5] Some of the more important criticisms or concerns about auditor performance expressed in submissions to us or in the course of hearings or private interviews were as follows:

- Competitive pressures on the level of audit fees were leading, or could lead, to cutting corners in audit procedures.

- Auditors rely too much on junior staff.

- Auditors are too inclined to follow a rule book and do not rely sufficiently on professional judgment or give sufficient weight to the overriding goal of achieving a fair presentation of financial information.

- Auditors may fail to be sufficiently knowledgeable about the business audited, particularly in the case of specialized industries.

2.12   Although these criticisms were expressed by relatively few people, the Commission believes the profession should not take too much comfort from that fact. It is difficult for a layman to evaluate professional competence at any time, and few have a real opportunity to evaluate or even come in contact with an auditor's work. It is our belief that a healthy profession will continually monitor the general level of competence of its members and strive to enhance it.

PUBLIC EXPECTATIONS FOR FINANCIAL DISCLOSURE

The Auditor Is Expected to Ensure that All Pertinent Financial Information of which He or She Is Aware Is Reported

2.13   The public, with justification, regards the auditor as its representative—the person who bears its interest in mind in determining what financial disclosure is needed. It also seems probable to the Commission (although we have not sought evidence to substantiate this impression) that at least some members of the public think that the setting of accounting standards is in the hands of auditors. It would be easy to gain that impression, since virtually all the auditors of public companies are chartered accountants and it is a committee of the national association of chartered accountants that sets accounting standards.

2.14   It follows from these two observations that perceived shortcomings in the extent and quality of financial disclosure will be regarded as evidence of a failure on the part of either the auditor or the auditing profession. If accounting standards are perceived to be inadequate, a "standards gap" exists. If the auditor fails to compensate for an apparent omission or inadequacy of standards in a particular case, that will be seen as a "performance gap." These two kinds of expectation gaps related to accounting standards are considered more fully in the next three sections of this chapter.

The Auditing Profession Is Expected to See that Accounting Standards Governing the Information in Financial Statements Are Adequate

2.15   The information to be presented in financial statements is governed by accounting standards. These standards have been developed over the years largely by a due and orderly process sponsored by the CICA and designed to implement a collective judgment as to what represents appropriate financial disclosure.

2.16   The Decima survey suggests that the public does not have a highly developed understanding of accounting standards (also known as "GAAP"—see paragraph 1.8) other than knowing that they exist. For example, approximately 45 percent holds the incorrect view that, because these rules exist, little judgment is required in the preparation and presentation of financial statements.[6] Members of the financial community appear to have a better understanding of the character of GAAP, although they generally lack knowledge of the standards themselves (except, of course, for those members who have an accounting background). Overall, the general impression derived from the Commission's inquiries is that accounting standards in Canada are reasonably satisfactory and the standard-setting process is well designed.

2.17   Four specific concerns were expressed to the Commission, principally by public accounting firms and regulators:

- There are holes in the coverage of accounting standards in the *CICA Handbook*, often related to accounting issues in specialized industries. These leave the auditor without the benefit of a collective judgment on the best accounting treatment of certain issues and lessen the strength of his or her arguments should there be any disagreement with management as to the best accounting treatment.

- The "due process" in setting accounting standards is time-consuming. As a result, it is harder to close up the holes in the *Handbook*, and it is very difficult to give authoritative guidance to "emerging issues" in a timely manner. Emerging issues in accounting stem principally from new types of business transactions, new forms of financial instruments, and changes in legislation. This problem is becoming more important as financial and other transactions are increasingly structured to achieve or avoid a particular accounting treatment.

- The CICA accounting recommendations, and accepted practice in areas not covered by the recommendations, occasionally permit alternative accounting treatments that can result in widely divergent reported figures. Members of the public who become aware of this find it difficult to understand and, as a result, tend to lose some confidence in accounting standards. The flexibility can also weaken the auditor's influence on a client company's accounting and lead to a suspicion that the auditor always acquiesces in the selection of the alternative that suits management best.

- CICA accounting recommendations are often (and deliberately) stated in terms of general objectives and principles rather than being stated as specific rules. The intention is that companies should use good judgment in selecting an accounting method that best reflects the general principle in their particular circumstances. The problem is that the choice of one particular method over another is often not based very clearly on genuine differences in circumstances. As a result, an impression may be left that companies can take advantage of the flexibility permissible in accounting treatments to manage the financial results reported by them and that there is very little the auditor can do about this.

The Public Expects Better Warning in Financial Statements of Risks, Especially of Imminent Business Failure

2.18 Sometimes a business fails not long after audited financial statements have been issued accompanied by an unqualified audit opinion. When this occurs it is common to hear remarks critical of the auditor. It almost seems as though the public equates a business failure with an audit failure.

2.19 The significance for financial disclosure of this popular concern about business failure may not be immediately obvious. For example, in the Decima survey each person interviewed was told that some companies are normally exposed to particular kinds of risks, such as wide fluctuations in interest rates or product prices, and was then asked to indicate the degree of adequacy of present disclosure of such risks. Sixty-five percent of those questioned indicated present disclosure was adequate or very adequate and 5 percent expressed no opinion. Thus, the answers to this question did not suggest a cause for serious concern.[7]

2.20 This result, however, has to be viewed in context. A large majority (78 percent) agreed with the statement that financial statements provide a very good indicator of the state of health of a company.[8] Thirty-nine percent expressed medium to strong agreement with a statement that an unqualified audit opinion means there is no possibility of serious financial problems with the company.[9] Thus, a significant portion of the public believes, incorrectly, that under present standards an unqualified audit opinion means that a company is not in financial difficulty.

2.21 A separate question asked about a situation where there is need to warn the reader about something in the statements but otherwise the company would receive an *unqualified* audit opinion. Forty-seven percent stated that the warning should be in the notes to the financial statements. However, 49 percent stated that the warning should be in the audit report.[10] The fact that some members of the public believe the auditor now has a responsibility to give them specific warning of any serious risks may explain why a stronger desire was not expressed for disclosure of risks in financial statements beyond that now being provided.

2.22 Members of the financial community believe that the financial statements must disclose material uncertainties and any failure to do so is grounds for qualification of the audit report. An uncertainty whether a company can continue as a going concern would usually be the most significant uncertainty of all. Here there seemed to be a fairly strong feeling that the audit report should be qualified if serious doubt exists on that score. Although there was some difference of opinion over the extent to which auditors should be expected to make predictions, there was some sentiment that the auditor should feel confident that a company will be able to meet its obligations for at least six months after the audit.

2.23 A number of individual submissions to us advocated increased disclosure of risks and uncertainties. Although the primary goal of this disclosure was seen to be a fairer, more balanced presentation of the information, some respondents, especially the public accounting firms, seemed to feel that such disclosure was one way to combat public misunderstanding. Better disclosure of risks and uncertainties, it is felt, should make it more evident to the public that businesses can fail for many reasons, some of which are relatively unpredictable.

The Auditor Is Expected to Monitor the Application of Accounting Standards in a Particular Case and Make Up for Inadequacies in Them

2.24 Given the flexibility in accounting standards, it is not unnatural that the public should expect the auditor to see that the flexibility is not abused. There is evidence that some members of the public expect the auditor to see that the most appropriate accounting policies among alternatives are adopted. The auditor is also expected not just to see that individual accounting standards are complied with by the client but also to "stand back" and assess whether the financial statements as a whole yield a fair impression of the state of affairs.

2.25 The previous sections have suggested that an important response to expectation gaps related to financial disclosure should be improvements in

accounting standards. This response is consistent with the fact that the law assigns primary responsibility for financial reporting to directors and management, not to auditors. The Commission believes that there would also be merit in a clearer public understanding of the respective responsibilities of all parties. An incidental benefit from this would be the reminder to directors and managements of their primary responsibility.

The Public Expects the Auditor to Plan Audit Work so as to Pay Significant Attention to the Possibility of Fraud

2.26 Present auditing standards indicate that an auditor should seek reasonable assurance through audit procedures that fraud or error material to the financial statements has not occurred, or, if it has occurred, is properly accounted for.[11] It is not entirely clear whether this satisfies public expectations. It is fairly clear from the inquiries we made that the public does not generally believe that an audit *guarantees* the discovery of fraud.[12] Beyond this, however, public opinion seems to be divided. A significant minority believes that the auditor has a responsibility to actively search for fraud, even at some considerable cost, and it may be that those holding this viewpoint would expect more audit effort directed to this purpose than is performed under present auditing standards.[13] There are also some questions, and some division of opinion, as to what the auditor should do if fraud or irregularities are discovered.[14]

The Public Expects an Auditor of Financial Institutions to Acknowledge a Responsibility to the Broad Public Interest as well as to the Shareholders

2.27 In recent years a number of failures of financial institutions have focused attention on the responsibilities of the auditors of such institutions. There is virtually nothing in auditing standards to suggest that auditors have any different responsibilities with respect to such institutions than they have with respect to ordinary companies. Some special responsibilities are, however, contained in the statutes and regulations relating to various kinds of financial institutions. The evidence we have gathered suggests that members of the public are virtually unanimous that the public interest in the well-being of financial institutions is so important that their auditors must look beyond their normal responsibility to shareholders. Not surprisingly, the practical effect of this general proposition is not well spelled out in public opinion. It is not conceivable, however, that the auditor should be assigned some broad and undefined

obligation to the public at large. Rather, the proper response to public expectations on the part of the auditor is to continue to fulfil the obligation to shareholders and to add to that an obligation to report fully to regulators of financial institutions those audit findings that are relevant to their responsibility.

References

1. Decima Research Limited, Executive Summary of *Public Opinion Survey* (1986), see Appendix B, p. 149.
2. For a discussion of the reasons see the report of the CICA Long-Range Strategic Planning Committee, *Meeting The Challenge of Change* (Toronto: CICA, 1986), p. 10.
3. Decima, *Survey*, Appendix B, pp. 149–50.
4. Ibid., p. 149.
5. Ibid., pp. 150, 151.
6. Ibid., p. 152.
7. Ibid.
8. Ibid.,
9. Ibid., p. 150.
10. Ibid., p. 151.
11. *CICA Handbook*, Section 5300, "Audit Evidence" (Toronto: CICA), par. 41.
12. See Decima, *Survey*, Appendix B, p. 151.
13. Ibid., p. 150.
14. Ibid., p. 151.

3

The Established Structure for Financial Reporting

3.1 Timely disclosure of reliable and understandable financial information plays an important role in our society. It is fundamental to the financial and other decisions that individuals and enterprises make on a day-to-day basis. In their totality, these decisions contribute to the efficiency of the capital markets and thereby to the economic welfare of society. These are the basic reasons for a public interest in financial reporting.

3.2 In view of the public stake in good financial reporting, it is common for the law to set minimum requirements for the content and frequency of financial communication to parties deemed entitled to receive such communication. In Canada, corporations law typically requires that corporations furnish to shareholders annual financial statements that have been reported on by auditors. (Most corporations statutes allow an exemption from the audit requirement to non-public companies under certain conditions.) In addition, securities legislation requires regular financial reporting by all companies once they have made a distribution of securities to the public. It appears from this that the provision of reliable financial information to facilitate the market for securities is now generally considered to be in the public interest. The strength of the public stake in the financial reporting of private corporations is less clear.

3.3 Annual audited financial statements of public companies are only one element, albeit a central element, in the present total corporate disclosure system. The total system comprises a combination of legally required financial disclosure and legally permitted, but not required, disclosure. A characteristic of the system is a balancing of maximum disclosure of relevant information against the costs of disclosure and the rights of corporations operating in a competitive environment to some measure of confidentiality. Any modifications or extensions of auditor responsibilities should fit within this established approach to corporate disclosure.

PARTIES RESPONSIBLE FOR FINANCIAL REPORTING

Directors

3.4 Under corporations law, the directors of a corporation have the duty to manage its business and affairs. Consistent with that responsibility is the obligation to provide an accounting to shareholders. For public companies that obligation entails the annual presentation of audited financial statements. Most Canadian jurisdictions also require public companies to distribute unaudited interim financial statements—statements that are less complete than the annual statements and contain much less detail. In addition to these mandatory financial reporting responsibilities, directors sometimes have an obligation to provide additional information, and have a general right to communicate anything that they consider significant. The vast majority of public companies provide explanations and commentary in their annual and interim reports that are over and above the required financial statements. Currently some consideration is being given by certain securities commissions to a requirement that management publish specified financial disclosure in the form of a Management Discussion and Analysis (MD & A) in the annual report.

3.5   Although directors have considerable discretion to decide on the nature and extent of financial disclosure, several factors limit the exercise of that discretion as a practical matter.

- Most corporations statutes require that the financial statements to be placed before shareholders at the annual meeting must be prepared in accordance with specified standards, generally described either as GAAP or as the standards set out in the *CICA Handbook*. When GAAP are specified as the applicable standards and a given accounting issue is not covered by the *Handbook*, it is necessary to have the auditor's agreement that the accounting treatment proposed by the company is "generally accepted." In view of these constraints, it is not wholly surprising that some members of the public think of the annual financial statements as being "the auditor's statements," as though the basic responsibility for the disclosure rested with the auditor and not with the directors of the company.

- With respect to financial disclosure that is not required under a particular statute, directors face a potentially powerful deterrent. The more financial information that is disclosed, the more opportunity there is for someone to allege that the information is misleading and that he or she suffered damage thereby. A cautious director might well decide that the advantages of additional financial disclosure are outweighed by this additional exposure to liability for alleged misinformation.

- In any event, most directors do not regard themselves as experts in financial reporting. They rely upon management to produce the data required to support additional financial disclosure. They are also likely to take the advice of management about the merits and difficulties of additional disclosure. In the end result, it is largely management and not the directors who determine the

nature and extent of financial disclosure beyond the minimum required by law. However, as a practical matter directors often look to the auditor for reassurance that what management proposes meets legal, and perhaps broader, disclosure requirements.

The Audit Committee of the Board of Directors

3.6   Some of the practical difficulties that a board of directors experiences in making effective decisions in financial reporting matters have been met by the creation of an "audit committee" of the board, a development of the past 10 to 20 years. Modern corporations statutes now normally require companies with publicly traded securities to appoint such a committee. Other companies may decide voluntarily to have an audit committee. To emphasize that the function of the committee is to represent shareholders, not operating management, a majority of the members (in public companies) must be "outside directors," not officers or employees of the company or any of its affiliates.

3.7   The personal experience of some members of the Commission and many submissions to it have emphasized the very great potential value of the audit committee. Extra effort on the part of audit committee members to become familiar with the company's operations, together with probing questions of management and of internal and external auditors, can significantly enhance the integrity of a company's financial reporting. It was often remarked, however, that realization of the value of the audit committee depends upon the members of the committee and its separation from management. A committee that does not take its responsibility seriously or tends to defer to management can be quite ineffective. We recognize that there is skepticism among regulators and others about the effectiveness of audit committees, based on occasions when directors have not faced up to problems. Nonetheless, we believe the combination of the changes we propose in this Report and a growing recognition by directors of their increased vulnerability to legal liability will overcome most, if not all, of the justification, perhaps legitimate in the past, for that skepticism.

3.8   Typically, the only statutory responsibility assigned to the audit committee is a responsibility to review the annual financial statements before they are approved by the board. However, many audit committees, with the consent or at the direction of the board and usually with the full cooperation of management, have taken on wider responsibilities. These may include, for example, reviewing the company's prospectuses before issue, reviewing the audit plan with the auditor, reviewing the auditor's recommendations with respect to the company's major internal controls, and assessing the performance of the auditors and of senior management involved in the preparation of the financial statements. In Chapter 4 we discuss the functions to be performed by the committee and desirable qualifications of its members.

Management of the Corporation

3.9 In practice, managers, particularly the chief executive officer and the chief financial officer, have a very strong influence on the nature and extent of financial disclosure. Most boards of directors will delegate to management the responsibility for preparing financial statements and other financial disclosure for the board's approval. The introduction of an audit committee enables a board to examine management's proposed financial information more critically, but does not change the basic situation in which management drafts the information and the board normally approves it.

3.10 The primary constraint on management discretion in financial reporting lies in the existence of established accounting standards and the related need to obtain the concurrence of the external auditor on the appropriateness of the company's accounting policies and the validity of management's estimated figures. If management and the auditor have thrashed out any differences of opinion before financial statements are presented to the audit committee and the board, the request for approval of the statements will not normally encounter problems.

3.11 Reliable records of transactions, assets, and liabilities are necessary to enable reliable financial reporting. Directors typically delegate to management the responsibility for seeing that such records exist. The policies and checks that management institutes to control the operations of a company are commonly known as a system of internal control. The

subset of that system that deals with accurate recording of transactions and safeguarding of assets is commonly described as internal accounting controls. Since directors bear the ultimate responsibility for financial reporting, they should have as much interest as management in the efficient functioning of the internal accounting controls (as well as the control system generally).

The Chief Executive Officer

3.12 The chief executive officer (CEO) is or should be the linchpin that holds the corporate organization together and interacts with shareholders and other third parties with a stake in the enterprise. The CEO bears the ultimate responsibility for the operation, control, and direction of the enterprise and is answerable to the directors for its success. The directors, in turn, to fulfil their responsibility to the shareholders, need to assess the CEO's performance and take action if it is less than satisfactory.

3.13 The CEO needs reliable information upon which to base decisions. The quality of the company's internal controls and internal financial reporting is, thus, vital to his or her performance. If these are satisfactory, the CEO should be well placed to monitor the company's external financial reporting. The CEO should feel able to take personal responsibility for the company's financial statements rather than simply accepting whatever is presented by the company's chief financial officer. At the same time, the CEO has the same legal and ethical obligations for fair financial reporting as any director. The CEO therefore has an important role in facilitating and ensuring full and candid communication between the company's financial officers, the board of directors, the audit committee, and the external auditor.

The Auditor

3.14 Corporations and securities acts generally require that annual financial statements of a public company presented to shareholders or included in a prospectus be accompanied by the report of an auditor. The obvious reason is that the opinion of an independent auditor after an examination complying with professional standards makes the financial information more dependable and therefore more valuable. It also reduces the risk of officer and director liability for inadequate or misleading financial disclosure. Both legislation and professional ethics generally require that the auditor maintain independence from the company and its affiliates and from directors and officers of the company and affiliates.

3.15   Corporations statutes do not typically outline specific procedures to be followed by auditors or how they should relate to management, the directors, and the audit committee. In some Canadian jurisdictions, however, the legislation requires the auditor to report in accordance with GAAS and specifically links GAAS with the *CICA Handbook*. In some other jurisdictions there is a direct requirement that the auditor report in accordance with the *Handbook*. One way or the other, therefore, most statutes require that the auditor follow auditing standards recommended in the *Handbook*. Even when the law does not contain such a direct connection to the *Handbook*, any CA appointed as auditor would be expected to follow the standards.

3.16   The auditor must plan procedures to provide reasonable assurance that in all material respects:

- Assets and liabilities reported in the financial statements exist and there are no other assets and liabilities that should be reported.

- The accounting policies selected by the company are within GAAP.

- The amounts at which assets and liabilities are stated in the financial statements have been measured in accordance with the company's accounting policies applied on a consistent basis with the previous accounting period (unless a change in policy has been adopted and is properly disclosed).

- Management's judgment estimates made in measuring assets and liabilities are reasonable.

- Assets and liabilities are correctly categorized and described in the balance sheet and related notes.

- Changes in assets and liabilities in the accounting period are correctly categorized and described in the statements of income and changes in financial position, and disclosure is provided of all the detail required by accounting standards.

- Sufficient explanation and disclosure is provided to assist the understanding of readers of the financial statements, all as called for by accounting standards.

- Management's selection of accounting policies is appropriate to the company's circumstances.

As noted in paragraph 1.6, no matter how well-planned it is, an audit cannot give a guarantee of the accuracy of the financial statements. It does, however, provide a basis for a professional *opinion* that has value to shareholders, creditors, and others.

3.17   A variety of procedures are performed by the auditor to provide evidence to support the audit opinion. They include physical inspection of assets, confirmation of the existence of assets and liabilities with outside parties, reference to source documents to establish prices, computations of various costs, analyses seeking out anomalies in the information, and inquiries to explain them. Normally, any single piece of audit evidence is not conclusive. The auditor, therefore, often seeks evidence from different sources or of different types to support an audit conclusion. The accounting records themselves represent some evidence of the state of affairs displayed in the records but, because of the possibility of error or fraud, that evidence cannot be conclusive. A strong system of internal controls strengthens that evidence. An auditor may place some reliance upon certain of the company's internal controls in planning the program of audit procedures, but only if the actual functioning of those controls has been tested. Thus, trade-offs are made in planning the audit in the interests of economy and efficiency. A decrease or increase in direct audit procedures may be justified by evidence that the internal controls are strong or weak. However, because a failure in internal controls is always possible—e.g. management may override them—the auditor will never place complete reliance upon the accounting records and internal controls.

3.18   The auditor's legal responsibility is to report on the financial statements presented for audit, not to prepare them. If not satisfied with the statements, the auditor will attempt to persuade management and the directors to make changes. An auditor may gain respect by taking a firm, yet constructive, stand on matters in question. However, there are times when disagreements cannot be resolved. The auditor must then consider whether the disagreement is sufficiently serious to warrant a qualification of the audit opinion. In coming to a decision on this the auditor is likely to consider the following:

- Securities commissions, as a matter of policy, are unwilling to accept financial statements accompanied by qualified audit reports if it is possible to change the financial statements and thereby remove the reason for qualification. Thus the threat of qualification may be tantamount to forcing management to change its position.

- It appears that the practical result of this policy of securities commissions could, in some cases, modify or override the basic philosophy of the corporations acts. The corporations acts lay the primary responsibility for financial reporting upon the directors. The policies of the securities commissions may be perceived as a dilution of that responsibility by giving auditors what may be, in effect, a veto power in particular cases.

- The exercise or threatened exercise of this veto power puts a severe strain on relations between the management of a company and its auditors. Even if the auditor's action does not result in termination of his or her appointment at the earliest opportunity (as sometimes it does) it can make the conduct of the audit in future years more difficult by creating an adversarial relationship. As a practical matter, an auditor needs management's cooperation to obtain the evidence necessary to support audit judgments.

The result of the above is that the auditor will usually be reluctant to force a change in financial statement presentation except over a major issue. Auditors and management will often make compromises on lesser issues that may not be fully satisfactory to either party from its particular point of view. At the same time, the auditor must be prepared, where the position dictates it, to risk both the loss of management cooperation and the loss of the audit engagement.

3.19 For the most part, the law lays no responsibility on the auditor for financial information provided by companies outside the audited financial statements. One exception to this is the requirement under secu-

rities act regulations or securities commission policies that auditors provide some "comfort" with respect to such information included in prospectuses. Wisely, however, the profession itself has long encouraged individual auditors to review financial information that is outside the financial statements but is included in documents that also contain audited financial statements. The *Handbook* provides guidance to the auditor on the review of such information in company annual reports and in prospectuses and other offering documents. The principal procedure required is a critical reading of the information to see that it is not inconsistent with information contained in the audited financial statements.[1]

3.20 From the foregoing it can be seen that the auditor's legal right to insist upon financial disclosure other than that which is required by law to be included in financial statements is quite limited. If the audit report on financial statements is qualified or otherwise modified the auditor may be in the position of providing such information. But no significant amount of information can be conveyed in this way. In practice, the auditor's ability to promote financial disclosure beyond that required by law rests upon his or her persuasive powers coupled with good and, when required, forceful communication with management and the audit committee or board of directors or both. Given good and forceful communication, an auditor can make a substantial contribution to the quality of a client company's financial reporting.

PUBLIC EXPECTATIONS AND INSTITUTIONAL ARRANGEMENTS FOR FINANCIAL REPORTING

3.21 As we have described above, the law responds to public expectations for financial reports in two principal ways. It places primary responsibility upon the directors for providing financial information to shareholders, and for making information publicly available when the company has issued securities to the public. In addition, it requires that an auditor make an examination to add credibility to the financial information and that the auditor be independent of the company and its directors and officers. Over a long period of time the accounting profession has strengthened these legal requirements in two ways:

- It has made recommendations for accounting in specific situations in order to lessen uncertainty as to what is appropriate and to promote "general acceptance" of desirable accounting policies.

- It has set standards for auditors to observe in the conduct of their audits.

Since the law originally gave very little guidance on the content of financial disclosure or the detailed responsibilities of auditors, this guidance by the accounting profession has been necessary to the effective implementation of the law's intentions.

3.22   We have also described the recent trend towards additional financial disclosure outside the audited financial statements through the medium of the MD & A. Practice is evolving with respect to the extent of this disclosure, auditor involvement with it, and the manner in which standards are set for the information supplied.

3.23   We must ask whether there are any aspects of this framework for financial reporting that can permit or contribute to gaps between public expectations as to the information it should receive and the information it actually receives. From submissions to us and our discussions, we can identify several features that could contribute to such gaps.

- As described above, in practice management is very largely responsible for proposing and preparing the financial information to be disclosed. However, forces exist that can tend to bias management's attitudes to the disclosure. It must be recognized that to some extent financial information provides a "scorecard" on management's performance. There can be a temptation to make that scorecard look as favourable as possible to the extent that accounting standards permit. In addition, management compensation is often tied to reported results or to share price performance, both of which are or can be affected by the accounting. It would not be surprising if these potential influences on management's judgment sometimes adversely affected the conveyance of completely unbiased financial information to the shareholders, and beyond them to the public at large.

- Directors, who represent the shareholders' interest, may be less subject to bias than operating management, but even they may be led to feel that it is better for shareholders if some disclosure is not made to the public. In addition, the audit committee of the board, in the absence of strong leadership and involvement and of clear standards for performance, may not play its role as effectively as it could. Also, in many companies directors are effectively appointed by major shareholders or management. Accordingly, there is danger that in some cases they may not bring to their duties that objectivity of mind and full independence in action that they ought.

- The auditor is in a peculiar position in the existing scheme of things. Although the audit appointment is nominally made by the shareholders, it is usually proposed by the directors and that proposal, in practice, is highly influenced by the recommendations of management. Thus, the auditor is called upon to examine critically the assertions of the very people who are instrumental in the audit appointment. On top of this, auditors may sometimes be reluctant to press their views as far as they should because their only sanction—qualification of the audit report—is so drastic. It not only can have a highly adverse effect on relations with a client company's management. It also can harm the business of the company and, by extension, the shareholders' investment in the company. Moreover, a qualified report on a sizeable financial institution could affect confidence in the whole financial system, not just in the one institution.

- Accounting standards necessarily represent generalizations on the subject of desirable accounting. They have been described as being like ready-made suits rather than made-to-measure suits. They fit most situations reasonably well, but they do not provide an excellent fit for every individual situation. If accounting standards are taken as the only criteria of fair presentation to the exclusion of professional judgment, there is some danger that financial information that may be important in an individual situation will not be disclosed adequately.

POSSIBLE CHANGES IN THE INSTITUTIONAL STRUCTURE OF FINANCIAL REPORTING

3.24 With this background we are in a position to consider what changes in the structural arrangements for financial reporting might help bring actual financial disclosure closer to public expectations. In the remainder of this chapter we consider whether some significant change in the present established structure for financial reporting could contribute to that end. First, we explore whether a change in the method of audit appointment could help overcome the weakness in the auditor's position caused by the influence of management on that appointment. Second, we assess an even more radical suggestion—namely, that the auditor be given the basic responsibility for preparing the financial report. Third, we consider a more moderate idea—that the auditor be given the right and obligation to provide information in the audit report that he or she considers desirable to supplement or explain the information contained in the financial statements prepared by management.

Modifying the Audit Appointment Arrangement

3.25 The first idea for exploration is one intended to reduce the threat to audit independence resulting from the fact that the audit appointment is so subject to the influence of management. There could be a number of variations of this basic idea. All would require that the power to appoint the auditor and negotiate fees be removed from anyone associated with the enterprise (whether shareholders, directors, or officers) and be vested in an outside party. The appointing agency would need to have government sanction, since presumably the independent audit appointment would be justified on the basis that it is in the public interest. The appointment could be made, for example, by the government itself, an agency set up by the government for this purpose, or a self-regulated professional association to which powers of appointment were delegated by the government.

3.26 We see powerful objections to any such arrangement.

- In Canada, at least, action along these lines would have to be taken both in federal and provincial jurisdictions, with the usual possibilities for incomplete coverage, conflicts, and overlaps.

- The arrangement would make changes of auditors, for whatever reason, much more difficult. Directors and management would justifiably resent a restriction on their ability to discharge an auditor who was not performing efficiently and effectively.

- Establishing fees for the audit function would be a problem because of the variability of conditions encountered. For example, two companies outwardly similar might require very different amounts of audit effort if the records and controls of one were not as strong as those of the other. A separate appointment agency would find it difficult to negotiate fees under these conditions.

- Establishing personal liability for the work done by the auditor would become much more difficult. If audit appointments and fees were not negotiated between the auditor and the auditee directly but rather were made by an appointment agency, it seems likely that an audit firm would be reluctant to offend the agency by refusing an appointment. In these circumstances, it might be unreasonable to hold the auditor liable if the appointment were subject to unusual risks (such as the existence of untrustworthy management). If, on the other hand, all audits were conducted by a single agency, individual auditors would effectively become employees. As such, they would surely refuse to accept penalties for bad work beyond those normally applicable to employees.

- It is fundamentally unsound for an outside agency that bears no responsibility for costs, risks, or performance to be in a position of determining or influencing the costs, risks, and performance of other parties.

- In any event, there is no basis for assuming that the auditor's need to ingratiate himself or herself with an outside agency would have any better results than the present arrangement. Indeed, the result might well be worse in that the auditor would feel a need to gain favour with both company management and the outside agency.

3.27   All this is speculative and necessarily stated in generalizations in the absence of a specific proposal for changing the procedures for audit appointments. No such proposals were made to us apart from suggestions for minor modifications in audit appointments, which are dealt with in Chapter 6. Nevertheless, we have felt it necessary to consider whether the performance of the auditor could be enhanced by a different means of audit appointment. Our conclusion is that any radical change along the lines explored above would likely carry disadvantages much more severe than those existing under the present system.

Assigning Responsibility to the Auditor to Prepare the Financial Statements

3.28   A second and even more radical idea is that the auditor should provide the financial information instead of merely expressing an opinion on the information provided by management. The independence of the auditor provides the main attraction to this idea. Typically, the auditor is the only person who is independent of the company and its officers and yet possesses—as a result of the audit examination—a high degree of familiarity with its financial affairs. As such, the auditor is in an excellent position to judge what would be desirable disclosure from the public's point of view and should be able to tailor the disclosure to its needs and wants, taking into account any important individual characteristics of the company's financial affairs.

3.29   Unfortunately, there are substantial practical drawbacks to the proposal.

- First, management, with its firsthand knowledge of the company and its economic environment, is almost certainly better equipped to make the estimates and evaluations that are so necessary for accountability. Additional cost, perhaps substantial, would be incurred if the auditor were given this responsibility.

- Second, information in a financial report comes largely from the books and records of the company. If an auditor were to decide that different

information should be provided than that which is available in the normal course from the company records, further cost would be involved. In extreme cases, management could frustrate the auditor's ability to obtain the desired information simply by failing to keep the records with the necessary degree of accuracy.

- Third, one of the strengths of the division of responsibility between management and the auditor is that the auditor is not checking his or her own work. If the auditor were providing information, there would be a need for a further check against error or misjudgment, and this would add to the cost. While the auditor is independent, this does not guarantee that he or she is always right.

- Finally, and above all, such a system would let management and the directors off the hook. It is the person responsible for action who should be held accountable. Conversely, it would be hard to justify a system in which management and the directors of a company had no effective say in how the financial results of their efforts were reported.

3.30   The Commission therefore concludes that the primary role of the auditor should continue to be that of adding credibility to the assertions of management.

Assigning Responsibility to the Auditor to Supplement Management Information

3.31   Acceptance of the basic conclusion just expressed means, under the present structure, that the audit report essentially conveys reassurance, not information in its own right. The only exception to this at present occurs when an auditor qualifies the audit report. On these occasions the auditor's explanation of the qualification may contain some measure of original information. But, the information content of a qualification is limited by the need to address directly the particular disclosure on the part of management about which the auditor has questions. Thus, an auditor's right to qualify the audit report is far from a general right to provide information.

3.32   While we reject the idea that the auditor should be given the primary responsibility for financial reporting, we have considered carefully whether there should be some more limited obligation to provide information in some circumstances. It is conceivable to us that there may be times when an auditor is certain that readers would feel entitled to certain financial information to assist a rounded understanding of the enterprise's position and progress, and yet that information is not adequately disclosed in the audited financial statements. That is to say, we have asked ourselves whether there are times when the financial disclosure provided by management is satisfactory so far as it goes, but nevertheless is incomplete. If such a situation exists, some might argue that the auditor should have an obligation to add some commentary in the audit report. The type of situation that warranted such action would, of course, have to be carefully defined and delimited to avoid confusion over the question where management's reporting responsibility ended and the auditor's began.

3.33 *The accounting framework and professional judgment.* In essence, this idea presupposes that management can meet all the standards for accountability and yet not provide all the financial information that is necessary or, at least, highly desirable. It may be helpful to explain how this could occur. The achievement of accountability rests upon a framework of accepted objectives and concepts. That framework has evolved over a long period of time. Although it is explained in many studies and texts, a written statement of the framework has never been formally incorporated in the *Handbook*.[2] In spite of this lack of authoritative expression, there is little doubt that a framework of objectives and concepts exists or that its major elements are generally accepted. One way or another, most formal accounting standards are based upon the framework. Conversely, the pattern of the framework itself can be inferred from the standards that have been adopted.

3.34 One of the basic tenets of the present accounting framework is that figures reported are initially derived from transactions—buying, selling, financing, and investing—in which the enterprise has engaged. Subsequent to the transaction dates, figures initially recorded for assets and liabilities are modified or combined by various cost accounting and other procedures so as to arrive at "book values" at which the various assets and liabilities are reported in the financial statements. Although the procedures

adopted for recasting the figures subsequent to original transactions have a major impact upon them, it is still possible to say that the figures stem from actual transactions. Additional departures from the original transaction figures occur when assets are written down or losses are recognized based on what are essentially valuations, rather than records of actual transactions or events. These, however, are exceptions rather than the general rule. That is to say, the present accepted accounting framework is transaction-based, not valuation-based. The name customarily given to this transaction-based framework of concepts and resulting accounting procedures is "historical cost accounting."

3.35 There can be little doubt that an accounting system based on transactions does not provide all possible significant information about an enterprise. For example, there are many times when current values of some or all assets and liabilities are considerably different from "book values." This was particularly true during the highly inflationary period of the 1970s. Yet, in spite of the obvious criticisms that could be made of historical cost accounting under conditions of rapid price change, sufficient support could not be gathered for a change in the basic accounting framework, or even for the general provision of value figures as supplementary information. Majority opinion seemed to be that the benefits of current value information, given the uncertain precision of many valuations and doubts as to their relevance in many specialized situations, did not justify the cost required to furnish them on a wholesale basis. In effect, if value information was considered very important in specific situations, it was up to accounting standard setters to provide a standard that would address those particular situations. No wholesale revolution in the basis of financial reporting was generally acceptable.

3.36 This history suggests a problem with any proposal that the auditor should provide information independently of that provided by management. The problem is that there is a large amount of information that conceivably could be provided, but is not called for under a transaction-based framework. Yet, the fact that it is not called for by accounting standards may be evidence that there is, or has been, no widespread agreement that the information is essential. An individual auditor, however, might feel that some particular type of information is important, as some accountants do feel about current values. Is the individual auditor, then, to provide information not called for by accounting standards or the accepted accounting framework simply on the basis of individual judgment as to what is important, especially when he or she knows that such judgment would not be supported by a majority of the profession? It is clear to us that such an obligation should not be placed upon the auditor. He or she should not be asked to second-guess the collective judgment embodied in the existing accounting framework.

3.37 *Accounting standards and professional judgment.* Having concluded that an auditor's obligation to communicate information must fall within the accepted framework for financial reporting, we come to a second question. Even though the auditor should not be expected to provide financial information that is outside the accepted framework of accountability, should he or she be permitted or obliged to provide information that is not called for by individual standards within the framework? To a large extent, standards represent guidance to the implementation of the basic framework in the different situations that may be encountered. Although standards are thus expressed largely as rules to be applied in specific situations, they may be seen as collective judgments about the best way to achieve accountability within an overall accepted framework.

3.38 Once again, we encounter the question of a possible conflict between an auditor's individual judgment and the collective judgment. That is to say, if the auditor thinks a particular accounting standard is ill-advised or wrong, should the auditor have an obligation to restate the figures to show what they would be if a different accounting policy were followed? We do not think so. Experience has shown that opinions can be strongly at variance concerning the merits of individual accounting issues, even given common acceptance of a basic accountability framework. Accounting standards have been developed by a collective process to avoid the chaos in financial reporting that would exist if everybody chose accounting policies to fit their own personal opinions. We do not think it useful to control a problem in management's reporting of financial information only to reintroduce it in information provided by the auditor. In other words, if any information were to be

provided by the auditor, we think it should be clear that such information should be consistent with the accepted accounting framework and individual accounting standards within that framework.

3.39 Even after adoption of this basic principle, some questions remain. It is common knowledge that more than one way frequently exists for implementing a particular accounting standard. Sometimes, the choice of specific accounting method has a major influence on the figures reported. If so, should the auditor be asked to express an opinion on which alternative is the better? This would not appear to be unreasonable if experienced professionals would agree on the answer. But such agreement would be evidence that the different accounting methods are not really alternatives. Each is appropriate in a particular situation. In such a case, management should use the method appropriate to the situation. If it does not, the auditor's proper course is to qualify the audit report.

3.40 The problem we are posing here is somewhat different. It arises in cases when alternative accounting methods are both recognized as acceptable *in identical circumstances.* Such a situation usually exists because strong arguments can be made as to the merits of both alternatives and no consensus, informed or otherwise, has been reached as to which is preferable. In such a situation, an individual auditor's expression of preference would have little value since another equally qualified expert could easily express an opposite opinion. This is a fact of life that cannot be avoided. The Commission's conclusion is, therefore, that auditors should not be asked to express what can only be individual opinions on issues of accounting method on which practice has demonstrated there is no agreement. The Commission believes, rather, that the problem should be attacked on two fronts. First, the CICA should make a vigorous effort to reduce the number of alternative accounting methods. Second, disclosure should be required, as an integral part of the audited financial statements, of the existence of alternative accounting policies that might have been selected, with some indication of the possible effect had they been chosen. (See further discussion in paragraphs 4.47 to 4.54.)

3.41 Having concluded in the preceding paragraphs that the auditor's duty must be carried out within the generally accepted framework and standards for financial reporting, we should comment on the application of this principle. For example, it is quite possible that a literal interpretation of a standard applied in a specific situation (especially when not accompanied by explanatory disclosure) may produce an accounting result that is inconsistent with the spirit and intent of the standard and accepted framework. We have no doubt that in such a situation an auditor should be expected to take exception to the accounting. That is to say, the auditor has a responsibility to "stand back" to see that methods adopted to interpret accounting standards are not misleading in their result. We would add that this responsibility should be applied broadly. It is not enough to see that what is actually stated in the financial statements and notes is not misleading. It is equally necessary to ensure that statements are not misleading because of the *omission* of information that ought to be provided to meet the spirit implicit in our accepted accounting standards.

3.42 It is here that we believe the real need for professional judgment lies. It is undeniably important that the profession have a well-understood and generally accepted framework of concepts to guide accountability. It is also helpful if this framework is explained in standards that speak to its appropriate implementation in the wide variety of situations that are encountered in the real world. But none of this would be effective if the preparers of financial statements do not observe the spirit and intent of the framework and standards and not just their words. Given the variety of economic transactions and events, it is a practical impossibility to express standards that provide specific and unmistakable guidance to the accounting for every possible transaction and situation. Auditing therefore requires much more than mere familiarity with a book of rules. Auditors forget this at their peril.

3.43 *Conclusion on the auditor's reporting responsibility.* We return now to the question raised in paragraph 3.32. Should the auditor have a right and obligation to "speak with his own voice" in the audit report, apart from the obligation to qualify the audit report if not fully satisfied with management's presentation? In effect, an affirmative answer to this question implies that there is a class of information that is not called for by accounting standards but

nevertheless ought to be provided. Given the fact that detailed accounting standards will always be incomplete and imperfect—they must strive to keep up with an ever-changing world, and also inevitably contain compromises in order to reach consensus—such an answer is not inconceivable. After careful consideration, however, we think it would be impractical to lay such an obligation on the auditor for several reasons that have been discussed previously:

- We think it would be unreasonable to ask auditors to make judgments as to what information beyond the accepted framework of accountability ought to be provided in specific cases.

- We also think it unreasonable to require individual auditors to pick and choose among accepted alternative accounting methods so as to ensure that the results of the method they favour are reported, when the profession has been unable to specify which alternative is preferable in what circumstances.

- We do think the auditor should be expected to see that accepted accounting standards are not interpreted in a misleading way. However, in this situation we believe the auditor's proper course is to qualify when information is misleading, not to provide additional information that, in effect, contradicts the information provided by management. In essence, we are saying that, if the results of applying an accounting standard appear to be contrary to the intent of the standard, then the auditor ought to take the position that the accounting is *not* in accordance with GAAP.

- If the auditor takes this obligation seriously, as we intend, we think it would be very difficult to describe a class of information that readers of the financial statements are entitled to know, but the omission of which is not grounds for qualification.

3.44 For these reasons, we do not at this time recommend that the auditor be asked to provide information independent of that provided by management, except in conjunction with a qualification of the audit report. The essence of the problem addressed here is the difficulty in articulating what information ought to be in management's statement of its accountability. We believe this problem will be attacked more effectively by a number of recommendations made in subsequent chapters. These include recommendations for extra effort to see that holes in the coverage of accounting standards are filled, that accounting problems are addressed on a more timely basis, and that additional information be provided both within and without the audited financial statements.

3.45 We do not regard this conclusion as a licence for auditors to hide behind literal interpretations of GAAP or absence of guidance in GAAP. In an ideal world, the accountability framework and GAAP would be well thought out and comprehensive, so that their application in an honest manner would almost inevitably provide the information that users need to know. But the auditor must know that we do not live in a perfect world. There are, and probably always will be, ambiguities and lack of completeness in GAAP. The auditor is expected to have a good sense of the basic concepts of fair presentation. He or she should be aggressive in seeing that they are applied, notwithstanding the absence or lack of clarity of guidance and, if not satisfied, the audit report should be qualified. This is particularly so when accounting is proposed that appears to be unreasonably optimistic. Users of financial information will be much more critical of accounting practices that paint an unwarranted picture of prosperity than of accounting that proves to have been conservative. An auditor needs an acute sense of danger. If the auditor encounters a dubious accounting presentation and has a sense of danger, we are confident that grounds will exist for qualification of the audit report.

SUMMARY

3.46 This chapter has described the legal environment of financial reporting and the parties who have responsibilities for accountability. In our present system directors and management bear the primary responsibility for preparing the information to be reported. The responsibility of the auditor is to attest whether the information is fairly presented. Accounting standards governing the fair presentation of information in financial statements have evolved over a long period of time. Latterly, the CICA has

taken on the responsibility for the formal expression of accounting standards, after "due process" procedures that allow all interested parties to be heard. The authority of these standards has been given legal recognition in regulations to corporations and securities acts in a number of Canadian jurisdictions.

3.47 There are some distinct disadvantages to the system from the auditor's point of view. The auditor's primary obligation is to report on the fairness of the accounting rendered by directors and management in financial statements. That obligation, at least in public companies, is primarily for the benefit of shareholders and other parties external to the company. Yet, the audit appointment is usually effectively controlled by management, the very people whose accounting the auditor is asked to assess. Moreover, the auditor reports in black and white terms. Either the financial statements are fairly presented or they are not, for reasons which can be stated only briefly.

3.48 These problems with the structural basis of the audit function are contributing factors to the expectation gap. Many members of the public have limited understanding of the division of responsibility for financial reporting in our system. They do not realize that it is the directors and management who have the accountability obligation and that the auditor's function is primarily to add credibility to the information reported. At the same time, they do accurately see the auditor as "their man," who is in the job to look after their interests. As a result, if the public perceives that financial reports are not satisfactory, it will assign significant blame to the auditor as well as, or perhaps even more than, to management or the directors. In effect, the public may expect management, and even the directors, to be self-interested. They expect auditors to act in the public's interests.

3.49 The Commission has been unable to think of major changes to the present system that would be free from serious objections far outweighing their presumed benefits. Nor do present public expectations indicate a necessity for major changes. This means the profession must find ways within the present structure to fortify its independence and maintain its professionalism. In subsequent chapters the Commission sets out its suggestions to this end.

References

1.   See *CICA Handbook*, Section 7100, "The Auditor's Involvement with Prospectuses and Other Offering Documents," and Section 7500, "The Auditor's Involvement with Annual Reports" (Toronto: CICA).

2.   The CICA Accounting Standards Committee issued an exposure draft of a statement of basic concepts in February 1988. This was preceded by a series of Statements of Financial Accounting Concepts issued by the U.S. Financial Accounting Standards Board over the period 1978 to 1985, and by a study, largely patterned upon the FASB statements, by The Accounting Standards Authority of Canada, a body sponsored by the Certified General Accountants' Association of Canada.

4

Strengthening the Audit Environment

4.1 In the previous chapter we rejected as impractical ideas for far-reaching change in established institutional arrangements for the audit appointment and for the responsibilities assigned to the several parties concerned with financial reporting. We are left, then, with the problem of devising practical suggestions for counteracting the weakness in the auditor's position that is implicit in the present established structure. We have concluded that two modifications or improvements in that structure could make a significant contribution towards improving the auditor's basic position. First, we advocate strengthening the performance of each of the parties responsible for financial reporting and much greater emphasis on their mutual dependence in the provision of financial reports that meet public expectations. Second, we advocate increased efforts to provide comprehensive, effective, and timely standards for financial reporting. In the next chapter we also advocate expanded disclosure with which the auditor would be associated. This should provide a fuller context for disclosure in the financial statements and thereby reduce the risk of their being misinterpreted.

STRENGTHENING THE PERFORMANCE OF PARTIES RESPONSIBLE FOR FINANCIAL REPORTING

4.2 We believe that some adaptation of the present established structure for financial reporting is desirable to enhance the auditor's independence and ability to influence the content of financial reports. To achieve this improvement we advocate building upon the community of interest and shared exposure to legal liability among those responsible for financial reports, especially the directors, auditors, and, where applicable, regulators. Directors and auditors bear a special responsibility for fair financial reporting. If a company is successful it is in everybody's interest to tell its story fully and fairly since this builds confidence in the company and lowers its cost of capital. If a company is relatively unsuccessful, sooner or later its position must come out. Unpleasant surprises resulting from previous overly optimistic reporting could then damage it even more seriously. Moreover, those who share the responsibility for the previous bad financial reporting will suffer a loss of reputation and possibly other penalties (financial, or worse) in our increasingly litigious world. Directors and auditors both need to be conscious of the risks attaching to inadequate financial reporting and the benefits from good reporting.

4.3 For the most part our suggestions consist of reinforcement of mechanisms already in place. Our primary objective is to strengthen the recognition on the part of directors and auditors of their mutual self-interest in good financial reporting for the company. The mechanism for strengthening their interdependence, namely the audit committee, is already in existence. Indeed, what we recommend here is to a large extent no more than a more widespread adoption of practices already followed by the management and audit committees of leading companies.

4.4 In 1981 the CICA published a research study prepared by a small independent group of people who were knowledgeable on the subject of audit committees.[1] The study included the results of a questionnaire survey of chief executive officers, chairmen of audit committees, other directors, and internal and external auditors. Based largely on the results of this survey, the authors of the study (the Study Group) identified five specific objectives for an audit committee: (1) to help directors meet their responsibilities, especially for accountability, (2) to provide better communication between directors and external auditors, (3) to enhance the external auditor's independence, (4) to increase the credibility and objectivity of financial reports, and (5) to strengthen the role of the outside directors by facilitating in-depth discussions between directors on the committee and management and external auditors.[2] The Commission agrees with these objectives. They confirm the Commission's belief that an effective audit committee can help meet public expectations of audited financial disclosure. In the following paragraphs we discuss more fully how the effective use of the audit committee can improve the quality of financial disclosure and the auditor's performance.

The Audit Committee's Role in Discharging the Directors' Accountability Function

4.5 In an ideal world the audit committee would review all financial disclosure before its release by the company. Practical limitations are imposed by the time availability of outside directors. The CICA Study Group suggested that the audit committee should perform the functions listed below:[3]

- Review the annual audited financial statements with management and the external auditor before making recommendations to the board.

- Review changes in accounting principles and practices followed by the company.

- Review all financial reports that require board approval before their submission to securities commissions.

- Review the financial content of all sections of the annual report to ensure consistency with the audited financial statements.

Other functions, such as a review of interim reports to shareholders before issuance, were considered by the Study Group to be of lesser urgency and therefore could be left up to individual boards to decide.

4.6 We agree with the Study Group's list of functions designed to meet the board's accountability responsibility. We would, however, go beyond them in certain respects. We note the existence of a long-term trend to more nearly continuous financial reporting. The starting point of much of our discussion in this Report has been the legal requirement for publication of annual audited financial statements. We must recognize, however, that companies are called upon to provide financial information more often than annually. Abbreviated statements are published quarterly, and other financial information may be published irregularly in such documents as prospectuses and press releases. The capital markets increasingly demand and act upon such interim information. To meet this demand, as well as management needs, companies require continuously up-to-date and accurate financial information and, through technological and systems development, are increasingly competent to provide it.

4.7 Because of these possibilities, there seems to be a trend toward a more active oversight of all financial information by audit committees. For example, the audit committees of some companies now review interim financial statements with management before their publication in the presence of the auditor, or will ask the auditor to make an independent review. We think the time has come to ask all audit committees to review and approve interim financial statements before they are published. A committee may determine its own procedures for fulfilling this responsibility. The important principle, we think, is that the committee remain conversant with, and have some participation in, the public financial reporting of the company more often than once a year.

4.8 In performing its role, we think the audit committee, as representative of the board, should develop its own financial disclosure philosophy. It should vigorously present this philosophy to both the auditor and management to ensure the best disclosure is made. An effective way to do this would be to conduct, from time to time, a formal review with management and the external auditor of all the company's major accounting policies. We also think the audit committee should be more involved in assessing key management estimates and judgments that can be material to reported figures.

4.9 At present, there is no requirement that the auditor review quarterly statements or some of the other financial disclosure that is published irregularly. That is to say, there is often a 12-month gap between the publication dates of audited information. If an error made in financial information published between the audited statements is subsequently discovered, its ultimate disclosure can be embarrassing to those responsible and can even cause difficulties for the auditor, notwithstanding his or her lack of involvement with the interim information. If the error is significant it can also affect the interests of shareholders or other third parties. Boards of directors and audit committees will want to consider, in the light of cost/benefit and other factors, whether a degree of auditor involvement in the review of interim financial information is desirable.

The Audit Committee's Role in Strengthening Audit Effectiveness

4.10 The CICA Study Group advocated the following functions for the audit committee in relation to the external audit:[4]

- Recommend to the full board the appointment of external auditors after obtaining management's view of the competence of the incumbent auditors.

- Review estimated and actual audit fees.

- Discuss the scope and timing of audit work with the external auditors, that is, the "audit plan."

- Review any problems encountered by the auditors, any restrictions on the auditors' work, the cooperation received in performance of the audit, and the audit findings.

- Review with the auditors any significant recommendations made by them to management on the subject of internal control, and management's response to the recommendations.

4.11 Once again we agree with the Study Group. We think the discussion of the scope and timing of the audit program can be particularly beneficial, for the auditor as well as the audit committee. Each can benefit from the other's views about the major risks to the company's finances and the audit procedures that seem appropriate in relation to those risks. In addition, we think the audit committee should review with the internal and external auditors the scope of their inquiries into the company's internal controls. While we would not expect the audit committee to acquire an in-depth knowledge of details of the internal controls, we do think its knowledge of the company's operations and business judgment should enable a fruitful dialogue with the auditors.

4.12 Above all, the audit committee should be conscious that a good audit is not a standardized commodity to be purchased off-the-shelf. The committee should have as much, or more, concern for the effectiveness of the audit as it has about its cost. Indeed, in difficult or risky situations the primary concern of the committee should be to see that a sufficiently thorough audit examination is carried out, even though the end result of that concern may be additional audit cost. The committee must always remember that its overriding obligation is to ensure fair reporting to shareholders and other third parties.

Enhancing the Independence of the Auditor

4.13 The CICA Study Group also recommended that the audit committee should deal with conflicts between management and the auditor, should conflicts arise that cannot be resolved amicably between the two parties.[5] In view of the importance of the auditor's independence, we would be more specific concerning the committee's responsibility.

- The audit committee should request to be informed on a timely basis of any serious difference of opinion between management and the auditors whether or not the difference has been resolved.

- The committee should request to be informed of any case in which management has sought accounting advice on a specific issue from an accounting firm other than the one appointed as auditor.

• The committee should be informed about the nature of and fees for any non-audit services performed for the company by the audit firm and consider whether the nature or extent of such services could detract from the audit firm's independence in carrying out the audit function.

Other Audit Committee Functions

4.14 The CICA Study Group also commented on audit committee functions related to the internal auditor and to corporate governance. With respect to the former, the Study Group recommended that the audit committee should inquire into the degree of independence of the internal audit department from financial management, its goals and plans, its experience in completing its program, and its significant findings and recommendations.[6] In other words, the recommendations cover much the same ground as those in relation to the external auditor. With respect to corporate governance, the Study Group recommended that the audit committee review the adequacy of staffing for accounting and financial responsibilities. The Study Group also recommended that the audit committee be charged with the responsibility for inquiring fully into activities and transactions that may be illegal, questionable, or unethical and into the company's control procedures against them.[7] (See further comment below on corporate codes of conduct.)

4.15 The Treadway Commission, in its recent report, made three additional recommendations.[8] First, all members of the audit committee should be outside directors (not merely a majority, as is the Canadian requirement). Second, a letter from the committee describing its responsibilities and activities should be included in annual reports. Finally, the audit committee should monitor the company's code of corporate conduct and report its findings annually to the board.

4.16 The last of these suggestions presumes acceptance of a prior recommendation that all companies should adopt a written code of conduct—a practice not now universal either in the United States or Canada. The Adams Committee recommended in 1978 that all enterprises with public accountability be required to set out a code of corporate conduct in their by-laws.[9] A code of conduct sets out company policy concerning such matters as compliance with laws and regulations, questionable activities and ethical conduct generally, and avoidance of conflicts of interest by officers and employees. The advantage of a written code of conduct communicated to all employees is said to be that it demonstrates the dedication of management and the board to ethical standards. On the other hand, some people question the effectiveness of such a code without a formal procedure for reviewing compliance with it, and are skeptical that any such procedures can be effective without incurring unreasonable cost.

4.17 We support the first two of the Treadway recommendations (that is, that the audit committee be composed entirely of outside directors and that it provide a description of its responsibilities and activities to be included in the annual report). Indeed, we would go somewhat further. We advocate a publicly stated mandate from the board to the audit committee. The committee's annual reporting to the shareholders would then describe specifically what it did to discharge its mandate.

4.18 We also support the intent of the recommendation concerning a corporate code of conduct but are less certain that it needs to be formalized to the degree suggested by Treadway and Adams. We think it desirable that a code of conduct be expressed in writing by the board and communicated to officers and employees. We think the audit committee should (1) inquire into any possible breaches of the code of conduct that come to its attention, (2) request internal and external auditors to report to it any matters of which they are aware that might appear questionable under the code, and (3) encourage management to discuss with the committee any matter that might be considered unethical or "on the fringe" by a disinterested observer. The important goal, we believe, is that the board, through the audit committee, act so as to demonstrate that it is concerned to maintain ethical standards, not just to maintain appearances. We question whether a legislative requirement for corporate codes of conduct would be effective unaccompanied by firm commitment by the board. We therefore do not consider such a change in the law to be important in itself.

The Effective Audit Committee

4.19 The functions we suggest an effective audit committee should perform are important and not to be taken lightly. Members of the committee need to be well qualified by nature and experience to understand the financial significance of business activities and to devote more energy to the work of the committee than is required from the average member of the board. The opinion survey in the CICA Study Group's research study listed the following qualities of committee members in order of their importance to the success of the committee: (1) basic soundness of judgment, (2) independence from management, (3) ability to devote necessary time, (4) broad business background, and (5) knowledge of finance, auditing, and accounting.[10] Those responsible for the composition of boards of public companies, especially of financial institutions, should ensure that their boards have an adequate number of members with the experience, character, and commitment to play a strong and active role on their audit committees. An auditor can also help the effectiveness of an audit committee by communicating to its members the fruits of experience gained in working with other audit committees and by passing on publications providing guidance to the work of audit committees. Committee members, of course, need to be adequately remunerated for their responsibilities, which are likely to become more, rather than less, onerous as time goes on.

4.20 Notwithstanding the central role and value of an effective audit committee, such a committee is not a panacea. There is a limit to the amount that can be accomplished by outside directors, no matter how able, in a relatively few meetings a year. It is all the more important, then, that auditors take full advantage of the opportunity for communication when these meetings do take place. If unsuccessful in obtaining appropriate action from an audit committee, an auditor may have to perform additional work and his or her sense of danger should be alerted. In addition, there may well be occasions when concerns should be communicated to the full board of directors as well as the audit committee even if such action entails some risk of dismissal.

4.21 When a company does not have an audit committee the auditor may also be faced with the problem of inadequate communication with the board of directors. In such situations the auditor should attempt to establish a relationship with the full board similar to that recommended here for the relationship with the audit committee. An auditor should assume that the absence of an audit committee may have the effect of increasing audit risk unless it is clear that the full board is able to act as an adequate substitute.

4.22 This raises the question of what the auditor should do when an audit committee is ineffective, perhaps, as is now permitted, meeting only once a year and performing a perfunctory review of the annual financial statements. When this occurs, the auditor's task is made more difficult and the auditor personally may be much more at risk. We advise auditors for their own self-protection to be aggressive in their attempts to keep the audit committee fully informed in a timely manner of the matters it should know about. Examples include failures on the part of management to deal promptly and adequately with serious weaknesses in internal controls or serious disagreements on accounting matters, especially if the company is in a weak financial position, is exposed to significant risks, or has engaged in any apparently irregular transactions.

4.23 Similarly, auditors should be diligent in bringing to the attention of the audit committee important questions involving estimates and valuations. Auditors should not unilaterally assume risks in relation to measurements and disclosures when members of the audit committee and other directors also have responsibility to bring their knowledge and judgment to bear. Indeed, auditors who do not take full advantage of their opportunities to communicate with the audit committee and board may, depending on the circumstances, be perceived by that very fact to have been negligent in the full performance of their duties.

4.24 We have considered whether the duties of audit committees should be expanded by law. At present, corporations statutes typically require only that the committee review the annual financial statements before they are approved by the board. The CICA Study Group also considered the question whether additional functions should be required by law and recommended against this on the grounds that the role of the audit committee was still evolving.[11]

4.25 We tend to agree that the inflexibility of legal requirements could hamper the adaptation of board committees to best fit their company's particular situation. Nevertheless, we believe boards of directors should formally spell out the functions assigned to the audit committee, making use of the recommendations made by the Study Group and ourselves, as set out in previous paragraphs. It is, of course, true that no list of rules or procedures can substitute for active commitment to standards on the part of every party with responsibility in the corporate disclosure system. Each party must always bear in mind that failure of one party increases the risk of others and may require additional effort on their own part. Their response to such a failure may be crucial in determining whether they are found to have discharged their own legal obligations in a proper manner.

4.26 Most of the advantages we see in improved communication and cooperation between parties responsible for financial reporting can be obtained without changes in the law or in auditing standards. Indeed, the improvement we envisage can only be achieved through the good judgment and active dedication of all parties to objectives held in common. Such cooperative behaviour cannot easily be legislated. In fact, it might be inhibited by attitudes oriented toward literal compliance with a set of rules. What is really needed is an ever-present consciousness of the advantages of good communication in the conduct of relationships between audit committees, boards, regulators, and auditors.

4.27 Nevertheless, we believe certain changes to the law should be implemented. While we think that the board should retain the discretion to determine what specific functions should be assigned to the audit committee, we advocate that the board's legal duty be extended. The law should require the board to draw up a formal statement of the responsibilities of the committee and publish that statement to the shareholders. We also advocate that the law specifically require that the audit committee review a company's interim financial statements before issuance as well as the annual financial statements. We further recommend that the law require the audit committee to report annually to the shareholders on

its discharge of its mandate from the board of directors.

4.28 In summary, we urge the CICA and individual audit firms to encourage the development of effective audit committees in every possible way, perhaps involving other interested organizations in joint educational programs. The following recommendations are directed to more specific action:

RECOMMENDATIONS

R-1 The CICA should enlist the support of provincial institutes and other interested bodies in seeking legislative amendments that would require all public companies to have audit committees composed entirely of outside directors.

R-2 The CICA Auditing Standards Committee should provide guidance in the *CICA Handbook* to matters that should be raised by an auditor with an audit committee (or in the absence of an audit committee, with the board of directors) and to actions an auditor should take when not satisfied with the results of such communication. The guidance should stress the need for timeliness in communication.

R-3 The CICA and provincial institutes of chartered accountants should press for changes in the law to require that (1) boards of directors draw up and publish to the shareholders a formal statement of responsibilities assigned to the audit committee, (2) audit committees report annually to the shareholders on the manner in which they have fulfilled their mandate, and that (3) audit committees review both interim financial statements and annual financial statements before publication.

All of the Commissioners share a belief in the importance of more active and effective audit committees bearing increased responsibility along the lines discussed above. However, two Commissioners would have preferred not to set out specific requirements in the law to this end. Rather, they would leave it to boards and audit committees to fulfil their responsibilities in a manner that best fits their circumstances.

4.29 If the audit committee is composed solely of outside directors, it will need ready access to detailed information about operations of the company. We suggest that a member of management who is also a member of the board should be designated as special adviser to the committee, to attend all meetings except when the committee requests his or her absence. There are two reasons for this. The first is that inside directors may have knowledge which the committee should know. The auditor will not have complete information on every subject and should not be the only source of information for the committee. The second is that at least one inside director should have ongoing responsibility to facilitate the work of the audit committee. Such responsibility should be no less than that of a full member of the committee.

STRENGTHENING ACCOUNTING STANDARDS

4.30 It is clear to the Commission that the assignment of responsibilities for financial reporting described in Chapter 3 can put the auditor in a difficult position in individual cases. A company's position on disclosure in the audited financial statements may not clearly offend any specific accounting standard, but nevertheless may, in the judgment of the auditor, fail to present relevant financial information in a manner that best suits the legitimate needs and expectations of users. Under the present structure of responsibility for disclosure, the auditor has little opportunity to provide information independently. The auditor's principal recourse is a qualified audit opinion. This position has been compared to that of a government deciding whether to press a nuclear button. While this analogy may seem overdrawn, it does convey the sense of the auditor's dilemma. There may even be circumstances, as in the case of financial institutions where confidence in financial viability is central, when the comparison seems quite apt. The problem is that a qualified opinion or denial of opinion on fairness of presentation may send a more extreme signal than the auditor intends, with potentially serious ripple effects. Failure to qualify, however, risks a failure to meet legitimate user expectations as well as exposure to legal liability for the auditor, directors, and management.

4.31 The unpleasantness of such a choice thrust upon the auditor is increased if, as some perceive (including some serious and thoughtful members of the profession in Canada, the United States, and the United Kingdom), the auditor is in a weak position vis-à-vis management. In these circumstances the quality of accounting standards is most important. A well-reasoned and established accounting standard can give the auditor leverage in disputes with management even though standards cannot cover every conceivable question. On the other hand, if GAAP are not clear on a subject, the temptation for management to try to override the opinion of the auditor by seeking a second opinion from another accounting firm may be increased. Also, when a matter is not apparently covered by GAAP, the auditor is generally in a weaker position in urging improved disclosure. Finally, if the financial statements proposed by management appear to conform with the literal wording of accounting standards but the auditor believes the end result is misleading, the auditor faces a difficult task in describing the grounds for qualification of the audit report, notwithstanding the professional obligation to make such a qualification.

4.32 For all of these reasons we believe shortcomings in accounting standards are or can be important contributing factors in expectation gaps. We have therefore looked for evidence of the overall quality of accounting standards without attempting to assess the merits of individual standards. Although a number of criticisms of individual standards and their application were made to us, our overall impression is that the public is not dissatisfied with their general quality. The same cannot be said, however, about the standard-setting process. The Commission has received many comments to the effect that (1) important gaps left in accounting standards often create difficulty, (2) it takes too long to arrive at a standard once a project is undertaken, and (3) guidance usually comes too late when a new accounting problem arises as a result of changes in business practice, new forms of financial instruments, or changes in the economic environment. We discuss each of these criticisms in succeeding paragraphs. After that, we discuss the issue of flexibility in accounting standards and comment on the cost of standard setting.

Gaps in Accounting Standards

4.33 CICA accounting recommendations originated as attempts to deal with individual problem areas in financial reporting, not as an attempt to build an all-embracing set of rules. Thus for many years the CICA accounting recommendations were fragmentary. Once the recommendations were pulled together in the *Handbook* in 1968, they took on more of the appearance of a unified whole. Nevertheless, large gaps remained.[12] For example, until quite recently no attention was given to the special situation of financial institutions, non-profit organizations, and governments. Problems peculiar to a particular industry, for example, the oil and gas industry, were ignored. This was partly based on the idea that it should be possible to state accounting standards in terms of broad principles and, if that were done, specialized industries could adopt accounting methods suited to their individual circumstances that were consistent with the broad principles. In addition, some issues of broad application were ignored if they did not seem to present significant problems in practice. For example, although an early recommendation was made on the subject of how to calculate the cost of goods in inventory, no recommendation was ever made on the precise basis of valuation of goods in inventory that needed to be written down below cost.

4.34 The drawback to a policy of merely giving guidance in problem areas is that no guidance is available when difficult questions turn up in an area not previously thought to be troublesome. For example, the growth of service industries in recent decades raised numerous revenue recognition problems that resulted in questionable accounting in a number of instances in the 1970s. As another example, increased public interest in both property and casualty and life insurance companies in recent years highlighted the absence of any recommendations dealing with accounting issues peculiar to them.

4.35 We believe the time has come for the CICA Accounting Standards Committee to close the gaps in its coverage of accounting standards. This means that it must examine the universe of economic activity and see that standards are in place to cover questions of revenue and income recognition, costing of manufactured assets, asset and liability valuations, and so on, for all important types of activity. In addition, experience has shown that many acute problems are confined within the boundaries of a narrow industry. To achieve the sort of coverage we envisage, we believe the CICA must be prepared to study the accounting problems of particular specialized industries in some depth. We fully recognize that the foregoing is an extremely demanding task that cannot be accomplished overnight. We are encouraged, however, by the fact that the Accounting Standards Committee has been embarked upon such a program for some time. We suggest that it now undertake a survey of the universe of accounting, identify the gaps in coverage of accounting standards including those that are peculiar to specialized industries, assign priority on the basis of importance and urgency, and intensify its efforts to provide guidance where gaps exist.

RECOMMENDATION

R-4   The CICA Accounting Standards Committee should make a comprehensive survey of the existing body of accounting theory, identify important issues for which accounting standards are unstated or unclear, determine priorities, and intensify its efforts to give guidance on those issues, all with a sense of real urgency.

4.36 A second cause of gaps in the coverage of accounting standards is simply the fact that differences of opinion on some issues are so strong that the Accounting Standards Committee is hesitant to impose a standard even if the committee could reach the necessary degree of consensus within itself. A clear-cut example is provided by the question of accounting for investment tax credits. That issue arose in the early 1960s, but it was not until 1984 that the Committee felt itself able to grasp the nettle and prescribe a single basis of accounting.

4.37 There is no specific recommendation we can make to meet this situation. It must be conceded that if the Committee were to establish a long series of unpopular accounting standards, no matter how right they could be argued to be in theory, the legitimacy of the CICA's right to set standards could be threatened. Nevertheless, obvious unaddressed problems, for whatever reasons, must damage the CICA's credibility and may pose the greater immediate threat to its standard-setting role. We may observe that, as a matter of tactics, it probably is better to tackle an issue like the investment tax credit quickly. The longer that divergent practice exists, the greater will be the polarization of opinion and the difficulty in changing positions. In the last analysis, however, how controversial accounting standards are dealt with must come down to the wisdom and judgment of the standard setters.

Timely Production of Accounting Standards

4.38 Accounting standards set by the CICA are given special legal status under corporations and securities legislation in a number of jurisdictions. It is, therefore, essential that all interested parties be allowed an opportunity to put forward their points of view before a decision is taken. The "due process" procedures are designed to accomplish this and inevitably mean that the production of an accounting standard from start to finish can be time-consuming. The time-consuming aspect of due process is compounded by the extreme complexity of some issues with which the Accounting Standards Committee has to deal.

4.39 Although we do not think this problem has any easy solution, we believe the CICA Board of Governors must see that the standard-setting process is expedited. Possible actions include: (1) more formal attempts to identify developing problems early and initiate background research if considered necessary, (2) greater use of task forces (especially in connection with projects requiring specialized knowledge) to draft recommendations for the Accounting Standards Committee, (3) some full-time members of the Committee, and (4) a procedure for quick examination and, if thought fit, adoption without wording modification of some of the more specialized standards produced by the U.S. Financial Accounting Standards Board (FASB). These are possibilities only, not firm recommendations based on extensive consideration. Our only considered suggestion is that the process of standard setting must be expedited within due process. We are aware that the Joint Steering Committee of the CICA's accounting and auditing standards committees is looking at the possibilities. Our message is that the Committee should regard this task as one of great urgency if public expectations are to be met.

RECOMMENDATION

R-5 The CICA should move decisively so that the process for production of necessary standards is expedited without sacrificing due process.

4.40 It also should not be overlooked that expediting the production of standards requires good judgment and determination in managing the process just as much, if not more, than changes in the process. A standard-setting committee needs a good sense of the possible. Those likely to be particularly affected by a new or changed standard need to be identified early, and their points of view well understood. Perhaps a complex subject can be subdivided and dealt with in manageable sections. Sometimes a standard calling for greater disclosure in a certain area can precede and pave the way for future standards designed to reduce the range of alternative accounting methods in that area. (Our recommendation R-8 in paragraph 4.54 recognizes this point.)

4.41 Those occasions in which a new standard project is undertaken and then has to be interrupted or abandoned after a considerable expenditure of effort represent failures in the planning or management of the standard-setting process. No doubt some failures are unavoidable, as in any worthwhile human activity. Nevertheless, the CICA Board of Governors, as the body responsible ultimately for the standard-setting function, should monitor the committee's progress regularly. The purpose of this should not be to interfere with the technical responsibility delegated to the committee, but rather to satisfy the Board that the committee's efforts are being adequately performed and funded. The CICA has no more important function than that of standard setting. It is vital that this function be performed well and be seen by the public to be performed well. That is why we think it of first importance that the CICA take every possible means to respond to public concerns over the apparent slowness of the standard-setting process.

Emerging Issues

4.42 No matter what improvements are made in the established standard-setting process, it is unlikely that it can be made capable of providing quick answers to rapidly "emerging" accounting issues. Such issues seem to have greatly increased in number in recent years. They stem from a variety of sources, and their highly individual character makes them somewhat unsuited for a normal standards committee project. The normal project is broader in scope and is designed to establish broad principles rather than deal with a single narrow issue.

4.43 Many submissions have been made to us critical of the CICA's apparent inability to provide timely guidance for emerging issues. It is clear to us that this is one area in which the profession is failing to meet expectations and something must be done about it. What is required is some body composed of widely knowledgeable accountants that (1) can arrange to learn about new accounting problems very early on, (2) has the resources to obtain quickly a good understanding of the legal, economic, or business dimensions of the problem, and (3) has the technical expertise to make recommendations for dealing with it in a practical, even if not always theoretically perfect, way.

4.44 There may be various means by which the CICA can achieve the goal of providing timely guidance. We have not conducted the study necessary to suggest one particular way. However, the job needs to be done well, and we therefore are not certain that it can simply be assigned as an additional responsibility of the existing standard-setting apparatus, unless, at a minimum, its resources are significantly increased. Indeed, since we are already concerned about the overload and slow pace of the existing standard-setting process, we would fear that the responsibilities for dealing with long-run projects and emerging issues could interfere with each other. Moreover, the "due process" style and the urgency and practical "street-smarts" style required for guidance to emerging issues are two different styles that could clash. For this reason, as well as the overload problem, it would probably be better to have two separate groups.

4.45 There is also the question of the authority to be attributed to guidance on emerging issues. The present policy is that an accounting standard must clear due process. We believe that policy is necessary in view of the legal significance that attaches to *Handbook* standards. Accordingly, guidance on emerging issues will lack the authority of an ordinary *Handbook* recommendation. In view of this, it is important that it receive adequate publicity so that the profession is fully aware of it. It will then be up to individual members of the profession to see that the guidance is given due weight in practice. The courts are also likely to take note of the guidance, but the ultimate weight given to it will, no doubt, depend on the particular circumstances of the case.

RECOMMENDATION

R-6 The CICA should sponsor a separate committee or task force to express considered opinions on new accounting issues that are likely to receive divergent or unsatisfactory accounting treatment in practice in the absence of some guidance. These opinions should be developed expeditiously and be given wide publicity so that members of the profession can give them due weight when dealing with the issues in question.

4.46 The emphasis in this recommendation is upon quick, practical advice to nip bad accounting practice in the bud. It may well be, however, that some emerging issues are indicative of a more deep-seated inadequacy in accounting theory. In such a case, the Accounting Standards Committee should be prepared to undertake more intensive research and/or initiate a full-fledged *Handbook* project. The emerging issues group should notify the Committee of any such cases it encounters, but should still express its opinion on the case in question to the extent possible.

Flexibility in Accounting Standards

4.47 We turn now to the issue of flexibility in accounting standards. A number of concerns were expressed to us about this. Knowledgeable members of the business and financial community are by now aware that the actual methods used in implementing particular accounting standards may differ, sometimes with quite dramatic effect. Two consequences follow. First, the financial statements of different companies are less comparable than they could be and therefore are less useful to readers. Second, the value of the audit could be diminished. If management has great scope for choice of accounting policies, it may select methods designed to suit its own ends, auditors will lack leverage in disagreements with management over accounting policies, and, in the end result, audits will appear to be less worthwhile and their credibility will be undermined.

4.48 More than one explanation can be found for the coexistence of alternative ways of accounting for the same event or transaction. Most alternative methods can be traced back to a time when accounting standards were less regulated than they are today. When the test of appropriate accounting was "general acceptance," it was common to find that apparently reasonable arguments could be made for more than one way of accounting in a particular situation. If so, each possible alternative would be used by its proponents and all would be deemed "generally" acceptable. Many of the existing differences in available accounting method are not significant to results reported by an entity if one method is used consistently from year to year. However, there are a few cases where this is not so.

4.49 Two examples may be cited to illustrate the problem. The first concerns the costing of goods sold. When goods are sold from inventory it is necessary to assign a cost to the goods sold in order to write that cost off. Several methods are found in practice for costing goods sold, including identifying the actual cost of the specific goods sold, making an assumption that the goods sold were the goods in inventory that were received earliest (the first in, first out method), and assuming that the goods sold were the last goods to be received in inventory (the last in, first out method). There can be a drastic difference between figures for cost of sales using the last in, first out method and those resulting from the use of other methods. Hence the question of which method is more appropriate is not of minor importance.

4.50 Another example of contradictory accounting methods is provided by the oil and gas industry.

There can be a very large difference between the amounts of exploration and development costs capitalized and written off depending on whether the "successful efforts" or "full cost" accounting basis is used. This subject is not addressed in the *CICA Handbook*, although a Guideline was issued recently intended to reduce the diversity in ways of applying the full cost basis. Any suggestion that one of the two basic methods should be adopted in preference to the other would undoubtedly be highly controversial since both are used so widely in the industry. Some years ago, the FASB proposed to permit the successful efforts basis only in the United States. Full cost proponents were able to persuade Congress to overrule the Board and, as a result, contradictory accounting continues.

4.51 Another explanation for flexibility in accounting standards can be found in the philosophy of the Accounting Standards Committee. It has been a long-standing policy of the Committee to strive to express its recommendations in terms of general principle. Several advantages are seen to this policy, including the proposition that it leaves room for the adoption of different specific methods of implementing the general principle when professional judgment suggests that differences in circumstances justify a different method. There is merit in this policy provided alternative accounting methods do represent an appropriate response to possible differences in circumstances and provided professional judgment is, in fact, applied to match the accounting alternative with the circumstances.

4.52 We wonder, however, whether these provisos are always, or even usually, effective. We consider that, if the Accounting Standards Committee has a policy of encouraging adaptability of accounting methods to circumstances, it has a corresponding obligation to see that the resulting flexibility in accounting standards is not abused. The profession cannot retain its credibility if it is inconsistent, especially if the inconsistency is perceived by the public to facilitate management-dominated reporting objectives at the expense of fair and unbiased financial reporting to the shareholders. The profession cannot stress the importance of judgment in the application of standards, and then permit auditors to claim that they cannot effectively exercise judgment to arrive at conclusions that differ from those of management because the standards do not entitle or enable them to do so.

4.53 We therefore believe that the role of professional judgment needs to be thought through if the present policy of leaving room for flexibility in the application of accounting standards is to be justified. We note the Accounting Standards Committee has taken a first step by commissioning a research study on the role of professional judgment in accounting. We suggest the Committee could go beyond this by monitoring the use of alternatives in practice. It is conceivable that, in particular areas, the range of alternatives permissible by professional judgment is so wide as to seriously impair the significance of the figures reported. In the interests of comparable financial reporting and strengthening the position of the auditor, it might be preferable to prescribe the use of a single accounting method, arbitrarily chosen if necessary. It would still be open to management, in such a case, to provide additional information on other bases that management considered useful, always assuming that information was clearly stated and not misleading.

4.54 We also believe that the CICA should attempt to eliminate alternatives that are not justified by substantial differences in circumstances whenever possible, and require better disclosure with respect to alternatives that remain in use. In order to be meaningful, that disclosure should give some indication of the effect of having chosen one acceptable alternative over another. An approximate indication is all that should be required when, as often will be the case, a precise calculation would be onerous, or even a practical impossibility. Also, there need not be disclosure of the effect of not choosing an apparently acceptable alternative that is only rarely used in Canada, unless that alternative is used by one or more significant companies in the same industry. For example, most Canadian companies would not need to disclose the effect of using sinking-fund depreciation versus straight-line depreciation for buildings, but at least some real estate companies would need to do so.

RECOMMENDATIONS

R-7 The CICA Accounting Standards Committee should undertake a review of GAAP to identify situations in which alternative accounting methods are accepted under GAAP, and should make every effort to eliminate alternatives not justified by substantial differences in circumstances. When it is thought such justification exists, the criteria for selection of the appropriate policy should be stated clearly.

R-8 If, in some individual area, support cannot be mustered for the elimination of alternatives not justified by substantial differences in circumstances, accounting standards should require disclosure that the choice of policies in this area is arbitrary. That disclosure should indicate the accounting result that would have been obtained by using the alternative. When disclosure of the result in quantitative terms would be impractical or excessively costly, the indication may be in approximate or general terms (at a minimum stating whether the alternative is more or less conservative than that actually adopted). (See also Recommendation R-23 in Chapter 5.)

4.55 Since disclosure given to the existence of acceptable alternative accounting policies will be made in the financial statements, it will automatically come under the review of the audit committee. We expect that the committee will have exercised its business judgment with respect to the choice of alternatives from the perspective of its philosophy and approach to disclosure, as we have recommended in this chapter. The auditor has a proper role in providing professional input to the committee to assist it in this task. The audit committee should ensure that it explains its rationale for the particular accounting methods it has selected as part of the accounting policy disclosure that we recommend.

Meeting the Cost of Standard Setting

4.56 In the preceding paragraphs we have made a number of strong recommendations for improvements in the substance and timeliness of accounting standards. If the production of standards is expedited, as we have urged in paragraph 4.39, it will be easier to achieve these improvements. Nevertheless, we are conscious that their achievement will almost certainly involve increased cost. The current standard-setting effort is highly dependent on volunteers from within and without the profession. Such people are in scarce supply. If a greater output of standards or other guidance is expected, it seems probable that staff support will need to be stepped up significantly with a corresponding increase in out-of-pocket costs.

4.57 Current standard-setting activities are almost entirely financed through the annual fees levied on the 44,000 individual chartered accountants in public practice, industry, government, and academe. Clearly there is a limit on how much those fees can be increased. That limit may well be insufficient to meet the accelerating demands for guidance on accounting and auditing matters in the complex and dynamic business environment of Canada today. At the same time, we are concerned that the improvements in standard setting must be made. This leads us to propose that the CICA conduct a study of possible different approaches to providing resources for its standard-setting activities.

4.58 We suggest that the study also examine the ways and means of maintaining the admirable and well-established tradition of reliance on volunteer expertise in standard setting. Are there better methods of utilizing volunteer time so as to maximize volunteer input and control of the process while maintaining at present levels, or even reducing, the time demands placed on individual volunteers? It is possible that more well-qualified volunteers could be attracted if ways could be found to reduce their heavy time commitments and make them feel the time they spend is genuinely productive.

RECOMMENDATION

R-9 The CICA should study how to increase the output of its standard-setting activities. As part of this study, it should consider the possibility of obtaining additional financial support from sources other than membership fees without jeopardizing the independence of the standard-setting function.

SUMMARY

4.59 In this chapter the Commission suggests two principal responses to the weaknesses in the auditor's position in the present established structure of financial reporting. First, measures should be taken to strengthen the auditor's relationships with other parties responsible for financial reporting, in order to compensate, so far as possible, for the weakness in the relationship with management alone. Second, means should be sought to improve the quality and adequacy of information in financial statements.

4.60 The Commission believes the following two measures would be of significant assistance in achieving these objectives.

* Improved communication between the board of directors and the auditor—principally through the medium of the audit committee where such exists—can both strengthen the auditor's independence and help the quality of financial reports. The board of directors has the responsibility for fair financial reporting. Its greater involvement in the actual information presented should help to mediate and reconcile differences of opinion between the auditor and management. An audit committee can also bring to bear a broader philosophy of disclosure encompassing more than mere compliance with minimum legal disclosure requirements. On particular issues its judgment and experience can greatly assist reaching the most appropriate conclusions as to what the public is reasonably entitled to look for.

* Improvements in the coverage of accounting standards and the timeliness of their production, together with clear explanation of criteria governing the manner of their application in order to reduce unjustified alternatives, should directly contribute to improved financial statements. They should also reduce the number of serious differences of opinion between management and the auditor, and strengthen the hand of the auditor when such differences exist.

References

1. *Audit Committees* (Toronto: CICA, 1981).
2. Ibid., Chapter 5.
3. Ibid., p. 26.
4. Ibid., pp. 27-28.
5. Ibid., p. 28.
6. Ibid., pp. 29-30.
7. Ibid., pp. 28-29.
8. National Commission on Fraudulent Financial Reporting, *Report* (n.p.: The Commission, 1987), pp. 35, 40, 46.

9. The Adams Committee, "The Report of the Special Committee to Examine the Role of the Auditor," *CAmagazine*, April 1978, par. E5.
10. *Audit Committees*, p. 86.
11. Ibid., p. 25.
12. For a discussion of the historical development of Canadian accounting standards see Ross M. Skinner, *Accounting Standards in Evolution* (Toronto: Holt, Rinehart and Winston of Canada, 1987), pp. 34-35.

5

Financial Reporting: Content, Communication, and Audit Contribution

5.1 This chapter focuses on three aspects of public expectations of financial reporting:

- Public desires for information that is not at present supplied.

- Public expectations as to what the auditor can contribute to financial disclosure.

- Possible ways of communicating to the public the limits to what can be achieved by an audit of financial information, so that misunderstanding or unrealistic expectations concerning the quality of information or the auditor's responsibility for it are lessened.

To provide a background to our consideration of these three matters, we begin with an explanation of the way in which the Commission looks at the problem of financial disclosure.

ANALYSIS OF FINANCIAL DISCLOSURE

5.2 As we have already pointed out, any sizeable enterprise engages in a mass of transactions and is subject to the influence of a wide variety of economic events. The result is that the amount and detail of financial information that could be reported about its affairs is large enough to overwhelm almost any recipient. That is why some classification, compression, and summarization of the information is necessary. At present, financial statements represent one end product of that process. At some future date financial information may be conveyed in some other fashion—e.g. by computer access to a database—but we can be sure that some means of classification and summarization will continue to be necessary to promote understanding.

5.3 A well-designed basis of classification and summarization contributes to an understanding of the pattern of events that cannot be obtained just by looking at the raw data. However, classification and summarization can also suppress information that would be apparent if greater detail were available. Financial reporting, therefore, requires that choices be made concerning the degree of classification and summarization to be performed and the extent of detailed information to be made available. Logically, these choices should be made based on the needs and capabilities of the people who are going to use the information.

5.4 We have already stated (in paragraph 1.10) the Commission's view of the audience to which general-purpose financial reports should be addressed. That audience consists of persons with a reasonable understanding of business and economic activities, but not necessarily the degree of expertise that is possessed by a professional financial analyst. Thus, the Commission sees a need for subdivision of financial disclosure, admittedly on a judgmental basis, between that which is suitable primarily for the professional analyst and the remainder which may be described as general-purpose financial disclosure. It is the latter type of disclosure with which the Commission has concerned itself and which is the concern of accounting standards as we know them today.

5.5   A conclusion that general-purpose financial communication should be understandable to reasonably well-informed users, of course, can only be interpreted in a subjective fashion. The conclusion also does not tell us what information should be disclosed. It is possible that understandable information may be useful, but not be worth its cost. Financial disclosure does have a cost, which is borne in the first instance by those who provide the information but may ultimately be passed on in prices to purchasers of goods or services. Theoretically a specific requirement for general-purpose financial disclosure should be justified on a cost/benefit test. A judgment whether it will pass that test, however, is extremely subjective. The best that those who set standards for financial disclosure can do is be aware of the costs and attempt to form an opinion whether these are exceeded by the benefits, intangible though the latter may be.

5.6   The next question to be addressed is how general-purpose financial disclosure is best conveyed. Information bearing upon the financial affairs of a company now reaches the public by a variety of means.

• The board of directors is required to provide annual financial statements to shareholders. Proxy statements to voting shareholders also contain a limited amount of financial detail.

• Public companies customarily include the audited financial statements within an "annual report." Only Quebec, among Canadian jurisdictions, requires that a minimum amount of additional financial information accompany the audited financial statements distributed to shareholders. However, in all jurisdictions management normally provides a substantial amount of financial

information in the report in addition to the financial statements. Such information may include, for example, analyses of operations, financial highlights, and a multi-year history of financial data, company statistics, and ratios based thereon.

• Public companies are also required to provide interim financial statements, which are considerably less detailed than the annual financial statements.

• Securities legislation requires companies to file special notices of events that have a potentially significant impact on the company's operations.

• Many companies issue press releases concerning important events, not confined to events that require notification under the securities acts.

• Upon those occasions when a company sells securities to the public, the law also requires the provision of audited financial statements, more recent unaudited information, and a wealth of additional information.

5.7   These various forms of financial disclosure can be classified as (1) information included in financial statements and (2) information provided by other means. It is natural to ask what basis exists for choosing between financial statements and other means for conveying information. Some considerations bearing on this question are as follows:

• Financial statements are designed to report the results of a company's transactions and other events affecting the business in terms of assets and liabilities at a point in time and revenues, expenses, gains, and losses for a period. The figures in the statements are grounded in actual transactions and events and consist primarily of measurements of the financial impact of those transactions and events. Apart from historical summaries and highlights drawn from the financial statements, information outside the financial statements is commonly a description, analysis, and interpretation of events that have had financial consequences, rather than a more or less factual measurement of those events. Still other information outside the financial statements may consist of forecasts expressed in financial terms, rather than reports of actual transactions and events. One can argue that financial statements should be confined to measurements (with accompanying classification and necessary description) of actual transactions and events. Analytical and interpretive information, and especially forecasts, should be outside financial statements. This division, in addition to being suited to the nature of financial information, permits the use of more descriptive language and less technical terms in the information outside the financial statements.

• A somewhat related criterion for choice between vehicles of communication is the relative "hardness" of the information. It is arguable that it is useful to restrict financial statements to information that is factual or, at least, capable of measurement (estimation) with a reasonable degree of reliability. Financial information that is more completely a matter of opinion or interpretation is better presented apart from the financial statements.

5.8   In the Commission's opinion it is better not to overload the financial statements with all financial disclosure that may be desirable. The discussion above suggests the criteria we think appropriate to govern the choice of a vehicle for dissemination of financial information. Information that consists of measurements and classifications of the results of transactions and events that have taken place, together with appropriate explanations of the measurements, should be in the financial statements. It is desirable that these measurements be as reliable as possible even though many judgments and estimates go into them. Information that consists of analysis and interpretation of the measurements reported in the financial statements, and financial information that is largely a matter of subjective opinion, should be outside the financial statements. We recognize, however, that the application of these criteria will not be open and shut in every case.

5.9   Few formal standards exist in Canada for financial information that is presented outside the financial statements. The *CICA Handbook* contains only one example—the recommendation on *Reporting the Effects of Changing Prices*.[1] Moreover, except for

information in prospectuses and similar documents, there are no legally recognized standards for information outside the financial statements. As a result, auditors have little leverage on such financial disclosure. The Commission believes, as we have indicated, that some financial information for the ordinary reader is best conveyed outside the financial statements and that the need for such information is likely to increase over time. In an increasingly complex world, effective accountability becomes a moving target that requires ingenuity and effort to attain. The Commission feels, therefore, that the CICA should be alert to public needs for additional financial disclosure and active in developing standards to meet those needs. As such standards are more likely to be effective if they receive legal support, the CICA should normally seek the cooperation of securities commissions or other regulatory authorities in the achievement of desirable disclosures outside the financial statements.

PUBLIC EXPECTATIONS FOR SPECIFIC ADDITIONAL DISCLOSURE

5.10   The Decima survey of the expectations of the general public did not disclose strong desires for additional information in financial statements, as such. Seventy-two percent of those surveyed did not see any need for additional information.[2] Moreover, the description of additional information desired by the remainder of those surveyed showed no concentration on any particular types of information desired. Among members of the financial community there were stronger expressions of desires for more disclosure, principally from some public accounting firms and from those concerned with the capital markets including financial analysts, stock exchanges, and securities regulators. Again, a wide range of possible additional information was mentioned, which included both more detailed data supplementing the financial statements and better indication of the accounting policies and the judgments, assumptions, and estimates necessary in financial reporting.

Disclosure of "Going-concern" Status

5.11   Nevertheless, in the course of our inquiry we received many representations concerning the need for warning the public about the risk of business failure and the auditor's responsibility in that connection. Recent well-publicized failures have increased the urgency of that concern. At present, detailed standards for accounting for individual assets and liabilities of an enterprise are based on the assumption that the enterprise can continue as a going concern. That assumption does not mean that individual assets will not need to be disposed of and therefore should not be written down to some "market" or "recoverable" value. It merely means that the basis of valuation adopted need not assume forced liquidation of the business and/or sale of assets under distress conditions.

5.12   In the real world, businesses frequently do fail and are liquidated or reorganized. In such cases, the usual going-concern assumption becomes inappropriate. However, there are no written accounting standards that give guidance to financial reporting when an enterprise has failed, or when there is a considerable probability that it will do so. The *Handbook* does not even mention the going-concern assumption in its accounting section.

5.13   The auditing section of the *Handbook* contains a discussion of the auditor's responsibility when doubts exist as to the validity of the assumption.[3] This material contains no specific recommendations; it merely reiterates that the auditor's responsibility is to review the accounting treatment, disclosure, and presentation by the enterprise to see that the financial statements are fairly presented in accordance with GAAP. There is a clear implication that GAAP require explicit disclosure to the reader of the possibility that the enterprise may be unable to continue in the normal course of business. No indication is made of any other change from the normal accounting treatment for a going concern that may be required by GAAP in these circumstances. If the auditor is satisfied with the disclosure, no specific reference to the going-concern doubt is required.

5.14   We have already indicated that a substantial percentage of the public at large and the financial community think the auditor should render a qualified opinion when there is substantial doubt whether an enterprise can continue as a going concern. The Commission is of the opinion that new or amended accounting and auditing standards are needed to lessen the present confusion on the subject of financial reporting for enterprises in danger of failure. The new standards should be consistent with the existing philosophy of financial reporting explained in Chapter 3. That is to say, it is management's responsibility to provide information—including disclosure of doubts about the company's going-concern status if such exists. It is the auditor's responsibility to see that such explanation meets the standard.

5.15   The purposes of the new accounting standards would be twofold:

- To give explicit expression to the principles governing the presentation of financial information for failed enterprises. Presumably historical cost should no longer be the principal basis of valuation. But what basis should be substituted for it— e.g. immediate liquidation value, value realizable in orderly liquidation, the discounted value thereof, or some other basis?

- To give guidance to the manner in which doubts as to going-concern status should be expressed. For example, what degree of probability is required to cause disclosure of the existence of doubts concerning ability to continue as a going concern? Is it a black-and-white question? That is, should doubts be expressed only when the probability of failure exceeds a certain level or a significant probability exists that cannot be estimated closely? Or, should there be some attempt to indicate the *degree* of probability of failure in the disclosure? If the probability of failure is high but not certain, is there a need to provide any supplementary information concerning how the valuations reported in the financial statements would be altered if they were prepared on a liquidation assumption?

5.16   There is also the question of the length of time ahead that should be covered by management's and the auditor's warnings concerning going-concern status. The future is always uncertain and is all the more so for a company that is not financially strong. How far ahead should management and the auditor be expected to foresee potential serious financial difficulty? Conversely, how far ahead can management and the auditor feel confident that a company is *unlikely* to experience financial difficulty? (It must be remembered that if warning is expected of doubts about a company's going-concern status, absence of warning will imply that there is little doubt on that score.)

5.17 Obviously, the answer to these questions will vary from one company or industry to another. However, if guidance is to be provided, it must be workable in the most difficult situations. It follows that the time horizon must be quite short. Inevitably, opinions will vary to some degree, but we would think that six to nine months ahead is ordinarily the maximum period for which it is reasonable to expect the expression of going-concern doubts.

5.18 The action we suggest with respect to auditing standards depends, in part, on what is done with respect to accounting standards. If an accounting standard can be developed that will result in reasonable disclosure of the probability of business failure when there is a significant measure of doubt on that score, we believe it would be wrong to require qualification of the audit report as well. A qualification implies that the financial disclosure is deficient, or that the auditor is unable to come to a conclusion that it is not deficient. If the auditor is satisfied that the disclosure is fair and in accordance with accounting standards, it is illogical to qualify the audit report.

5.19 We are concerned, however, about the strength of the opinion that there should be some warning in the audit report on something as fundamental as doubt concerning the future going-concern status of the company. In view of that strong opinion and the present belief by a considerable segment of the public that the auditor does have a duty to call specific attention to the possibility of business failure, we have concluded that the auditor should provide that warning. This should not be a qualification, which we think illogical, but additional disclosure to be set out in an extra paragraph of the audit report. We should emphasize that this is an exception to our general position. In Chapter 3 we have given reasons why we

support the position that it is directors' and management's obligation to provide information and it is the auditor's responsibility to attest to that information, not to interpret it or provide new information. Therefore, our recommendation concerning the auditor's comment on going-concern status is not intended to establish a precedent for auditor commentary on other matters. It represents emphasis of management's disclosure only, not a separate disclosure by the auditor.

RECOMMENDATIONS

R-10 The CICA Accounting Standards Committee should study the question of financial reporting when an enterprise is in financial difficulty and issue explicit standards giving guidance to:

- The basis of reporting appropriate for a company that has failed.

- The disclosure that should be made by management in financial statements when an enterprise is a going concern at the reporting date but there is significant danger that it may not be able to continue as such throughout the foreseeable future. Since every enterprise carries some risk of failure, the standard should be as clear as possible concerning (1) how serious the risk of failure must be to require special disclosure of that risk, (2) whether or how gradations in the degree of risk should be indicated in the disclosure, (3) the length of the period ahead for which the risk of failure must be evaluated, and (4) whether or to what extent there is a need for indication of the extent of changes that might be required in the figures reported in the event of business failure.

R-11 The CICA Auditing Standards Committee should hold to its present position that qualification of the audit report is not required if financial statements give adequate warning of a serious risk of business failure. It should, however, issue a new standard requiring the auditor to highlight the risk by calling special attention, in an additional paragraph in the audit report, to the financial statement disclosure.

Disclosure of Risks and Uncertainties

5.20   The question of disclosure of risks and uncertainties is closely related to the subject of disclosure of going-concern uncertainty. We noted in Chapter 2 that the public did not express a strong desire for more disclosure of risk and uncertainty than is provided at present. However, the public also appears to rely on auditors to a considerable extent for warnings of serious risk and that may account for some apparent complacency on its part. Members of the financial community, on the other hand, appear to be much more aware of the need for better disclosure of risks, and many representations to us raised the matter.

5.21   On the basis of the evidence presented to us, the Commission has been convinced that there should be better disclosure of risks and uncertainties, both because such disclosure adds a needed dimension to the portrayal of financial position and because it should reduce the naïve belief that an unqualified audit report means that a company is, and will remain, in good financial health. Just how that disclosure should be made, however, is not a simple question.

5.22   There are different types of risk. A company may be at risk because of actions it has taken or events that have taken place before the reporting date. For example, there may be a lawsuit against the company creating a risk, but not a certainty, of loss. Such conditions are known in accounting as contingencies, and their accounting treatment is covered by present standards. Alternatively, a company may be exposed to risk and uncertainty simply because of the nature of its business. For example, it may be exposed to commodity price risks or foreign currency risks with respect to a substantial portion of its sales revenue or purchase costs.

5.23   Finally, a company may face risks greater than those experienced by other companies in its industry because of the way in which it operates and manages its business. For example, a company may, either de-

liberately or by oversight, not insure its property or not hedge significant foreign currency or interest rate exposure when it is customary to do so. Or, a company may undertake a leveraged acquisition without having completed or arranged necessary equity financing or realization of cash through divestitures.

5.24   Some types of financial institutions, by the nature of such activities as commodity and currency trading, are subject to even more serious and volatile risks than the ordinary business. The existence of these risks demands extremely well designed and monitored systems of internal control. In Chapter 8, we propose an expanded role for the auditor in relation to the internal controls of financial institutions. We have not, however, been convinced that a similarly expanded role is required in relation to all other types of companies.

5.25   An auditor's present responsibility is to examine and test internal controls only to the extent that it is proposed to place reliance upon them for the purpose of the audit report. It is obvious that an auditor must do this minimum. However, to expand his or her responsibility to review internal controls would involve additional cost to all companies, and we are not yet ready to recommend such a step. Nevertheless, we do point out that the risk environment of some companies may necessitate exceptionally strong internal controls for their own protection. The need may arise from the character of the business, as in the case of financial institutions, or from the special circumstances of the company, such as financial pressures upon it that increase the risk of some misfeasance. The wise auditor, in such a case, will want to obtain sufficient knowledge of the internal controls to make sure that control weaknesses do not, in themselves, put the company at serious risk that might itself need disclosure.

5.26   Since uncertainty is pervasive in the business environment and there are many different types of risk, it will not be easy to provide guidance to the disclosure of risk. With respect to the location of disclosure, for example, one possibility might be to disclose those risks that are specific to the enterprise—that is, contingencies and any risks that are peculiar to the way its business is operated and managed—within the financial statements. Other risks that are inherent in the business carried on might be disclosed by some other means outside the financial statements since the risks are not peculiar to the individual company. However, risks that ordinarily would be described outside the financial statements might, upon some occasions, need to be flagged within them as well. For example, if a company clearly is going to have to raise substantial additional financing in the near term (even if it can get by for six months or so) and if there are sufficient question marks concerning its ability to finance successfully, a need would exist to form a judgment whether some caution should be expressed about its going-concern status. The study of risk and uncertainty disclosure that we propose below will need to explore such issues in considerable depth.

5.27 We expect that the question of a time horizon for risk disclosure should largely answer itself. We think that risks to be disclosed will be largely risks that exist at the financial statement date and that are continuing, such as risks pertaining to uninsured or unhedged positions. Any business will be subject to a large variety of other risks that *might* affect it in future. However, we would think that disclosure of such risks need be required only when there are specific indicators at the date of release of the financial statements that such risks could cause problems in the foreseeable future. While there will, on occasion, be present indication of potential long-term problems, for the most part an emphasis on specific indicators of problems will limit risks to be disclosed to those that may affect the enterprise within a year or less.

5.28 Other topics on which guidance would be desirable include the question of how far to go in risk disclosure considering the very large number of possible risks and how to indicate the immediacy and magnitude of particular risks. Because the matter is so complex, we recommend that the appropriate committee within the CICA commission a special study of risks and risk disclosure before attempting to frame standards. Notwithstanding our recognition of the need for study, we stress the urgency of this question in our present environment of risk and auditor vulnerability.

RECOMMENDATION

R-12 The CICA should initiate and complete as soon as possible a study of risks and uncertainties leading to conclusions as to how they may best be disclosed in financial statements or elsewhere (e.g. in Management's Discussion and Analysis in the annual report). Such a study should:

- Describe the nature of uncertainties and risks in some depth.

- Attempt a classification of different types of uncertainties and risks and provide guidelines for assessing their significance, particularly in terms of magnitude and probabilities.

- Consider how each category might best be disclosed and provide guidance on the form of disclosure.

- Indicate how and when gains and losses should be recognized in the financial statements (along the lines of present recommendations with respect to contingencies).

Handbook recommendations based upon this study should be issued as soon as possible after its completion.

Disclosure of Commitments

5.29 The typical business today enters into a large number of medium and long-term contracts—a much greater number than did an enterprise of yesteryear. Examples include sales of assets with repurchase options or obligations, joint ventures, a variety of leasing arrangements, long-term product purchase and sale agreements in resource industries, throughput and take-or-pay commitments entered into by pipelines and public utilities, and agreements for sale and repurchase of securities in financial institutions. These contractual relationships convey valuable rights and give rise to obligations. To a considerable extent, these rights and obligations are not valued and recorded in the accounts. Hence, they are sometimes described as "off-balance-sheet."

5.30 At one time the distinction between transactions that were reflected in the balance sheet and those that were not was fairly clear. A transaction would result in the recording of an asset largely based on legal or physical tests—such as transfer of title to the asset or its physical delivery. Similarly, recording of a liability would depend principally upon the criterion of performance or partial performance of the other party's obligation in the transaction. A commitment that was unperformed by either party, or that was contingent upon some future event that might or might not occur, was not recorded. These tests for the recognition of assets and liabilities in the balance sheet have become less satisfactory today with the increased complexity of business arrangements. For example, under leasing arrangements risks and rewards that once attached to ownership of assets may now be transferred partially or completely from one party to another without transfer of title to the asset. As another example, one may find actual obligations and contingent obligations bundled in a single transaction with consequent difficulty in valuing and recording each aspect of the transaction.

5.31 These complexities pose challenges for accounting standard setters. There are times when consideration of the substance of a transaction leads to a conclusion that it should result in the recognition of assets and liabilities in the balance sheet even though the traditional tests for recognition are not clearly met. There are many other times, however, when the contingent aspect of a transaction or difficulties in valuation or other reasons preclude any workable general rule to guide the accounting. The problem is sometimes intensified when a principal reason for the particular legal form of a transaction is the desire to prevent the contractual obligation being recorded as a liability in the balance sheet. Because of these difficulties, there is a danger that the traditional balance sheet will become less and less able to provide a rounded portrayal of all the factors relevant to an enterprise's financial position.

5.32 The Commission is in no position to suggest a solution to this general problem in accounting stan-

dards. It does, however, consider that one general principle should be adopted. Because of the risks associated with material commitments, the Commission believes that whenever the capitalized value of a commitment is not recognized as an asset and liability properly disclosed in the balance sheet, there ought to be full disclosure of the nature and existence of the commitment in a schedule or note accompanying the financial statements. Present *Handbook* guidance on this seems not to be sufficiently forceful or specific to be satisfactory.[4] We therefore make the following recommendation, in addition to our recommendation for a study of the treatment of risk and uncertainty in general.

RECOMMENDATION

R-13 *CICA Handbook* recommendations with respect to disclosure of commitments should be amplified so that material commitments, when not capitalized as assets and liabilities in the balance sheet, will be disclosed in fuller detail than is customary in today's practice.

Need for Emphasis in Disclosure

5.33 In view of the importance of disclosure of doubts concerning business continuance, we have considered how it can be emphasized apart from the auditor's report. For example, the present required statement of accounting policies could begin with a positive assertion that the financial statements have been prepared on the basis of accounting policies accepted for a going concern and then continue with the disclosure of any doubts on that score, if such exist. However, disclosure of going-concern doubts may be closely related to disclosure of specific risks. In addition, there may be other disclosures in notes to the financial statements that are as important as the disclosure of risks.

5.34 The general question, then, is whether there ought to be some means for highlighting particularly important disclosure so that it does not become buried in information that is more routine in character. At present, for example, a good deal of information is called for in notes to supplement figures and descriptions in the financial statements themselves— such as details of changes in share capital during the year, and schedules of debt maturities and lease payments for the next five years—and this information is repeated on an updated basis year after year. There could be merit in separating such recurring disclosure from disclosure that is related particularly to the results and financial position in the current year.

RECOMMENDATION

R-14 The CICA Accounting Standards Committee should consider how financial disclosure in notes supplementing the financial statements might be arranged so as to highlight matters of particular importance—including disclosure of risks and doubts as to going-concern status— and provide guidance in a standard on disclosure.

Accounting Estimates and Valuations

5.35 The core of present GAAP is the historical cost accounting theory. One of the basic ideas embodied in that theory is that costs incurred in a company's acquisitions of goods and services should be classified according to the different types of assets acquired and then should be "matched" with revenues—that is, should be written off—as the benefits from the costs expire. (Some costs are written off when incurred because their benefit is transitory or they cannot be clearly associated with identifiable assets.) This system is considered to have certain strengths. First, original or historical cost represents objective evidence of the value of an asset when it is first acquired because the cost is established in a market transaction. Second, the various methods for matching costs with revenues, if well devised, recognize that the benefit from an asset expires when it is sold or otherwise used up. In this way the need for regular revaluations of the assets—a process in which precise results may be difficult to achieve and which can be costly—is avoided.

5.36 The historical cost system is at its strongest in relation to the operating assets of the business—that is, assets acquired for production or sale. It has less merit when applied to monies laid out on investments and loans. For the most part, the principal amount invested in such assets is expected or hoped to be recovered eventually. Therefore, there is little question of matching the cost against revenues from the investment. Moreover, over time the realizable value of the asset may come to differ substantially from the original cost. The recovery of the amount invested may become uncertain; conversely, the realizable value of some investments may become far greater than their original cost. The usefulness of financial reporting can be questionable if these changes in value are ignored.

5.37 In fact, modification of amounts assigned to assets based on historical cost is not completely ignored under the so-called historical cost system. Even with respect to operating assets, writedowns below historical cost-based carrying values are called for if it is felt these values cannot be recovered. The same is true of investments in securities and loans. Writeups of assets before sale, however, are generally not permitted except in the case of investment companies that account on a market value basis rather than historical cost.

5.38 One trouble with existing practice is that the basis for asset writedown is not always well described in accounting standards. This is especially true in the case of specialized industries. For example, it was only recently that a guideline was issued with respect to the writedown of costs of exploration and development carried forward by oil and gas companies using the "full cost" accounting method. Also, because the *Handbook* has just begun to give special attention to financial institutions, guidance to appropriate bases for valuation of the different types of assets held by such institutions is far from complete.

5.39 There is a second problem with asset valuation not based on cost. Even if a basis for writedown is decided upon, the actual amount of writedown may be hard to establish within a narrow range. For example, if it is decided that the valuation should be based upon current realizable value, there can be practical difficulties if reliable market prices are not readily available. Alternatively, if it is decided that valuation should be based on estimates of future recoverable values, possibly with some provision for discounting, the valuation necessarily will be uncertain because future recoverable amounts cannot be known with certainty and the choice of discount rate may be arbitrary.

5.40   Estimation problems are not confined to valuations. Estimation is also required in many figures based on historical costs. For example, depreciation rates applied to the cost of plant and equipment are based on estimates of useful lives of assets. Problems in estimation and valuation present a challenge to financial disclosure. Assets and liabilities are traditionally stated at a single figure in a balance sheet. An impression of precision is conveyed to the uninitiated by the fact that the balance sheet is in balance. That impression may be corrected to a degree by stating all figures to the nearest thousand or million dollars. Yet, even rounding to the nearest million dollars can be somewhat misleading if a particular figure might have been estimated by different experts, each fairly exercising his or her judgment, at tens of millions of dollars more or less than the balance sheet figure.

5.41   In today's practice the reader of financial statements has no way of knowing the possible lack of precision in the figures reported, although a knowledgeable person will be aware that the figures must be variable to some degree. Uncertainty as to the possible range of estimated carrying values compounds the real uncertainty that a reader may feel on account of the risks to which a business is exposed. In the extreme, the possible range in estimates of values may mean the difference between an appearance of solvency and an appearance of insolvency.

5.42   What we are suggesting in these few paragraphs is that guidance as to the basis of valuation used to establish writedowns represents one of the gaps in the coverage of the *Handbook* that should be rectified as soon as possible. How to best explain the bases and possible variable results of estimates and valuations also deserves consideration.

RECOMMENDATIONS

R-15   The CICA Accounting Standards Committee should give priority to defining more precisely the bases for writedowns of assets below cost-based figures, particularly in relation to the assets of specialized industries where the valuation placed on specific classes of assets is highly material to the reported net equity of the enterprise.

R-16   The Committee should also consider whether there is a need for better guidance with respect to disclosure of the bases used in making accounting estimates and the possible range in the valuation figures that could have resulted within the exercise of reasonable judgment.

Management Discussion and Analysis

5.43   Having dealt with the questions of disclosure of doubts about the going-concern assumption and disclosure of risks, we have covered the additional information most often suggested to us as needed in financial reports. Strong desires for financial information beyond this are confined, for the most part, to financial analysts. We have already suggested that detailed information for analysts might be conveyed, if authorities such as securities commissions consider it desirable, by reports filed separately from those that at present are sent to all shareholders. The reason for the separate treatment is the desire not to overload general-purpose financial reports, thereby possibly making them less usable by persons who do not have the time or incentive to study matters as deeply as do professional analysts. The special reports, of course, should be available to shareholders upon request.

5.44   Notwithstanding the desire not to confuse the ordinary reader, we believe some analytical and interpretive material may be included in general-purpose financial reports without making them too complex, and would represent a valuable addition. The sort of information we have in mind is already required by the U.S. Securities and Exchange Commission (SEC) to be included in a "Management

Discussion and Analysis" (MD & A). We, therefore, do not need to go into great depth in our description of the sort of information that is desirable. In essence, the information that might be useful can be inferred simply by asking ourselves the question: "What information would help the intelligent reader to understand what conditions brought about the financial position portrayed in the financial statements?" Based on that understanding, the reader could then make sensible predictions of the company's future financial health, given various assumptions as to the external economic environment. The answer given to this question by the SEC takes the following form:[5]

- An analysis of results of operations for the past three full fiscal years. The objective is to describe and explain significant components of revenues and expenses so that the reader may understand what forces produced the results that actually occurred. Particular attention would be given to any unusual or infrequent transactions that affected those results. Trends and uncertainties that could have a material effect on future operations would be highlighted.

- Information about the company's liquidity, i.e. its present and future ability to generate sufficient cash for its needs. This information has two elements. There would need to be consideration of trends or uncertainties that could have a material impact upon the company's cash flow from operations. There would also need to be consideration of the impact on liquidity from the company's commitments and plans for future capital expenditure and its means of financing. All this information would be relevant to management's disclosures of risks and uncertainties and going-concern status that we have recommended earlier.

- Forecast data beyond the disclosures already required under the preceding headings. The SEC encourages disclosure of this additional forward-looking information but does not require it.

5.45 We repeat that a widespread demand for information of this sort was not voiced to us. Therefore, we cannot say the absence of such information contributes to an expectation gap at present. Nevertheless, we believe that, in the longer view, expectation

gaps will be minimized to the extent the CICA is able to anticipate changes in public expectations rather than merely react to them. We believe the MD & A information, particularly that about operations and liquidity, could be widely useful and therefore is appropriate for general-purpose financial reporting. We think reference to specific trends that are evident in the data is valuable. We are less impressed with the need for, or usefulness of, overall financial forecasts. Their accuracy is necessarily limited by an inability to predict the future, and their numerical precision conveys a sense of assurance that can only be misleading.

5.46 In total, however, we think that the Management Discussion and Analysis is an example of financial disclosure outside the financial statements that the CICA should look on favourably. That approval could be evidenced by an expressed willingness to advise and assist in developing standards for the information.

RECOMMENDATION

R-17 The CICA should look favourably on additional financial disclosure of a softer, more subjective nature in a Management Discussion and Analysis section of the annual report. The CICA should assist and cooperate with securities commissions in the development of standards for information in the MD & A.

PUBLIC EXPECTATIONS OF THE AUDITOR'S WORK

5.47 We turn now to the contribution that the auditor can make to the quality of financial reporting. A direct contribution is ruled out by the fact that the auditor does not supply information but rather attests to the accounting rendered by management. Nevertheless, the individual auditor does have an important role to play in reviewing and possibly influencing management and audit committee judgment. As one whose training and experience has concentrated on good financial disclosure, the auditor should be able to offer valuable advice on the most desirable reporting to shareholders.

5.48   Management exercises judgment in the preparation of financial statements in at least two important ways. Judgment is used in the selection of accounting policies from among alternatives that may be available. Judgment is also required in making the estimates necessary to implement accounting policies. Examples are: estimates of recoverable value, judgments concerning whether there has been long-term impairment of asset values, and estimates of useful lives over which assets should be written off. The decisions taken by management in the exercise of these judgments can have a major impact on the reported financial results. We believe it can be said fairly that the public expects the auditor to take responsibility for seeing that management judgment is exercised in a reasonable manner and that the audit committee plays its proper role in that respect.

Selection of Accounting Policies

5.49   Accounting policies are defined in the *Handbook* as "...the specific principles and the methods used in their application that are selected by an enterprise as being most appropriate in the circumstances."[6] The *Handbook* instructs the auditor to consider whether management selection of accounting policies is appropriate to the particular circumstances of the enterprise being audited. In this task the auditor is to exercise "professional judgment."[7] On the face of it, this injunction requires the auditor to do precisely what the public expects so that there should be no expectation gap here.

5.50   The matter, however, is not so simple. In paragraphs 4.47 to 4.54 we explain that alternative ways often exist for accounting for the same event or transaction. This poses a problem for auditors. How can they decide what method of accounting is appropriate in the circumstances when the existence of alternatives indicates that expert opinion is divided on the subject?

5.51   Notwithstanding this difficult problem, we believe the general principle should stand that the auditor should be satisfied with management's selection of accounting policies or else should qualify the audit report. It is often argued that accounting recommendations should be stated in terms of their general objectives, leaving room for judgment in the

adoption of accounting policies that are appropriate for the individual business. If this is accepted, we believe the auditor must take a measure of responsibility for seeing that management's judgment in the selection of accounting policies is not biased or ill advised. While there inevitably will be room for some difference of opinion and the choice of policies may not be critical when the effects of differences are not material, there must be some point at which a policy can be seen to be well outside the norm in its degree of optimism or pessimism.

5.52   Accordingly, we believe the present recommendation in the *Handbook* that "the auditor should exercise his professional judgment as to the appropriateness of the selection and application of principles to the particular circumstances of an enterprise," should be continued. However, the meaning of "appropriateness" should be clarified. It should be indicated that there can be room for some difference of opinion as to what policy is reasonable in the circumstances. It should also be indicated that the auditor is not expected to express a general or purely personal preference for one accounting alternative over another when it is clear that the Accounting Standards Committee itself, or accepted practice when a matter is not covered by the *Handbook*, are unable to define the circumstances in which each method is acceptable. (See recommendations in paragraph 5.73 on the subject of the disclosure of management judgment when this situation prevails.) With these cautions, the wording should be strengthened to emphasize that the auditor is not relieved of an obligation to consider whether a method is appropriate *in the circumstances of the enterprise* just because the method is used by other enterprises in their particular circumstances.

5.53   In addition, we believe the auditor has a particular responsibility, when faced with situations for which there is no clear precedent, to be satisfied that the accounting proposed is reasonable in relation to the substance or economic reality of the thing or transaction accounted for. In such cases, the ingrained tendency of the auditor to ask what is "generally accepted" should not be relied upon to provide an answer. It is conceivable that a precedent can be found or an analogy can be made to existing practice that suggests one answer to the accounting, while consideration of the substance of the matter and ordinary prudence suggests another. We believe the auditor ought to be, and is entitled to be, aggressive in indicating his or her preferences in such a situation. It will be better for the accounting profession if less desirable practice does not become entrenched before standard-setting committees have a chance to look at the problem.

RECOMMENDATION

R-18 The general principle that the auditor should be satisfied that the client's accounting policies are appropriate should be continued. The CICA Auditing Standards Committee should amplify that standard to emphasize that:

- When an accounting standard is stated in general terms and judgment is required as to the accounting policy to be adopted for implementation, the auditor should be satisfied that the accounting policy used is a fair and reasonable interpretation of the spirit of the standard.

- When new accounting policies are adopted in response to new types of transactions or new kinds of assets or obligations, the auditor should be satisfied that the accounting policies adopted properly reflect the economic substance of the transaction, asset, or liability in accordance with the broad theory governing present-day financial reporting and the established concept of conservatism in the face of uncertainty.

- When the selection of an accounting policy is arbitrary in certain named areas, the auditor is not expected to object to the selection of an established alternative, notwithstanding that the auditor may have a personal preference for one of the possible alternatives.

Estimates of Amounts of Assets and Liabilities

5.54 Accounting attempts to be a measurement science. However, it does not, and inherently could not, achieve the precision of a science. Measurement of the financial activities of any business entity is based on many estimates. Some of these estimates result from activities as routine as splitting the continuous flow of business activity into discrete periods of time. Others are less commonplace. In all estimates management must exercise judgment, and the auditor must be prepared to evaluate that judgment.

5.55 It is sometimes questioned whether it is appropriate for the auditor to second-guess management. It is argued that no matter how much time and effort an auditor spends on an annual audit engagement, management will always have more knowledge of the business. It seems to follow that management's decisions will always be more accurate. This is not necessarily an appropriate conclusion. Every auditor should acquire a knowledge of the client's business and, although perhaps lacking in some of the intimate knowledge available to management, the auditor has the advantage of an objective view that management cannot possess. Thus, the auditor not only can, but must, second-guess management's estimations. Resources critical to the auditor's activity include professional skepticism and the use of outside information such as industry norms and technical experts.

RECOMMENDATION

R-19 The CICA Auditing Standards Committee should amplify auditing standards to emphasize the auditor's responsibility to come to an independent opinion on the reasonableness of management's estimates.

The Auditor's Overall View

5.56 Many comments have been made to us to the effect that auditors should "stand back" after their work is done and decide whether the financial statements really provide a balanced presentation of what the auditor knows about the financial affairs of the company. If the auditor has indeed monitored management's judgment every step of the way in the selection of accounting policies and in the making of estimates, the occasions in which the financial statements cannot meet this test should be rare. Nevertheless, we believe that encouragement of the stand-back point of view is warranted as a final test of the individual conclusions reached by the auditor in the course of the audit.

5.57   What the auditor should be concerned about are the possibilities that:

• Accounting policies adopted, although complying with the letter of *Handbook* recommendations (or GAAP not codified in the *Handbook*), depart in important respects from the spirit of the recommendations. Although unusual, it is possible that a *Handbook* recommendation may be quite inappropriate for a particular type of situation or transaction that was not contemplated when the apparently applicable accounting standard was drafted. Transactions may even be deliberately structured so as to receive a particular treatment under a literal reading of a standard when common sense suggests that there is no chance the standard was intended to be applied in that way. This may be saying no more than that transactions should be accounted for according to their substance rather than their form. However, there may be a tendency to overlook that basic concept when a transaction appears on the surface to be directly covered by a *Handbook* recommendation.

• Judgment estimates made by management, although each individually falls within a zone of reasonableness, are all biased with the result that the cumulative bias is materially misleading in the context of the real financial strength of the company.

5.58   The question the auditor must always ask himself or herself is, "What is going on here?" A stand-back look at the overall impression conveyed by the financial disclosure complements the auditor's verification of the individual figures and descriptions in the financial statements. But the injunction that the auditor stand back and consider the overall impres-

sion has to be interpreted very carefully. The reason we have accounting standards is to provide a collective judgment on what is important to report. In the last analysis, accounting standards have to be broadly acceptable to achieve compliance. This occasionally means that information that some would regard as important may not be reported.

5.59   Accordingly, when we say the auditor should stand back and evaluate the overall impression provided by the financial statements, we are not suggesting that the auditor should step outside the framework of accounting theory that is implicit in present accounting standards. The auditor is not expected to substitute personal judgment for standards that are established collectively through due process procedures. What the auditor should be asked to do is to see that (1) application of the principles and judgments called for under the present governing theory of financial reporting does not produce figures that are misleading under any reasonable interpretation of the objectives of that theory, and (2) gaps in principles required to implement those objectives also do not permit misleading results. (See also our comments in paragraphs 3.33 to 3.42, especially 3.41 and 3.42.)

RECOMMENDATION

R-20   The CICA Auditing Standards Committee should amplify auditing standards to stress the auditor's responsibility to be satisfied that the end result of the client's application of accounting principles, judgment estimates, and disclosure is not materially misleading.

Auditor Association with Information outside the Financial Statements

5.60   Accounting literature contains a considerable number of ideas about additional services that might be offered by auditors. Sometimes the authors of such literature argue that additional responsibility should be assigned to the auditor in the public interest. For example, it has been suggested that auditors should provide some measure of assurance with respect to interim financial information, current cost or current value information when included in the annual report, management forecasts, and so on. The ideas propounded could be described generally as recommendations that the auditor take some measure of responsibility for all financial disclosures of the company, not just for the annual financial statements.

5.61 The most immediate concern, we think, should be with information contained in annual reports, especially information with natural direct links to the audited financial statements. The audited financial statements are included in the annual report. We consider it likely that some members of the public do not distinguish between the auditor's responsibility for information in the financial statements and information elsewhere in the annual report, in view of the confusion we have found as to the responsibility of the auditor for the financial statements themselves. If such confusion exists, its importance will be magnified if a Management Discussion and Analysis is included in the annual report. We also believe that it would be valuable if the somewhat subjective information in that report received some review by the auditor.

5.62 At present, the *Handbook* calls for auditors to arrange to read drafts of annual reports before they are printed. The purpose is to identify inconsistencies between the financial statements and other information in the annual report that might indicate errors either in the statements or the other information.[8] The *Handbook*, however, also suggests that the main purpose of this review is to prevent any undermining of the credibility of the information in the audited financial statements, not to provide assurance as to the general accuracy or reliability of the other information. We think this goal is too limited. We also note that there is a difficulty in implementing even this limited goal, since the auditor has no legal right or obligation to see the annual report before its issuance.

5.63 We think the CICA should adopt a more positive position concerning the auditor's responsibility for financial disclosure in the annual report but not part of the audited financial statements. We think the profession should take the position that an auditor should not accept an engagement to report on financial statements without having the right to examine

and comment on the document in which those statements are to be included before it is published. The auditor should also require the right to refuse consent to publication of the audit report if the auditor seriously objects to the other financial disclosure in the document. These rights could be implemented by appropriate wording in the auditor's contract with the client. It will be noted that this recommendation is based upon the link between audited financial statements and the document in which they appear. Its principle is not restricted to information in annual reports, although that is the situation in which it will most often be applicable.

RECOMMENDATION

R-21 Auditing standards or provincial codes of conduct, whichever is the more appropriate, should be amended so that auditors will accept an engagement to report on financial statements for public distribution only on the condition that they have a right to (1) review and comment on financial disclosure outside the financial statements that is intended to be included in the document in which the audited statements are to be published, and (2) refuse consent to publication of the audit report in association with that disclosure if the latter is seriously objectionable.

5.64 Some financial disclosure, such as interim financial statements, is included in documents that do not contain audited financial statements. An argument can be made that the auditor should have some involvement with all financial disclosure of a client in the interests of contributing to its quality. This argument is not as strong as the argument that the auditor should have a responsibility to review financial disclosure outside the audited statements that is included within the document that contains the statements. The Commission, therefore, does not suggest that the CICA go so far in this case. Nevertheless, it is probable that an auditor's review of financial disclosure in documents other than those containing audited financial statements would often be worthwhile. In such cases, auditors should be prepared, on request, to perform the additional work necessary to provide some added credibility to that disclosure.

5.65 The possibility of acceptance of additional responsibility by the auditor for financial information outside the financial statements requires that consideration be given to (1) the procedures to be taken by the auditor to fulfil that responsibility, and (2) the form of report that the auditor should make (if any) to acknowledge and describe the responsibility. For example, depending on the circumstances, the procedures performed by the auditor might consist of one of the following:

- A simple comparison of the financial information outside the financial statements with the statements to ensure that there is no conflict between them.

- The preceding procedures together with a reading of the whole document in which the financial disclosure is contained to see whether anything in the document is contrary to knowledge that the auditor holds as a result of his audit engagement.

- The foregoing enhanced procedures together with more active inquiry of management or other sources as to the basis for the financial disclosures and accompanying explanation, but without necessarily verification procedures.

- Verification procedures similar to those employed in an audit examination.

The auditor's communication might correspondingly vary from:

- No report at all.

- A statement, conveyed privately to the audit committee and/or the board of directors, that the auditor's work did not discover any misrepresentations.

- A similar statement published along with the information to which it relates.

5.66 In framing recommendations for some auditor responsibility for, and reporting on, information outside the financial statements, we expect the CICA will give careful consideration to the legal effect of such possible extension of auditor responsibility. There may be times when the financial information to be reviewed is so "soft"—i.e. hard to substantiate—that an auditor cannot realistically do anything that adds to its credibility. In such a case, the auditor simply should not be associated with the information in any way. There will be other times when an auditor can add some credibility to the information, but there necessarily remains a significant possibility of error in it. In such cases, the auditor should not accept any responsibility for the information unless it can be made clear, by law or contract, that the auditor's responsibility is limited to unmistakable failure to do what was required to add the measure of credibility requested.

5.67 The recently adopted Section 5020 of the *Handbook* dealing with a public accountant's "association" with information supplied by others provides a context for consideration of these matters. U.S. standards, existing and proposed, give much more detailed procedural guidance for auditor involvement with various types of information such as interim financial statements, information supplemental to the audited financial statements, and Management Discussion and Analysis.[9] This guidance could be adapted for Canadian use with little difficulty.

RECOMMENDATION

R-22 The CICA Auditing Standards Committee should provide more guidance to appropriate procedures to be undertaken by the auditor, and the appropriate form of communication of the auditor's involvement and findings, with respect to all types of financial disclosure outside the traditional financial statements. This includes both information with which the auditor is required to be involved by auditing standards, and information with which the auditor may be involved by special engagement with a client.

IMPROVING PUBLIC UNDERSTANDING

5.68 In the first part of this chapter we have made recommendations for additional financial disclosure both inside and outside the audited financial statements. In the second part of the chapter we have considered possible extensions of auditor responsibility with respect to financial information provided outside the financial statements. In several places we have commented on the confusion on the part of members of the public as to the respective roles of management and the auditor in the provision of financial information. Very little that we have recommended has spoken directly to public misconceptions of the role of the auditor. But, if such misconceptions exist, they can obviously contribute to a gap between public expectations concerning what the auditor should be doing and what the auditor is actually doing in particular circumstances.

5.69 Many people urge that the profession should mount a campaign to educate the public so as to remove these misconceptions. We are frankly skeptical that any such efforts would be effective in reaching users of financial information, let alone the public at large. Moreover, the educational campaign would need to be repeated regularly. Even then, it would be quite possible that in some difficult case an aggrieved group of users could claim that they were never adequately informed about, for example, the limitations of an audit opinion.

5.70 Accordingly, we believe that the most constructive action that can be taken by the profession is to ensure that the separate responsibilities of management and the auditor are spelled out in communications accompanying the financial information. Even this will not be fully successful if the users of financial disclosure do not read and absorb this communication. But, at least the communication will be before the readers. We suggest three ways to reduce public misunderstanding: (1) better explanation in the financial statements of the inevitable role of judgment in financial reporting, (2) inclusion of a Statement of Management Responsibility in annual reports, and (3) expansion of the standard audit report.

Disclosure of the Role of Judgment in Financial Reporting

5.71 Our survey and inquiries show that different segments of the public hold different views concerning the scope for exercise of judgment in financial disclosure. There were, however, enough representations made to us by people who believed that management bends the rules, that auditors do not stand up sufficiently against management pressure, and that the situation is getting worse that we think the profession should be concerned. It is of particular concern that some of those who hold these beliefs are securities regulators, legislators, and government authorities whose trust and goodwill is of great importance to auditors.

5.72 There are two possible benefits from action to improve the public's understanding of judgments underlying information in financial statements. First, removal of misconceptions about the need for judgment in financial reporting can lessen public disillusionment on those occasions when it becomes apparent that past judgments have been wrong. Second, increased disclosure of detail of management judgments actually made can convey an impression of what is known colloquially as "the quality of earnings" (more conservative judgments produce earnings figures of higher supposed quality) and can sometimes even help a reader make some very approximate estimate of what would be the effect on the figures should different judgments have been applied. The principal question is how these desirable results can best be achieved.

5.73 Present accounting standards require that management summarize, as a note or separate statement accompanying the audited financial statements, the significant accounting policies that govern the figures reported in the statements.[10] The purpose of this requirement is essentially the same as that we have been discussing—the improvement of readers' understanding of the basis for the figures presented to them. It therefore seems quite logical that management's statement of accounting policies might be expanded to become a more comprehensive explanation of the basis for financial reporting. Such an explanation could include:

- A statement (where applicable) that, in accordance with the "historical-cost" accounting theory, figures in the financial statements are derived fundamentally from amounts established by transactions in which the company has engaged, and that they do not (except when specifically disclosed) constitute realizable values or any other current valuation.

- A summary (similar to the present required explanation) of the significant accounting policies that the company follows to produce the figures reported in the financial statements.

- An explanation, where applicable, of alternative accounting policies permitted by GAAP that management might have selected, when such policies would have resulted in reporting significantly different figures. This explanation should be accompanied to the extent possible by an indication of what the effect would have been on the figures presented of choosing a different acceptable accounting policy. (See paragraph 4.54.)

- An explanation of the bases upon which management has exercised its judgment in matters of valuation and estimation or of implementation of accounting policies. This explanation could be made more pointed by bringing together disclosures of judgments made that are now required by accounting standards but are usually scattered through the notes (such as estimates of useful lives of fixed assets by types of asset). Some comment on the possible scope for variation in reasonable judgment would also be helpful. The general principle should be that there should be full but compact disclosure of all the areas in which judgments have been required that have a significant effect on the financial statements. As well as enhancing user understanding, this disclosure should have the incidental benefit of focusing the auditor's attention on the judgments and their significance to results reported, both separately and in their overall effect.

RECOMMENDATION

R-23 The CICA Accounting Standards Committee should amplify the present standard requiring disclosure of accounting policies, so as to emphasize:

- The underlying theory of accounting being followed.

- The judgments made in the selection of accounting policies and the effect, if significant, of choosing one alternative from two or more acceptable policies (see Recommendation R-8 in paragraph 4.54).

- The judgments and estimates made in the valuation of assets and liabilities and the implementation of accounting policies, together with the evidence supporting such judgments.

Detailed disclosure of actual judgments and estimates made by management could be usefully integrated with the disclosure.

Statement of Management Responsibility

5.74 The inclusion of a Statement of Management Responsibility in the annual reports of public companies has become quite common in the last 10 years. Such a report was recommended by the Cohen Commission in the United States in 1978 and subsequently received support in that country from the Financial Executives Institute, the AICPA, and the SEC. In Canada, the Adams Committee recommended the use of a management report, also in 1978. In 1981, a joint Study Group of the CICA and FEI Canada published recommendations for the content of such a report. Support for the inclusion of such a report in company annual reports has been provided by a notice of the Canadian Securities Administrators and by the regulations to the Quebec Securities Act. A survey of practice over the years 1981 to 1985 disclosed use of the management report by a significant number of leading Canadian public companies.[11]

5.75 We believe that such a management statement should be provided in the annual reports of all public companies containing, as a minimum, the following management assertions:

- Management has responsibility for preparing all the information in the financial statements, including any accompanying explanatory notes and schedules. Preparation of the information necessarily requires estimates, and these reflect management's best judgment. In addition, management might wish to state its responsibility for all information in the annual report and add that financial and operating data contained outside the financial statements in that report are consistent, where applicable, with the financial statements.

- Management is responsible for the records that provide the data included in the financial statements and for maintenance of internal controls that provide reasonable, but not absolute, assurance that assets are safeguarded.

- The accounting policies adopted are within GAAP and are judged to be appropriate.

5.76 There is some difference in practice in the positioning of the management statement within the annual report.

- Some companies include the statement of management responsibility within the audited financial statements. One attraction to this approach is that positioning the statement of management responsibility in close conjunction with the statement of accounting policies emphasizes management responsibility for the selection of those policies. It would be easy to obtain universal adoption of the management statement in this position because all that would be required would be a simple change in accounting standards.

- Other companies place the statement of management responsibility outside the audited financial statements. This would lessen the possibility of public confusion concerning the auditor's responsibility for management representations. On the other hand, provision of the statement cannot be required by accounting standards if it is outside the financial statements, and in this situation some companies will probably choose to continue not providing a statement of management responsibility. Only a change in the law is capable of guaranteeing that given information will be provided outside the financial statements.

5.77 The survey mentioned in paragraph 5.74 indicates that approximately one quarter of Canadian public companies now provide statements of management responsibility. Approximately three quarters of these place the statement outside the financial statements. This position was recommended in the 1981 Notice of the Canadian Securities Administrators. We agree that this position is logical in view of the fact that the management statement may refer to information other than that included in the financial statements.

RECOMMENDATION

R-24 The CICA should support a legal requirement that management clearly acknowledge its basic responsibility for the information in the audited financial statements. The management statement should be outside the financial statements themselves, but should be published in close association with them.

Expansion of the Standard Audit Report

5.78 For some considerable time there has been a debate between those who think the traditional two-paragraph audit report tends to be mere boiler plate, devoid of meaning, and those who believe that a simple report is desirable to clearly convey the message—that an audit has been done and the result is (or is not) a "clean" opinion. For example, the Cohen Commission heavily criticized the standard audit report as having become a mere symbol that is no longer read.[12] On the other hand, the Adams Committee said: "We have no particular objection to the standard report being treated as a symbol, as long as the meaning of that symbol is properly understood."

The Committee's inclination was towards a shorter simplified form of standard report.[13]

5.79 The principal concern of the Cohen Commission was that the audit report did not adequately inform the reader of the auditor's function, the nature of the auditor's work, and the responsibilities assumed. The following examples were cited as aspects of the audit that should be communicated more fully:[14]

- The fact that the financial statements are the representations of management, as explained in the management report.

- The nature of the work carried out in the course of audit examination.

- The fact that the auditor considers accounting policies adopted by management to be appropriate in the circumstances.

- The auditor's agreement or otherwise with management's assertions (in a management statement of responsibility) as to the strength of the accounting system and internal accounting controls, if management has made such assertions.

- A description of material weaknesses in the accounting system and controls if management has made no representations on this score.

- A description of the auditor's association with other financial information disclosed by management, if such association exists.

5.80 The threshold issue to be addressed is whether the audit report should be expanded in an attempt to convey more fully the nature of the auditor's responsibility for the information provided by management, the extent of the auditor's work, and the degree of assurance the audit provides.

5.81 The Adams Committee, as noted, stated a preference for a "shorter simplified form of standard report" rather than a longer, complex report.[15] It is hard not to be sympathetic to the desire for plain language and brevity. But we must ask whether such a report can do the job. The evidence is that the present

audit report is misinterpreted (whether or not it is read) by significant segments of the public. We doubt that simplification of the standard audit report would improve the situation. Removal of details concerning the scope of the audit or the facts that professional standards exist concerning the financial information presented and the work done by the auditor would hardly contribute to the lessening of misconceptions. We also suspect that simplification of the wording only would prove more difficult than one might think. It is hard to explain a technical process in non-technical language, especially if brevity is desired.

5.82 Given that public misconceptions do exist concerning the audit function and given our doubts as to the effectiveness of a program of educating financial statement users, we have concluded that the audit report should be made more explicit concerning what the auditor does and does not do. Thus we come down on the side of an expanded audit report.

5.83 We leave for detailed consideration by the CICA the question of precisely what should be the content of an expanded audit report. We have already referred to recommendations of the Cohen Commission. The American Institute of Certified Public Accountants (AICPA) has just adopted new and expanded standard audit report wording. In view of the internationalization of global capital markets we believe that coordination of accounting and auditing standards is of considerable practical advantage. We recommend that the CICA examine carefully proposals that are made in the United States and elsewhere and, in the interests of international harmonization, adopt the same wording as that recommended elsewhere so long as the CICA agrees with the intent of such recommendations.

RECOMMENDATION

R-25 The CICA Auditing Standards Committee should adopt an expanded standard audit report to explain more fully the nature and extent of the auditor's work, and the degree of assurance it provides. To the extent possible, the same wording should be used in the Canadian standard audit report as that used in other major industrial countries.

5.84 We note that the AICPA proposes to retain standardized wording in the audit report even though its content is expanded. According to the Decima survey, a majority of the public feels the audit report would be more informative, and therefore more likely to be read, if auditors had the flexibility to say what they thought was important without being constrained by a standard format.[16] This was the situation some fifty years ago before the profession began issuing recommendations based on collective deliberations. It is well to remember that an important reason why the profession recommended a standard audit report was that it was hard for the public to tell from the reports they were receiving whether the audits of companies were being conducted to some common standard. It was also sometimes hard to tell, based on the reading of a mixture of observations on the accounts and descriptions of audit procedures carried out, whether the auditor was rendering a clean opinion, a qualified opinion, or no opinion at all concerning fair presentation of the financial statements taken as a whole. A standard audit report using standardized wording was adopted to cure this problem. It did cure the problem. We would fear a regression to the former situation if standardized wording (whatever it says) were to be abandoned. Standardized wording, especially if it conforms to international norms, is also less likely to be open to misinterpretation in legal actions.

SUMMARY

5.85 This chapter focuses on the satisfaction of public expectations for financial disclosure. The focus is not confined to audited financial statements because the Commission believes that a significant segment of the public feels that the auditor has some responsibility for financial information provided outside the financial statements, particularly if it appears in the same document as that which contains the audited financial statements.

5.86 Conceivably there is a vast amount of financial information that could be disclosed. The Commission has assumed its mandate extends to consideration of disclosure to reasonably well-informed users of financial information but not to the special information needs of professional analysts.

5.87 The audited financial statements have been the traditional means of conveying financial information to the general reader. The long-term trend has been towards an increase in information within the financial statements and some presentation of highlights and interpretive information outside the financial statements, particularly in the annual report. The Commission believes that it is useful to provide information in these two ways. The financial statements can be reserved for classification and reliable measurements of the results of transactions and events that have taken place. Analytical and interpretive information, including forecast figures where appropriate, can be expressed outside the financial statements.

5.88 Based on the evidence it has gathered, the Commission has concluded that a limited extension of financial disclosure beyond that customary at present would be desirable. The Commission believes that accounting standards for financial statements should be amended to provide better guidance to disclosure needed when continuance of a business as a going concern is in doubt. Accounting standards should also be amended to call for fuller disclosure of (1) the specific risks and uncertainties to which an enterprise is subject, (2) commitments that have not received formal recognition in the balance sheet, (3) bases for writedowns of assets below cost-based figures, and (4) bases for accounting estimates and the range possible in estimated figures within the exercise of reasonable judgment.

5.89 The Commission also recommends that the CICA be responsive to developing public needs for financial disclosure outside the financial statements. A Management Discussion and Analysis analyzing recent periods' results and providing information relevant to a company's present and prospective liquidity is suggested.

5.90 The Commission believes the auditor can make a contribution to the quality of financial information provided by management. That contribution depends upon the auditor's willingness to exercise independent judgment concerning management's selection of accounting policies and the estimates made by management in fulfilling its accountability obligation. The auditor not only should examine the individual judgments made by management in these two areas but also should be satisfied that the impression conveyed by the financial statements as a whole is not misleading. The Commission recommends revision of auditing standards to emphasize these responsibilities of the auditor.

5.91 The Commission also believes that some degree of auditor review of financial disclosure outside the financial statements would be desirable. The auditor should review such financial disclosure contained in any document that also contains audited financial statements. The auditor should also be prepared, upon request, to review other financial disclosure. The CICA should provide comprehensive guidance to the appropriate procedures and reporting in the various situations in which the auditor is called upon to review information outside the financial statements.

5.92 The evidence gathered by the Commission leads to a conclusion that some part of the public expectations gap is caused by lack of public understanding of the extent of judgment required in presenting financial information. A further part is caused by misunderstanding of the auditor's responsibility for the information. To lessen these misunderstandings, the Commission recommends (1) better disclosure in statements of accounting policies of the accounting theory that forms a basis for the policies and of the possible impact of judgment on the information presented, (2) a separate statement of management's basic responsibility for financial information presented, and (3) expansion of the standard audit report to explain more fully what the auditor does and does not do and the degree of assurance provided by an audit.

References

1. *CICA Handbook*, Section 4510, "Reporting the Effects of Changing Prices" (Toronto: CICA).
2. Decima Research Limited, Executive Summary of *Public Opinion Survey* (1986), see Appendix B, p. 152.
3. *CICA Handbook*, Section 5510, "Reservations in the Auditor's Report," pars. 51-53.
4. See *CICA Handbook*, Section 3280, "Contractual Obligations."
5. See *Title 17, Code of Federal Regulations*, Regulation S-K, Part 229.303.
6. *CICA Handbook*, Section 1505, "Disclosure of Accounting Policies," par. 01.
7. *CICA Handbook*, Section 5400, "The Auditor's Standard Report," par. 13.
8. *CICA Handbook*, Section 7500, "The Auditor's Involvement with Annual Reports."
9. See AICPA Auditing Standards Board, *Other Information in Documents Containing Audited Financial Statements*, Statement on Auditing Standards No. 8 (New York: AICPA, December 1975); *Reporting on Information Accompanying the Basic Financial Statements in Auditor-Submitted Documents*, SAS No. 29 (July 1980); and *Review of Interim Financial Information*, SAS No. 36 (April 1981). See also the proposed Statement on Standards for Attestation Engagements, *Examination of Management's Discussion and Analysis* (December 1986). Certain other Statements on Auditing Standards might also be pertinent to an integrated philosophy with respect to the auditor's involvement with information outside the audited financial statements.
10. *CICA Handbook*, Section 1505, "Disclosure of Accounting Policies."
11. See CICA, *Management Reports in Annual Reports 1981-1985* (CICA: Toronto, 1986).
12. The Commission on Auditors' Responsibilities, *Report, Conclusions, and Recommendations* (New York: AICPA, 1978), pp. 72-73.
13. The Adams Committee, "The Report of the Special Committee to Examine the Role of the Auditor," *CAmagazine*, April 1978, pars. F1, F3.
14. Commission on Auditors' Responsibilities, *Report*, pp. 77-79.
15. Adams Committee, *Report*, par. F3.
16. Decima, *Survey*, Appendix B, p. 151.

6

Professionalism

6.1   A professional holds out a promise of special skills in an area in which the ordinary layman is often not competent to judge the quality of service. Many occupations are claimed to be professional; only a few make good their claim. Certain characteristics mark the true skilled or learned profession. First, a lengthy period of education and training for the profession is required to attain its special skills. Second, good judgment is necessary for competent exercise of those skills. Third, the skills must be exercised so as to meet the standards of the profession, which cannot be compromised for any reason of expediency.

6.2   In Chapter 2 we listed the chief public expectations of auditors. In addition to a number of specific expectations, we noted that the public expects the auditor to be impartial in opinion and competent in performing expected tasks. In effect, we are saying that the public expects the auditor to be professional. The public also does not expect to be forced to examine the auditor's work critically to determine whether it is up to standard. Because of the difficulty in evaluating the quality of service, members of any profession, including that of auditing, must earn the public's trust. To achieve this, some form of regulation of service is normally seen as necessary or desirable. Matters of concern include:

* Prescription of the educational program required to qualify for membership in the profession.

* Control over admission to the profession to see that entrants are qualified and trustworthy.

* Assurance of continuing competence after admission to membership, possibly requiring measures to monitor quality of service by members and

continuing education to see that they remain up-to-date in their skills.

* Codes of professional behaviour so that members continue to justify the public trust.

* A disciplinary process to deal with apparent unsatisfactory behaviour or performance by members.

Over the last one hundred years accountancy has gained the status of a profession and needs to be concerned to maintain it. For auditors, the obligation to be professional begins at the level of the individual and extends to the educational and quality control efforts of firms and to the leadership of firms. Accountants in industry and government must also recognize a personal responsibility to demonstrate professionalism. The efforts to this end of both auditors and accountants not in practice are furthered through professional development programs, practice inspection and advice, and other services provided by their professional associations.

6.3   Because of the specialized knowledge base of a profession, external regulation of such matters as education and standards of performance may not be very effective. Accordingly, most professions are granted broad powers of self-regulation by law. Some people believe there is an inherent conflict in such delegation of powers. For example, if a profession controls standards for admission, it is argued it has the power to restrict the supply of services and thereby raise the cost of service beyond that which would prevail in a free market. On the other hand, members of a profession will reply that admission standards set and monitored by competent professionals are necessary to maintain the quality of service. Members of the public are not ordinarily equipped to distinguish for themselves between good quality and poor quality service because a profession's body of knowledge is so specialized. Thus, a tension exists between those who believe in the virtues of unrestricted markets for services as well as goods, and those who believe that some interference in pure market forces is necessary to protect the quality of professional service. As in most matters of social policy, the truth is not all on the one side or the other. A balance needs to be struck in the public interest.

6.4   There are two possible sources of confusion in any reference to "the profession" in the context of accountants or auditors:

•   The first is the fact that there is not just one association of accountants in Canada or in a particular province. There are three sizeable bodies of accountants with different designations: the chartered accountants, the certified management accountants, and the certified general accountants. The history of the incorporation and development of each of the three bodies is different, but in the end result all are similar in that their members are at the same time members of both a provincial association and national body, with different functions being assigned to the provincial and national levels.

•   The second is the fact that the principal objectives of the three associations differ to some degree. Much of the impetus for the formation of the associations of chartered accountants came from members in public practice and, from early times, education for public practice has been a major interest. The association of certified management accountants, on the other hand, has from its inception been dedicated to helping its members perform effectively as part of management in industry or government. The association of certified general accountants also originated with an orientation to members in industry but now, like the chartered accountants, seeks to serve the interests of both members in industry and in public practice.

6.5   Because of the existence of several accounting associations and the broad division of function between accountants in public practice and accountants in industry, a simple reference to "the accounting profession" can be unclear. Some might take such a reference to refer only to those in public practice (especially those engaged in audit services). By extension, some think of the accounting profession as embracing all chartered accountants since all CAs have met the common standard required for qualification as a public accountant. Under the broadest usage of all, however, the accounting profession is taken to mean all those who have achieved a high level of accounting-related skills, whether they are occupied in public practice or not.[1]

6.6   Since this Commission is concerned with public expectations of auditors, the comments we have to make will largely be directed to those accountants who are engaged in public practice. For convenience we shall use the term "the auditing profession" in these comments, notwithstanding that the services of accountants in public practice embrace more than just auditing. Any recommendations we make that are directed to the auditing profession will generally apply to all who render audit services regardless of the accounting association to which they belong. However, a number of our recommendations deal with accounting and auditing standards that are established by committees of the CICA. For this reason, as well as the fact that the study was commissioned by the Board of Governors of the CICA, a number of our comments are specifically directed to all accountants who are CAs, even though many CAs are not engaged in auditing.

6.7   An additional source of possible confusion to the public lies in the existence of both provincial associations of accountants and national bodies whose names include the same accounting designation as do the provincial associations. Thus, for example, there are the Institutes of Chartered Accountants of Alberta, British Columbia, and so on, and there is the Canadian Institute of Chartered Accountants. This division has its roots in the peculiarly Canadian division of powers between provincial and federal governments. Since the self-regulatory powers of the institutes of chartered accountants stem from provincial legislation, it would be difficult to change the present organization in a fundamental way. In spite of this, virtually all accountants would agree that some professional functions are best performed on a national scale.

6.8 Appendix C provides a description of the means taken by the institutes of chartered accountants to maintain the professionalism of their members, particularly those members in public practice. In the remainder of this chapter we comment on coordination of the efforts of the provincial institutes, quality control within firms, current threats to the professionalism of auditors, auditing standards and standard setting, the quality of auditors' performance, and the impact of professional liability.

COORDINATION OF THE EFFORTS OF THE PROVINCIAL INSTITUTES OF CHARTERED ACCOUNTANTS

6.9 When the provincial institutes of chartered accountants were formed, and for some time thereafter, the practice of public accounting was largely local. Today, much of business operates on a national or international scale. It is obviously desirable that the quality of professional auditing service across the country be uniformly high. This means that there should not be major differences in the way that the several provincial institutes perform their functions.

6.10 The education function provides one example of interprovincial coordination. Because the Interprovincial Education Committee takes responsibility for the Uniform Final Examination, sufficient assurance is provided concerning the quality of education that persons admitted to membership in one institute are automatically eligible for membership in any other institute (with the additional requirement in Quebec of proficiency in the French language). We consider in succeeding paragraphs whether public expectations of auditors suggest a need for greater coordination of other functions.

Continuing Professional Education

6.11 Maintenance of the quality of professional service is, of course, of public concern. One possible way to affect quality of service is to introduce a requirement, as the British Columbia Institute has and the

Saskatchewan Institute is considering, that all chartered accountants engage in formal programs of continuing professional education (CPE). Such a requirement was advocated in the Report of the CICA Long-Range Strategic Planning Committee.[2]

6.12 The arguments against mandatory CPE are not based on opposition to the principle so much as they are on the question whether a *mandatory* plan is what is needed. Some feel that practice inspection, discussed below, is a more direct way to assure the quality of service of members in practice. A scheme of mandatory CPE would also require administration to see that its requirements were fulfilled. This could be complex because practitioners routinely participate in many conferences, seminars, and in-house educational programs. If the CPE requirement is to be effective, there would logically need to be some means to evaluate these programs to determine whether they qualified as fulfilment of the requirement. If the CPE requirements were to apply to non-practising members, the administration would be further complicated. The Commission has not made sufficient study to take a position on the question whether the additional cost of a mandatory CPE program is justified by its potential benefits.

Practice Inspection

6.13 A second way to encourage the maintenance of standards of service is through a practice inspection program. Existing procedures under the programs conducted by provincial institutes are described in Appendix C. There is some question whether practice inspection conducted on a province-by-province basis is the most effective way to proceed. The audit of a company of any size is a cooperative venture for which several people bear significant responsibility. The audit report is signed in the firm name, not by the individual partner in charge of the engagement. Quality control policies of a national firm will be laid down and monitored on a national basis.

6.14 Accordingly, it is somewhat anomalous that practice inspections of the offices of such a firm should be conducted by a number of different provincial institutes. It is true that every individual professional bears the ultimate responsibility for his or her behaviour. But it is only realistic that practice inspections should look beyond individual performance and consider as well those firm policies and procedures that are designed to maintain quality on audit engagements. Once again, the Commission has not made sufficient study to form an opinion whether present practice inspection programs are satisfactory as a practical matter. However, we can see that a need for interprovincial coordination of effort exists in principle.

Professional Discipline

6.15 Professional discipline procedures provide a further motivation to members to maintain their skills. The discipline function is performed by the provincial institutes since the legal authority to discipline members stems from the provincial acts by which the institutes are incorporated. Differences in the legislation mean that discipline procedures cannot be completely uniform across the country.

6.16 The Government of Ontario's Professional Organizations Committee, which reported in 1980, commented favourably on the discipline procedures of the Ontario Institute of Chartered Accountants.[3] We have not attempted a comparative study of discipline procedures country-wide. However, we have gathered the impression that most members of the public, including senior securities administrators and other government officials, have little knowledge of the disciplinary process of the profession. Although the outcome of discipline proceedings against members, when unfavourable, may be published in professional communications to members, as they are in Ontario, the public generally does not get to know about them. If the public were aware of the existence of disciplinary procedures, more complaints about auditors' services might be made to the institutes. As it is, the public ignorance of institute procedures for professional discipline permits, if not encourages, an impression that the profession is a closed shop that will naturally tend to protect its members against attack.

6.17 Even though we have no evidence to cause us to believe the disciplinary process is not basically sound, we think there is a need for improving public awareness of its existence. At the same time we think consideration should be given to making improvements in present procedures so that responsiveness of professional discipline procedures is enhanced

across the board. For example, such questions as the following should be addressed:

- Should complainants have a right of appeal if a screening committee decides that a complaint made by a member of the public should be rejected without reference to the disciplinary process?

- Should there be some lay representation in the disciplinary process?

- What public notice, if any, should be given to disciplinary hearings and their results?

- Should there be special publicity given to disciplinary proceedings in which there is a large public interest—say, proceedings related to the financial reporting of public companies—even if there is lesser publicity given to more routine cases?

- Are there any other procedures that can be adopted to assist the investigation of cases with a large public interest that involve complex issues?

Professional Ethics

6.18 The profession's code of conduct provides a final instance of the need for interprovincial coordination. We see no good reason why there should be different codes of conduct for chartered accountants in different provinces. We believe a national code would be desirable from the standpoint of the public posture of the profession. It may be that individual provincial institutes would desire some supplementary rules to fit their particular circumstances. This desire can be accommodated, so long as provincial supplementary rules do not contradict the national code; but we think a national code is desirable and should be attainable.

Coordination of Effort

6.19 The profession has recognized the need for interprovincial harmonization of certain functions and has taken steps to that end. As we have already noted, there has long been an interprovincial education committee. In 1984, an interprovincial agreement was reached whereby individual provincial institutes took on roles as coordinator with respect to certain other areas of interest. The areas assigned to date include: professional conduct, practice review, career information and recruitment, and public relations and information.

6.20 To date much of the effort of the provincial co-ordinating bodies appears to have been devoted to gathering comparative information about what is being done by each provincial institute in each area of interest, and sharing information and ideas with respect to specific problems. Although such activity is valuable, more positive steps will be necessary if any significant harmonization of provincial procedures is to be achieved. The greatest progress towards harmonization appears to have been made in the area of codes of professional conduct, and it is expected some amendments to provincial codes will be made shortly to bring them more nearly in line on a national basis.

6.21 We have not considered the question of inter-provincial coordination in sufficient depth to suggest how best it may be achieved. We do, however, think that the public does expect the profession to have high and uniform national standards of competence and behaviour, and will be intolerant of any failure to achieve those standards that is attributed merely to jurisdictional boundaries. We think the profession needs to find ways to achieve the goal of harmonization of its standards, and we raise the question whether present efforts are enough.

RECOMMENDATION

R-26 The provincial institutes of chartered accountants should seek effective practical mechanisms to promote country-wide uniformity in self-regulatory functions that are designed to ensure a high quality of service to the public. An incidental objective should be to find ways to increase public awareness of the profession's self-discipline procedures. Three subjects suggested for priority action are coordination or harmonization of (1) the profession's code of conduct, (2) the profession's practice review procedures, and (3) the profession's disciplinary procedures.

Discipline of Audit Firms

6.22 One matter, in particular, concerns us. Discipline proceedings are always taken by provincial institutes against individual members. This follows from the fact that institute disciplinary powers stem from their provincial statutes. The practice is quite unrealistic, however, in the context of audits of companies carrying on business in many jurisdictions and audited by firms that are regional, national, or international in scale. We have already pointed out, in paragraph 6.13, that any sizeable audit engagement is a cooperative venture. Responsibility may be shared by several partners in the firm, and the performance of staff on the engagement will be affected by the firm's training programs and standard operating procedures.

6.23 In these circumstances, logic suggests that discipline proceedings with respect to such large engagements should often be taken against the firm instead of, or as well as, individuals who worked on the engagement. We recognize that there may be impediments in the way of doing so under the present powers of an institute. We have not examined these in the depth necessary to make positive recommendations. We do recommend, however, that the several provincial institutes study how best to make firms as well as individuals accountable in discipline proceedings. It may be that there are means other than amendment of statute—for example, through the possibility of limiting the rights of firms to train students—to obtain results equivalent to those that might be obtained by direct disciplinary proceedings.

RECOMMENDATION

R-27 Provincial institutes of chartered accountants should study how to effectively bring audit firms as well as individual members within the ambit of disciplinary proceedings.

QUALITY CONTROL WITHIN FIRMS

6.24 Before leaving the subject of self-regulation, we should like to emphasize that the efforts of professional associations to promote good work are unlikely to be effective unless the normal quality of performance by individual practitioners and firms is high. Auditors of public companies carry a particular responsibility for the quality of work and reputation of the profession. This thought leads us to two observations:

- It has been pointed out that, as a matter of simple arithmetic, if a firm has one hundred audit partners whose careers as partners with primary responsibility for clients average twenty-five years, and if each partner makes only one serious mistake in judgment in his or her career, the firm as a whole will have to cope with an average of four audit engagements each year in which a serious mistake has been made. Obviously, large firms have significant procedures to minimize the adverse probabilities suggested by this statistic, in their own self-interest as well as that of the public. Among them, typically, is a requirement for a "concurring" or "colleague" partner review of the financial statements of clients that are large or are deemed to be particularly risky before the statements are "signed off." We note that the report of the Treadway Commission recommends a strengthening of the concurring partner role, including involvement of the concurring partner in the planning stage of the audit.[4] In addition, firms should make it easy, in fact should make it mandatory, that any serious difference of opinion between partners be resolved through a well-designed consultation process within the firm (and, if necessary, outside it).

- Because of their size, large firms have a special need for strong formal quality control procedures within the firm. In particular, they should ensure that regular firm quality control reviews cover a representative sample of work performed (possibly with more intensive scrutiny of risky audit engagements) and do not avoid the review of certain engagements because they are too large or are so specialized that a review would be arduous. In addition, there should be stringent follow-up of any procedural deficiencies discovered to see that they do not continue uncorrected.

6.25 We make these, perhaps obvious, points not because we are aware of deficiencies in the quality controls of any firms. We are simply aware that con-

stant vigilance is required to maintain quality, and sometimes the collegial atmosphere within an organization can hinder necessary self-criticism. In this connection, legal liability is an increasing concern of the profession. One must expect that the courts will be inquiring into the existence of procedures such as these in actions in which negligence is alleged. The presence or absence of effective quality control measures in a firm could affect the outcome of such actions.

THREATS TO THE PROFESSIONALISM OF AUDITORS

6.26 In Chapter 2 we reported the public's strong expectation that auditors ensure that the impartiality of their opinions is not endangered by considerations of self-interest. In Chapter 3 we noted that, ironically, the institutional arrangements for financial reporting and audit seem almost designed to make it difficult for the auditor to maintain independence. We concluded that some strengthening of the auditor's position was desirable. Among other things, we advocated more effective use of audit committees and improved accounting standards to that end. In the next few paragraphs we consider other suggestions for strengthening the auditor's position and assess current threats to professionalism.

Modification in the Manner of Auditor Appointments

6.27 We have argued that any radical change in arrangements for the audit appointment would entail severe disadvantages. We comment below on some minor modifications that have been suggested.

6.28 To begin with, we do not believe that the possibly greater safeguard of having two auditors (as banks now do) would justify the additional cost for the typical company. An alternative suggestion is that auditors be appointed for a longer term, say, five years, so that they would be less concerned about early loss of the audit appointment in the event of a disagreement with management. It seems to us, however, that auditors generally expect to have a long-term relationship with clients and vice versa. If so, we doubt that security of tenure for up to five years, which would become steadily less as the term expired, would have a large influence on their conduct. In addition it would be difficult to negotiate fees for a five-year term. Companies frequently change their scale of operations, buy and sell businesses, and make other changes that affect the audit effort required. If fees had to be renegotiated often during the term of the audit appointment, the apparent security of the longer tenure might well be illusory. In short, the suggestion seems to us both unworkable and likely to be ineffective in enhancing independence.

6.29 Another suggestion is that there should be a mandatory rotation of auditors after a three or five-year term so that the auditor would automatically be stripped of a concern for retaining the appointment. While this expedient might or might not have some such positive effect on auditor independence, which is by no means assured, we are persuaded its possible advantages would be more than offset by the additional costs and risks involved. Establishing a new audit relationship entails costs for both the auditor and the client. Moreover, some U.S. research shows that a disproportionate number of audit failures take place within a relatively short period after the appointment of a new auditor.[5] Also, the constant churning of auditor appointments could have a result opposite to that intended. If audit firms had to continually seek new appointments, they would not want a reputation of being hard to get along with—a reputation not easy to shake, however fairly or unfairly applied. Nor would there be the normal development of constantly improving standards resulting from familiarity with the client's business and the justified increase in mutual confidence between auditor and management that most auditors and companies do achieve over time.

6.30 In brief, we believe proposals such as these concerning the manner of the audit appointment are merely tinkering at the edge of the problem. They do not address the basic structural problem identified in Chapter 3, so that they fail to get to the heart of the independence issue. We regard our proposals for improving communication with the audit committee and improving the quantity and quality of information supplied in the audited financial statements, or in association with them, as being much more forthright and fundamental. In addition, we believe

there can be no substitute for the profession finding resources within itself to counter threats to the auditor's independence. Audit firms must be highly conscious that any backsliding from professional behaviour to gain a temporary commercial advantage, or a relaxation of standards merely to avoid loss of an existing audit appointment, will in the not-too-long run damage the firm itself and the profession. Although the obligation to be professional attaches to all chartered accountants in public practice, the larger firms have a particular responsibility. It is their work that is most in the public eye and has the major public impact, and it is the audits of public companies that are most obviously touched with the public interest.

Client Acceptance and Retention

6.31 Some threats to an auditor's professionalism stem simply from inadequate selectivity with respect to clients. To a considerable extent, an auditor's work in verifying the position shown by financial statements depends upon the cooperation of the client. If the client lacks integrity, perhaps to the point of actively wishing to mislead the auditor, the auditor's task is made much more difficult if not impossible. Such situations are very risky from the auditor's point of view. The risk is that the auditor may not succeed in obtaining fully satisfactory evidence of the state of financial affairs of the client and yet may give an unqualified opinion on the financial statements in reliance upon management assertions and in the absence of firm evidence that the statements are in error.

6.32 An audit firm's first line of defence against this possibility lies in its procedures for acceptance of clients. Some concern was expressed to us that, in the competitive environment of recent years, audit firms may have become less cautious than they should be in accepting new clients as a result of their eagerness to maintain and expand their client base. We have no basis for an opinion whether this concern is well founded. Even if we did, however, we would have no recommendation for collective action by the profession. We believe the cure, if it is needed, would lie with the firms themselves and would include:

- A systematic investigation of prospective clients to obtain reassurance as to the integrity of its owners, directors, and management.

- Acquisition of knowledge about the business of the client so as to gain a full appreciation of risks that could have an impact on its financial reports.

- Assurance that the audit appointment is sufficiently comprehensive to permit necessary verification. For example, if a company is one of a related group of companies, it will be convenient, and may even be necessary on occasion, to be the sole auditor for the entire group in order to obtain satisfaction that related party transactions are properly accounted for in the financial statements of individual components of the group.

- Communication with any predecessor auditor (as is called for by professional ethics and contemplated by most corporations statutes) to obtain any information he or she may have that is pertinent to the acceptance of the engagement. We also stress here the professional obligation of that predecessor auditor to be open with a professional colleague to the full extent consistent with the need to maintain confidentiality about the client's affairs unless released from the obligation by the client. (See further comments in paragraphs 7.47 to 7.48.)

6.33 If our advice is followed by all audit firms, it is conceivable that some public companies might be unable to fulfil their statutory obligation to have an audit because of lack of confidence by auditors generally in the management. We do not think this constitutes a reason for retreating from our advice that auditors should not accept untrustworthy clients. Rather, we think companies that have great difficulty in obtaining auditors must be prepared to make arrangements to enhance the integrity of their management. The point is that it is the obligation of public companies to have auditors; it is not the obligation of any auditor or of auditors generally to be any particular company's auditor. If, in future, deserving companies cannot get auditors, that will be the time to consider the nature of the problem and what an appropriate solution might be. In any event, a firm need not take on a risky engagement on the grounds that every company is entitled to an audit. There is no such obligation or imperative.

6.34 Notwithstanding an auditor's best efforts to screen out unacceptable clients, it is always possible that a client may be accepted whose management turns out, on better acquaintance, to be untrustworthy. It is also possible that a change in control of an existing client may introduce untrustworthy elements. In Chapter 7 we discuss the auditor's disclosure responsibility upon resignation or dismissal from an engagement.

Competitive Bidding

6.35 While auditing firms must be concerned not to accept clients lacking integrity, they naturally have a strong interest in obtaining new clients that are acceptable and retaining the clients they have already. We are aware that in recent years competitive bidding for audits, including competition on price, has become increasingly prevalent. There are divergent views on this development. Auditors generally believe that the competitive pressure has forced them to become more efficient and innovative. Some are also confident that the gain in efficiency is not at the expense of the quality of the audit. Some, however, see distinct dangers in the situation.

- There is concern that an auditor who has negotiated a cut-price fee may attempt to mitigate the adverse effect on firm income by reducing audit work.

- There is concern that competitive bidding may easily lead to unhealthy competition, in the sense that it will lead to deterioration in the quality of the audit.

- There is concern that acceptance of fees that are below cost or that cover incremental costs only and make no contribution to a firm's fixed overhead can destroy the economic base of the profession and leave it without the resources to attract the quality of entrants into the profession that is needed to maintain its standards.

- If, on the other hand, firms negotiate low fees to acquire an engagement in the hope of recouping losses on reappointment in future years, the Cohen Commission suggested that they thereby acquire a stake in the future prosperity of the client and compromise their independence.[6]

6.36 Both the Adams Committee and the Cohen Commission looked at the problem of competitive bidding as a problem in professional ethics. The Adams Committee recommended that firms' bidding practices should be included among those things looked at in professional practice inspections by the institutes.[7] That recommendation implies that proper and improper bidding practices can be reasonably easily distinguished. We are not so sanguine. Neither are we convinced that the institutes would be wise to attempt to set some guidelines for fee setting. Unlike some other professions, chartered accountants have never attempted to prescribe or recommend fee scales. We believe this policy remains appropriate.

6.37 Having said this, we should add that we do believe a problem exists. We believe that audit firms, particularly the larger ones, should make a critical review of their bidding and fee-setting practices. It should be obvious that if a firm sets its fees to cover only the incremental costs of an audit, it will only be a matter of time until it suffers heavy losses in its audit work. It has been suggested that this is not necessarily irrational since discounted audit fees may lead to an insider track on consulting work. Reliance on cross-subsidization in this manner, however, seems not only dubious ethically but also unwise in the longer term. In the long term a firm must cover all its costs. If it must charge enough for consulting services to help cover unrelated audit costs, it will be vulnerable to competition from consulting firms that do not have the same burden.

6.38 An alternative possibility is that efforts to cut costs will lead to audit failures—an outcome that could be disastrous for an audit firm. To avoid these unfortunate consequences, a firm may have to lower its growth targets for a period, but in the long run that may prove the wisest policy. We may add that a firm should consider the added legal risks it assumes when it negotiates an obviously non-compensatory fee, or even no fee at all, for an audit. As a minimum, the onus of proof to show that a good job was done, despite the fee-cutting, could well shift. Drastic fee-cutting is likely to be perceived by disinterested third parties, be they courts, insurers or the public, as counterproductive and inconsistent with other claims made on the part of the profession.

6.39 In short, we think audit firms cannot deny the benefits of competition to their clients. In pricing their services, however, they must remember their professional duty to do good work and their own necessity to cover their legitimate costs. Above all, they must remember that their ultimate obligation is to the shareholders and the public. They must do a proper audit, whatever it costs, or not do it at all.

Financial Dependence

6.40 A more obvious threat to an auditor's impartiality exists if the auditor is not financially independent of a client. That threat has long been recognized. Legal and ethical rules exist against an auditor or members of the auditor's family holding investment or other financial interests in a client. It has been suggested, however, that financial independence is not assured merely by prohibition of a financial stake in a client's business as such. In particular, if one client or associated group of clients accounts for much of the income of an auditor, he or she may lose some measure of independence merely because of the unfavourable impact on the auditor's livelihood from a loss of the appointment.

6.41 Little evidence was submitted to us to suggest that this is a problem in practice. On the other hand, the problem could exist and never be brought to light (except in the extreme case of an audit failure in which the auditor's judgment manifestly appears to have been subordinated to that of the client). From the profession's point of view, it is vital that auditors not only maintain their independence but also be seen by the public to do so. The Adams Committee recommended that institute rules of professional conduct specifically require that fees from one audit client or group of associated clients not exceed a given (unstated) percentage of the auditor's gross fees. Coupled with this was a warning to larger firms to ensure that their income-sharing arrangements do not leave individual members or offices of the firm equally vulnerable to the loss of individual clients or client groups for whose audit they are responsible.[8]

6.42 We can see problems in defining an associated group of clients. It could also be difficult to frame rules sufficiently flexible to allow smaller but growing firms to temporarily exceed a percentage limit of fees from one client group in order not to inhibit the firm's growth. Notwithstanding this, we think the profession needs to address the threat to the auditor's independence posed by commercial pressures. We would think that a possible loss of ten percent of the revenue of a firm (which could translate into a considerably higher percentage of net income for partners) would be a matter of concern to any firm. We think the profession should consider very carefully whether there should be some limitation on the percentage of revenue that a firm can derive from one client or associated group, or whether some other criteria could be found by which controls could be framed to limit excessive dependence on one client or client group.

RECOMMENDATION

R-28 Provincial institutes of chartered accountants should consider how to limit potential threats to the auditor's independent judgment caused by the fact that a significant percentage of revenue comes from one client or associated group of clients.

6.43 The independence of an individual partner of a firm can also be threatened in a less obvious way. To some extent, a partner's influence within a firm tends to be correlated with the importance of the clients for which he or she is responsible. Consequently, a partner could hesitate to be the cause of losing an important audit engagement, even though the fee revenue from it may be only a small fraction of the total firm revenues. There is no rule of professional conduct that could be effective against this subtle threat. The proper defence lies in the ethos of the firm itself. No partner should be thought less of for doing what has to be done—indeed, the contrary should be true. A partner should be expected to consult in difficult situations—not to escape responsibility, but to ensure the position taken is right. If that is done, the firm must be prepared to back up the partner, whatever the consequences.

Influence of Non-Audit Services

6.44 One of the most persistent concerns expressed about auditor independence in the last twenty-five years is that the performance of non-audit services

(i.e. consulting services of various kinds) for an audit client may jeopardize independence. We reported in Chapter 2 our finding that a significant segment of the public considers that the performance of non-audit services has a potential for affecting an auditor's independence. A 1986 U.S. survey of "key publics" indicated an even higher level of belief in the potential effect of non-audit services on auditor objectivity. The potential was considered to vary from little or no likelihood of an effect to a great deal of likelihood depending upon the specific type of service performed.[9]

6.45 No actual instances were cited to us of an auditor apparently not maintaining independence because of the performance of non-audit services. Rather, it was the potential threat that seemed to be of concern. That threat, it is felt, could stem from various aspects of such service:

- First, as a matter of economics, the more non-audit services a firm performs for a client, the more the firm potentially has to lose through the loss of the audit (although it does not necessarily follow that the loss of the audit engagement would automatically lead to a loss of all other work). This, it is feared, could influence an auditor to defer more to the client's judgment than is justified.

- Second, it is feared the desire to obtain an inside track on consulting services could lead an audit firm to discount proposed audit fees and thereby intensify the problem of competitive bidding discussed earlier.

- Third, certain kinds of non-audit services could have implications for the client's financial reporting. For example, an argument with respect to the appropriate basis of taxation of a company's income may be strengthened if it is shown that accepted accounting conforms with the position to be taken when filing the income tax return. In such a situation, it is feared that tax advice given by the accounting firm as to the most advantageous tax treatment could conflict with an auditor's impartial assessment of what is the most appropriate accounting. This may, however, be more a matter of the narrower concept of conflict of interest than of the broader concept of independence.

- Fourth, as a practical matter, consulting advice is likely to influence the actions and business decisions of the client. If that advice turns out badly, it is feared the auditor may be less vigorous in pressing necessary accounting action on a client—such as recognition of losses—because to do so would reinforce the dissatisfaction already felt by the client concerning the matter. This, too, could be more a matter of conflict of interest than of independence as such.

6.46 Public accounting firms are well aware of these concerns. Nevertheless, perhaps not surprisingly, they were virtually unanimous in submissions to us that the concerns were unfounded. Indeed, the firms suggested a number of reasons why the performance of non-audit services does not carry these dangers in practice, but rather is beneficial:

- An audit necessarily involves acquiring a good acquaintance with a client's accounting systems and controls. An audit firm is in a good position to perceive and suggest possible improvements. An assignment to perform additional study to enable detailed recommendations is likely to be less costly for clients, particularly smaller clients, than would be a consulting assignment by an outside firm which had to start from scratch.

- Conversely, consulting assignments may bring to light information that is helpful in planning and performing the audit.

- Moreover, the development within the firm of consulting skills, even skills unrelated to accounting, can assist the audit function. For example, a firm that has actuarial skills in-house is able to to call on these skills to assist in the audit of pension costs. The same is true of knowledge gained through consulting for different industries. We have already noted that a lack of knowledge about specific industries can be one of the sources of audit failure in a world that is increasingly complex.

- A further point is that the existence of a variety of skills within a firm provides greater opportunity for career development on the part of its members. As a result, it should be easier to attract and retain good people, and this should have a posi-

tive effect on the quality of audit service as well as other services.

- Finally, it has been put to us that the potential dangers seen in non-audit services may be more imaginary than real. In practice, non-audit services tend to be carried on by different people than those who are responsible for the audit. Frequently the consultants are not accountants. The auditors also have a stake in the good financial reporting of their clients, year after year. While the long-term relationship with a client can be endangered by bad consulting work, it is normally unlikely to change the audit firm's opinion on the financial statements because of the need to protect its reputation and credibility as auditors.

6.47 Over the years a number of study groups (among them the Cohen Commission and the Adams Committee) have given serious consideration to the question whether the performance of non-audit services may injure auditors' independence. In every case it has been concluded that, although a potential danger exists, there is virtually no evidence a real problem exists. Our conclusion is much the same. Based on the evidence, we believe it would serve no useful purpose to forbid performance of non-audit services for audit clients. Indeed, such a blanket prohibition would probably be harmful in its overall effect. This is particularly true for smaller businesses. The auditor's exposure to a wide range of business problems, coupled with familiarity with the affairs of a particular business as a result of the audit examination, makes him or her peculiarly well qualified to offer constructive advice to the small owner-managed company.

6.48 Nevertheless, the perception by a significant percentage of the public that auditors are or could be influenced in their audit judgments by the effect of non-audit services must be acknowledged and addressed. We have asked ourselves whether there is any effective way to improve the situation. One suggestion is that there should be disclosure in the financial statements of the value of non-audit services performed by the auditors so that users of the statements could form their own opinion as to the possible risk to audit integrity. There is no reason in principle why this should not be done, and we would not be against it. However, there is reason to doubt the practical value of such a requirement. The U.S. Securities and Exchange Commission required such disclosure in proxy statements for a number of years but then abandoned the requirement on the grounds it did not appear to be useful.

6.49 A more drastic suggestion is that rules of professional conduct be amended to prohibit an auditor from deriving revenue from non-audit services for a client that is very substantial in relation to the audit fee (say, equal to or greater than the amount of the audit fee). An even more extreme suggestion would be to forbid the performance of non-audit services for audit clients. In the absence of more compelling evidence of an actual independence problem, we are reluctant to advocate measures such as these that would interfere with the rights of business to obtain advice where it seems most advantageous. In any event, any such restructuring of the profession and its freedom of enterprise within a legal and professional framework should only be undertaken after a very detailed study including a careful analysis of all the consequences, and not just the perceived effect on auditor independence. At this point, there is no reason for us to recommend such a study or to expect such a study would come to a different conclusion than we have. Whether this continues to be the case will depend on future developments, including the behaviour of the profession, especially its major firms.

6.50 The fact remains that there are occasions when a client's actions following consulting advice may have to be evaluated for the purposes of financial statement presentation. This being so, auditors need to bear in mind that their professional responsibility is to maintain their impartiality when signing an audit report on the financial statements. They cannot let perceived advantage to the client company, or their own desire to avoid debate over the accounting consequences of a client's actions in respect to which they have advised, to interfere with that responsibility. Auditors may consider this fundamental proposition so obvious that it does not need to be stated. We think, however, that the growth of non-audit services has reached a point where the profession needs to make a public affirmation that an auditor will not permit any advice that his or her firm may have given on a consulting assignment to influence the impartial evaluation of evidence required for

the purpose of the audit opinion. The auditor's legal duty should also be borne in mind. There may be times when prudent auditors will wish to seek legal advice to ensure that they are meeting their legal responsibilities as independent auditors.

RECOMMENDATION

R-29 The profession's codes of conduct or interpretations of the codes should be amplified to speak to the potential consequences if non-audit services are performed for an audit client. It should be stressed that the auditor has a professional obligation in assessing audit evidence to avoid any bias or predisposition that could result from advice given to the client in a consulting capacity. Independent advice from third parties may be helpful on occasion to ensure compliance.

Pressures on Audit Performance

6.51 We turn now to a discussion of various pressures upon the auditor's judgment and objectivity that may arise in the course of an audit. The first of these is the practice known as "opinion shopping." Upon occasion a disagreement arises between management and an auditor as to the accounting treatment to be given to a particular transaction or event or class of transaction. The question at issue in essence will be a question of what is the generally accepted accounting principle governing the accounting treatment adopted—that is to say, it will be a question of interpretation. Such questions are often difficult to answer in practice for a variety of reasons. For example, more than one principle may appear to be pertinent to the issue and the accounting treatment to be adopted may differ depending on which principle is considered to be governing.

6.52 In such a situation management may wish to obtain an accounting opinion from a qualified expert other than its auditor. The derogatory description "opinion shopping" suggests that management is actively searching for some expert who will support its point of view. But that is not necessarily the case, although it may be so. Management has the primary responsibility for financial reporting. Accounting issues in practice are frequently not clear cut. Management is entitled to take steps to obtain the best possible advice, including second opinions, concerning how to fulfil its reporting responsibility.

6.53 Nevertheless, there are distinct dangers to the position of the auditor in the practice of opinion shopping. The auditor, too, has a professional obligation to arrive at an objective judgment on the merits of the client's proposed accounting treatment. An auditor does not lightly disagree with a client over an important issue. Too many such disagreements poison relations with a client which, in turn, makes performance of the audit more difficult. Serious disagreements are also likely, sooner or later, to lead to displacement of the auditor in favour of another.

6.54 Consequently, an auditor is highly motivated to research contentious accounting issues very carefully. If, after such research and consideration, the auditor must continue to disagree with a client, the odds are that the arguments favouring the auditor's position are strong. Another public accounting firm, in contrast, is under no such pressure. Indeed, an unconscious motivation may exist to try to find a way to agree with the position taken by management since a company in serious disagreement with its auditors may well be looking to retain a new firm in due course. Or, less questionably, the other firm may simply see it as an opportunity to demonstrate its superior professional ability by finding an acceptable answer that escaped the firm's regular auditor. In addition, the outside public accounting firm called on for an opinion almost inevitably lacks the depth of knowledge about the company in question that is possessed by its auditor. There is some danger that the outside firm may not obtain all the information that is pertinent to a judgment on the issue.

6.55 We believe that public accounting firms asked for an accounting opinion by a client of another firm will generally try to guard against these dangers. Even so, opinion shopping still represents a potential threat to the impartial judgment of the auditor. The auditor is charged with forming an independent opinion on the accounting treatment. Often issues are not black and white. If management can say to the auditor that another reputable accounting firm agrees with management on a particular issue, it may be

practically very difficult for the auditor to insist that his or her judgment is unalterable.

6.56 Every auditor knows that professional judgments by reasonable people can differ. Moreover, if the auditor remains fixed in the original position in the face of a contrary opinion by an equivalent expert, the relationship with the client, already strained, can be ruptured irrevocably. In the face of all this, it is quite possible that an auditor will accept management's proposed accounting treatment supported by the other firm on the grounds that it is "generally accepted," even though the auditor continues to be unconvinced as to its merits. When this happens, the role of the auditor has in effect been overridden, in this case with the assistance of another auditor.

6.57 How serious is the problem of opinion shopping? Our information is that it occurs relatively infrequently. On the other hand, we are led to believe that it is more common in the United States and it is not infrequent to find American developments repeated in Canada after a certain time lag. Moreover, a considerable number of accounting firms expressed concern about opinion shopping, indicating that they perceive it as a significant potential threat to their professionalism. We believe the problem should not be ignored by the profession, but the present evidence does not suggest the need for drastic measures.

6.58 Once again our primary recommendation was made in Chapter 4—namely to use the audit committee to strengthen the auditor's independence. We have suggested that the audit committee become familiar with the accounting policies of the company and review their appropriateness with the auditor as well as with management. As an extension of that we have suggested that the audit committee be informed of all disagreements between management and the auditor over matters of accounting policy and of any accounting advice sought by management from parties other than the auditor. If this function is performed responsibly by the audit committee, we believe it will be helpful in resolving accounting issues on their merits. It can also strengthen the tenure of the auditor in the most proper of all ways. This is by demonstrating to the audit committee as representatives of the whole board that they are being well served by their auditors. Unless they are heedless of their responsibility, audit committees and directors are most unlikely to acquiesce in any management proposal to replace auditors for reasons that could be attributable to issues on which the audit committee agreed with the auditors.

6.59   We believe also that the cure to the worst features of opinion shopping lies with the professionalism of the accounting firms themselves, especially those that are asked to provide opinions to clients of another auditing firm. With one exception, we do not believe that action is required by the profession collectively. The exception relates to the present provision in the rules of conduct having to do with advice sought from one public accountant by an audit client of another firm. The present rules direct that the accountant from whom advice is sought should inform the auditor that such advice has been requested, unless the client requests in writing that such disclosure not be made. This proviso represents an easy means of circumventing the intent of the rule.

6.60   We believe it is necessary that the accountant from whom an opinion is requested and the incumbent auditor should communicate openly and fully about the accounting issue. Thereby, misunderstandings as to facts and circumstances bearing on the issue will be removed so far as is possible. We do not believe the legitimate interests of the client are hurt by this, since the auditor will already be aware of the facts and the accountant from whom advice is requested is entitled to equal knowledge. We therefore recommend that the rules of conduct require that accountants from whom advice is sought refrain from giving an opinion unless the right is granted to communicate fully with the incumbent. The accountant should have the obligation to communicate with the auditor once the client grants that right. The incumbent auditor should have a corresponding obligation to explain his or her position to the other accountant.

RECOMMENDATION

R-30   The profession's codes of conduct should be amended to require an accountant from whom advice is sought by the client of an incumbent auditor to communicate with that auditor before expressing any form of opinion. In the course of that communication, the accountant requested to advise should confirm the pertinent facts of the situation with the incumbent

auditor. The auditor and the accountant consulted should each have an obligation to discuss fully the factors that lead them to the position they have taken or propose to take.

6.61   We do not suggest that the rules of conduct should spell out further the required behaviour of the accountant consulted or the auditor. Nevertheless, we believe fully professional behaviour on the part of both requires consideration of the responsibilities of the other. We urge firms to establish well thought-out policies to achieve that end and to establish internal procedures that ensure they are carried out. We believe, for example, the following would be appropriate:

- It should be a policy of a firm consulted that no member state an opinion, even a tentative one, on an issue raised by a client of another firm before the required communication with the incumbent auditor. The danger in stating tentative opinions is that it is all too easy to give an inappropriate opinion based on inadequate knowledge of the facts and, having given that opinion, be unconsciously influenced to stick to it to avoid losing face.

- In view of the sensitivity of a situation involving a professional colleague, it is highly desirable that the opinion requested be researched and formulated by the designated technical experts of the firm consulted. Those experts are likely to have personal acquaintance with the technical partners of the incumbent auditor. The latter will ordinarily have been consulted on any issue involving serious disagreement with a client and, therefore, will be well placed to communicate with the firm consulted.

- To facilitate the best resolution of the matter, it is essential that the incumbent audit firm be completely open about the reasons for its position. Equally, the firm consulted must be prepared to discuss the considerations that appear important to it with respect to the issue.

- If the issue is a particularly difficult or complex one, the two firms might well consider the desirability of obtaining the views of one or more other qualified experts who could be relied upon to be impartial.

• Ordinarily, the firm consulted should provide its opinion in writing including a description of the factual basis for the opinion. The incumbent auditor may well wish to explain its position in writing as well. Upon request, representatives of either firm should be prepared to attend a meeting of the audit committee to discuss the issue.

Other Issues

6.62 A number of other potential threats to the satisfactory performance of the audit exist. Most of these have been mentioned in previous studies and are reviewed only briefly in the following paragraphs.

6.63 Auditors are not required by law to conduct any examination of the interim financial statements of a client. Upon occasion some accounting issue has to be resolved for the purposes of those interim statements that is not governed by the existing accounting policies of the company and that could be open to debate. If the auditor is not consulted on the appropriate resolution of the issue at the time and subsequently concludes at the time of the annual audit that a different treatment would be preferable, a difficult situation results. Management will be embarrassed by any change that reflects on the interim financial statements already published. The auditor, on the other hand, is faced with the unpalatable choice between accepting the less desirable treatment (assuming that is even possible) and being the source of embarrassment to the management.

6.64 We believe the best way to deal with this problem is to avoid it. As we noted in paragraphs 4.6 to 4.9, the trend is toward more nearly continuous financial reporting by public companies. In such an environment, the Commission thinks it important that the auditor be consulted on a timely basis about any debatable question affecting financial disclosure. The arrangement could be formalized with respect to interim financial statements by asking the auditor to review the statements with management before they are presented to the audit committee. The objective would not be to obtain a full audit opinion on the figures, but merely to obtain the auditor's advice on

the accounting treatment and disclosure in the statements. Hence additional costs should be kept to a minimum.

6.65 Companies sometimes see early reporting after a fiscal year-end as a public signal of management efficiency. They not infrequently pressure auditors to accept deadlines that are not realistic in terms of the quality of the company's own records, the time that is required for its staff to perform necessary year-end accounting work, or the time to perform necessary audit procedures. The resulting overly tight deadlines for completion of an audit can lead to skimped audit work and sometimes errors in judgment, because adequate audit evidence cannot be obtained in time for the deadline. It has been suggested that it would be helpful if fiscal year-ends of companies were scattered more evenly through the year (by moving to a company's "natural" year-end when that is different from the calendar year-end), thereby lessening peak load pressures on auditors.[10] This idea has been advocated for many years, but unfortunately it seems very difficult to interest companies in it, and we doubt that it is achievable.

6.66 Pressures created by an audit firm's time budget, particularly if the firm is attempting to increase efficiency to improve its fee competitiveness, can backfire by creating incentives for audit staff to cut corners on necessary work. Good supervision and determination to perform the necessary work even at the expense of exceeding the time budget is necessary to counteract this danger.

6.67 The pressures described in the previous few paragraphs are familiar to all public accounting firms. We have suggested some measures to counteract or relieve them. However, it is unlikely they can be avoided completely. We believe the ultimate safeguard against the dangers mentioned must lie principally in the policies, quality control measures, and firmness of individual audit firms. No foolproof answers are to be found in modifications of the external environment of auditing.

AUDITING STANDARDS AND STANDARD SETTING

6.68 The Auditing Standards Committee of the CICA is responsible for the written expression of auditing standards. As already explained, the standards consist of broad guidance as to the necessary skills of the professional auditor, the work to be performed to fulfil the audit obligation, and the manner of reporting the auditor's conclusions. This broad guidance is supplemented by much more specific direction in a number of areas, but such specific direction does not attempt to cover what is already satisfactorily covered in a standard auditing textbook. Rather, the tendency is to concentrate on dealing with new challenges to the auditor as the need arises.

6.69 Unlike the Accounting Standards Committee, the Auditing Standards Committee is made up almost entirely of chartered accountants in public practice. This is quite natural, because the committee's work is highly technical. This is not to say that the public should have no interest in auditing standards. There could be a gap between the responsibility the public expects the auditor to take and the responsibility the profession acknowledges in its standards. The public also has an obvious interest in the auditing standards that govern the communication to the public through the auditor's report. This raises the question whether the public interest in auditing standards requires lay representation on the Auditing Standards Committee.

6.70 The Cohen Commission considered the need for wider participation in the setting of auditing standards.[11] It considered that corporate financial executives with appropriate experience and background might be suitable for membership in the standard-setting committee but did not go so far as to suggest that such diversity of background was essential. It also stressed the obvious need for obtaining participation of people knowledgeable about an industry when Industry Audit Guides were prepared.

6.71 The recent report of the Treadway Commission goes much further. It recommends that, in view of the public policy aspects of auditing standards, half of the standard-setting body should be persons not engaged in public accounting practice, so long as they are qualified and knowledgeable about auditing.[12]

The reasoning is that such persons would bring to the standard-setting body a strong sense of the public interest in such matters as the cost of audit procedures, the reliability of reported financial information, and the effect of auditor responsibility on auditor liability. One submission to us also suggested that the CICA Auditing Standards Committee be expanded to include members drawn from the business and financial community. The motivation in this case, however, seemed to be more to obtain a wider base of experience and knowledge than to obtain better representation of the public interest.

6.72 We naturally agree that auditing standards should be responsive to the public interest and reflect as wide a base of experience and knowledge as possible. The less easy question, however, is how these goals may best be achieved. There is no problem in principle with non-auditors being members of the Auditing Standards Committee. We doubt very much, however, that the inclusion in committee membership of persons who are not very well informed in the practical work of auditing would be successful. In Canada, all members of the Auditing Standards Committee are volunteers who dedicate three hundred hours or more a year to meeting their committee responsibilities. A person not actually engaged in auditing or closely conversant with it would have great difficulty in making an effective contribution to the technical work of the committee. Yet such work constitutes a very large percentage of the total. In these circumstances, it is hard to see how this involvement would, as a practical matter, strengthen the public interest component of auditing standards.

6.73 We nevertheless think it important that there should be some involvement by members of the lay public in the work of the Auditing Standards Committee. We suggest that a small advisory group be formed to meet periodically with the committee or with representatives of the committee. Members of the advisory group should be knowledgeable members of the business or government communities, but familiarity with technical auditing matters would not be a requirement. The group should be briefed periodically on matters on the Auditing Standards Committee's agenda. It should be expected to advise whether proposed standards will contribute to meeting public expectations for auditor performance, and appear to be reasonable from the standpoint of costs and benefits. The group should also be asked to suggest matters that should be placed on the committee's agenda for study. This proposal, we may note, is quite similar to one made by the CICA Special Committee on Standard Setting in 1980, but never implemented.[13]

6.74 There may be a question whether the group we suggest would be in a position to make a contribution often enough to warrant the formality of organizing the group, finding members, and holding meetings. If this were a concern, we suggest that the responsibilities of the group could be merged with those presently assigned to the existing Accounting Research Advisory Board. There might even be an advantage to broadening the mandate of the latter group to ask it to consider and advise from a public interest point of view on the direction, priorities, and performance of all the CICA's standard-setting bodies.

RECOMMENDATION

R-31 The CICA standard-setting structure should be broadened to provide a practical channel for effective advice on auditing standards from knowledgeable members of the lay public.

AUDITOR PERFORMANCE

6.75 The public expects auditors to be skillful as well as independent. We have not seen evidence that the public is disappointed on this score. Rather, the impression we gathered is one of general satisfaction with the work that auditors have performed to enable them to report. The public seems to believe that auditors are generally successful in gathering the evidence they need to perform their functions. If they have a problem, it lies in making sure that information is reported the way it ought to be and that all information that should be reported is fairly disclosed.

6.76 There has been a rising trend in lawsuits against auditors in recent years. This, however, is not necessarily an indication of deteriorating auditor performance. Counsel specializing in litigation involving auditors have expressed the opinion that the

rising trend is primarily a reflection of a more litigious environment. Research in the United States has also indicated that claims against auditors are more likely to be based upon questionable interpretations of accounting and auditing standards than upon an auditor's negligence in applying audit procedures.[14] We have dealt elsewhere in this report with questions of accounting standards and the exercise of auditor judgment concerning fair presentation.

6.77 Inevitably some critical comments about auditor performance were made to us. Since our inquiries were made over a short period, it is not possible to say whether the criticisms indicated any trend in performance. The following were the most important points made:

• Audit staff assigned to perform procedures are sometimes too junior and lack the training to perform them adequately.

• Rapid developments in certain specialized industries, such as the financial services industry, create a much higher degree of risk that the auditor who is not up-to-date will not understand, or will fail to verify, the financial consequences of some important business activity or commitment. Both partners and staff must be sufficiently knowledgeable to do an effective job.

• Auditors may not exhibit sufficient professional skepticism and obtain sufficient independent evidence to evaluate management assertions. They may also not exhibit sufficient firmness in questioning dubious judgments made by management.

The relative paucity of these critical comments suggests that deficiencies in auditor performance in the field are not major factors in any expectation gap.

6.78 While this conclusion may be some source of satisfaction, we do not think it is any justification for complacency on the part of the profession. On any larger assessment, the profession faces major challenges.

• Increased competitiveness threatens both the prestige and the perceived rewards of the profession. This can make it more difficult to attract high quality entrants to the profession and to retain trained staff and partners. The qualification and experience of a chartered accountant in practice still provide a foundation for success in many other lines of endeavour. A number of people have suggested to us that the profession is losing an undue number of good people and is failing to attract the number of qualified entrants that it needs. It is difficult to tell, of course, whether this is a temporary condition or part of a long-term trend.

- The auditing profession, in common with many other callings, is faced with the challenge of technological change. With new technologies, accounting systems are becoming, or are likely to become, increasingly merged with management information systems that continuously update information to facilitate decision-making. Technology also facilitates more complicated transactions which must be understood to enable appropriate accounting. As new technology affects information systems, the auditor must be equipped to acquire new competence very quickly—a daunting task in view of the need to sustain competence in diverse industry situations. Very careful organization will be required within audit firms to ensure that needed skills are available and applied as required.

- A review of the accounting literature suggests significant problems in education for auditors.[15] It is hard to reconcile the need for a considerable amount of technical knowledge to enable those entering the profession to be useful at an early stage in their career (consider the comments above about inadequately trained junior staff) with the need for a broad educational background appropriate for those expected to exhibit good judgment and reasoning skills throughout their careers.

- The issue of professional liability and insurance coverage represents a problem approaching, if not at, crisis proportions. We comment on this in the next section.

We have not considered these challenges in any depth in this report because they are not significant factors in any expectation gaps. They are, however, of vital concern to the profession and to its ability to attract and retain capable people. This in turn could affect auditors' performance and thus expectation gaps in the future. It is, therefore, undeniable that these challenges warrant the most careful study and considered action.

PROFESSIONAL LIABILITY AND INDEMNITY INSURANCE

6.79 Any person who owes a legal duty of care to another faces potential legal liability for negligence if he or she fails to exercise the degree of care that the law requires. The degree of care demanded of a professional is higher than that demanded of a lay person, in recognition of the special skills and expertise that the professional offers. When professionals practice in partnership, such as in a public accounting firm, all partners are liable not only for their own negligent performance but also for that of any other partner or staff member. Traditionally, it has been considered appropriate that a professional should bear the financial risk associated with such negligent performance, since this risk provides an incentive to good work and proper supervision, and will only give rise to loss when performance is deficient. Over the years, professionals have generally been able to find ways to mitigate this risk by carefully controlling the quality of work and by buying indemnity insurance, the cost of which is presumably covered in their fees.

6.80 In the past decade or so, this seemingly satisfactory arrangement has been disrupted. Several professional occupations have been affected, auditing among them. The disruption has been caused by a number of related factors: (1) an escalation in the number of lawsuits launched against professionals, (2) an escalation in the magnitude of awards for damages, (3) an escalation in legal and other costs associated with even a successful defence, (4) a consequent multiplication in the cost of insurance coverage, and (5) a reduction in the amount of coverage available so that it may well be below the amount of possible awards for damages. Lawsuits against public accounting firms can relate to any of their services, not just to their work as auditors. However, suits arising from the audit function may involve very large damage claims because of the number of third parties to whom the auditor and the firm may owe a legal duty of care. Our subsequent comments are particularly directed to this aspect of a firm's liability.

6.81 The situation described in the previous paragraph is potentially very serious for the auditing profession. A stiff penalty for negligence may well act as a desirable deterrent to bad work. But if that penalty runs to hundreds of millions of dollars and means personal financial ruin for all the principals of an audit firm, including those who are entirely innocent of the negligence, a reasonable person might well see it as far out of proportion with the gain that the audit firm receives from its fees. Indeed, it may not be too extreme to suggest that, should there be a case in which damages exceed the insurance cover, it could threaten the very continuance of the auditing profession. People with the ability to become highly skilled professionals will not choose a vocation that carries risks not commensurate with the rewards.

6.82 The insurance crisis was not generally mentioned in the submissions to the Commission, except for those from public accounting firms. Nevertheless, because of the significance of the problem to the profession the Commission felt it needed to be examined. Our inquiries with respect to indemnity insurance in Canada were limited, but were sufficient to confirm that a very difficult situation existed in the mid-1980s.

- Under a CICA-sponsored program (used generally by smaller firms) maximum coverage was reduced from the previous $10 million to $1 million in 1985. At the same time premiums were increased sharply, escalating by some 75 percent in the short period from 1984 to 1986.

- Coverage available for large firms in the normal insurance market was also reduced, with the maximum available being perhaps only one-half or one-third of what it was previously. The fact that the reinsurance segment of the industry has substantially reduced its participation in indemnity insurance is one factor in the reduction of maximum available coverage. In addition, since the industry's ability to accept risk is regulated on the basis of the ratio of premium income to capital, an increase in premium rates requires an

increase in capital for the same amount of risk coverage. Hence the sharp increase in premium rates in recent years operated to reduce the industry's capacity on its existing capital base to offer coverage.

6.83 Since 1986 the situation appears to have eased somewhat. Coverage limits under the CICA plan were increased to $2 million in early 1987 and again to $5 million in early 1988, while the upward trend in premiums has ceased. For the large firms, however, we understand coverage is still very tight, and the firms remain unable to obtain all that they desire. Throughout this period, for both smaller and larger firms, payments by insurers have formed a very low proportion of amounts initially claimed. However, some large claims have been asserted that are as yet unsettled.

6.84 The following summarizes our analysis of the problem:

- Members of the public who invest in an enterprise or otherwise entrust funds to it assume a financial risk.

- An audit of enterprise financial statements, as well as adding credibility to the accountability of management and the directors, also lessens the risks of third parties by assisting their decisions as to where to put their funds. To maximize the value of that risk reduction, it is important that audits be well performed.

- Therefore, it is reasonable to expect that auditors should not be negligent in the performance of their duties. If an auditor has carefully and conscientiously applied his or her skills in performing an audit, the exposure to adverse financial consequences should be minimal.

- In the real world, however, this will not always be true. There will always be a degree of uncertainty whether the auditor has satisfied the requisite standard of care, until a court has made a final determination. There are few precise boundaries within which an auditor's performance will be regarded as clearly satisfactory, and beyond which his or her performance will be regarded as clearly negligent. An audit cannot give complete assurance concerning the fair presentation of financial statements, nor would it be economical to perform the work necessary to give that assurance even if it were possible. The objective of an audit, therefore, is to provide "reasonable assurance" only.

- What is reasonable is a matter of opinion. To some degree, what is fair presentation in accordance with accounting standards is also a matter of opinion, since many accounting standards are necessarily generalizations. In view of these uncertainties, even where the risk of an adverse legal finding may be low, it is often prudent for auditors to make a financial settlement if the consequences of an adverse finding would be inordinate. Further, even in those cases where auditors are successful in their defence, they are unlikely to recover all of their legal costs, which may be substantial. Since auditors inevitably bear these several risks, it is reasonable for them to wish to carry insurance.

- In recent years, the rising tide of litigation indicates that auditor risks have increased. At one time auditors were liable only to those to whom they owed a contractual obligation. The long-term tendency seems to be toward a broadening in the scope of liability. It can now extend to a party whose identity was known to the auditor and who the auditor knew would rely upon the audited financial statements, regardless of whether there was a contractual obligation to that party. It can also extend to a party whose identity was not specifically known to the auditor but who belonged to a limited class that the auditor knew would rely upon such financial statements.

- There is also a perception that courts are increasingly liberal in awards of damages. Some believe that there is an unconscious attitude in assessing liability that victims should be compensated for their losses, even if they knowingly undertook the risk of loss. There may also be a feeling that no one is hurt when a damage award is covered by insurance. To the extent this feeling exists, it encourages litigation against auditors since they are usually the parties with the greatest insurance coverage and may therefore be seen as the only source of substantial funds.

- The first result of an increase in the number and size of damage awards and associated legal costs, even when the defence is successful, is a rise in insurance premium rates. Any perceived unpredictability in court decisions, however, has even worse effects. Insurance is based on the principle that risk of loss can be quantified, so that premiums can be established to cover the probable loss. If the loss becomes unpredictable, insurance companies will protect themselves either by increasing premium rates to apparently unreasonable heights to create a margin of safety or by restricting coverage offered or both. That all this has happened in the field of auditors' liability insurance is indicated by the facts set out earlier.

6.85   In the Commission's opinion, the threat to the profession from the increase in risk and the auditor's inability to obtain adequate insurance coverage is a matter for real concern. Only the future can tell the extent to which the pendulum may swing back in time. Professional liability was also a concern of the Adams Committee ten years ago, and, as noted, the situation became very much worse in the mid-1980s. Some feel strongly that the professional liability insurance industry, being largely centred outside Canada and to a considerable extent outside North America, has failed to allow for the fact that both legal procedures and the courts are more conservative in Canada than in the United States and are far less likely to make extravagant awards. However, the industry argues that it insures risks in the future, not the past, and the legal climate is showing sufficient signs of change in Canada in the direction of changes elsewhere to warrant its present approach.

6.86   Various interested parties have suggested possible changes to the law to protect the profession against the most extreme consequences of the liability crisis. Three of the more important of these suggestions are:

- A cap on liability for a specific audit engagement based upon a multiple of the fee. This would reflect in a rough way the idea that there should be a relationship between the risk the auditor is asked to assume and the reward for the assignment. If accepted, it should mitigate the insurers' problem of lack of predictability of loss. The cure might not be complete, however. Uncertainty might continue as to court findings with respect to the number of parties to whom the auditor is liable, and the degree of proof required that loss was properly attributable to the defective financial disclosure.

- A change whereby audit firms are enabled to practice in corporate form with limited liability to provide protection against financial ruin for all the principals in a firm (except for those proved to have been personally negligent). Some variations in this idea, such as the use of a limited partnership, are possible. A scheme involving limited liability would not impose a cap on the liability for any particular act of negligence, but would limit recovery to the amount of capital exposed. There would therefore need to be some public assurance that capital, together with insurance carried, was sufficient to provide a reasonable amount of protection to the public. Limited liability for auditors, however, would not change the risks taken by insurers. Hence any problems of coverage and high premiums would not be affected by such a change.

- A change to the procedures with respect to awards of damages. A loss to members of the public caused by reliance on misleading financial statements is often attributable to actions taken by management and possibly some directors to mislead. Coupled with this is a failure on the part of directors, auditors, and possibly some other party such as underwriters, to take the steps they ought to have taken to see that the disclosure was not misleading. If damages are awarded in an action, the responsibility for them is allocated by the court among the several parties to the action that are deemed at fault. Notwithstanding this, under present law the liability of each party is "joint and several." This means that plaintiffs are entitled to recover the full amount of the award from any one of the parties at fault, who then must attempt to recover their applicable share from the other parties held responsible. The practical effect of this is that plaintiffs will attempt to recover first from the party with most resources. That is usually perceived to be the auditors, whose insurance coverage is likely to be the greatest. The auditors must then proceed against the other parties, who

may by that time be unable to meet the full amount of the damage award allocated to them.

6.87 Ultimately, the answer to the profession's liability crisis depends on reaching some social and political consensus, together with better performance. On the one hand, the public is entitled to protection against misleading financial information. The audit forms an important line of defence and professional liability remains a potent means of ensuring full exercise of professional skills. On the other hand, the reasonable assurance provided by an audit will disappear if the profession withers away because of a perception that its risks exceed its potential rewards. Some balanced solution to the problem needs to be found.

6.88 The Commission, however, has not examined the subject sufficiently deeply to feel qualified to propose a solution. The nature of the solution depends upon one's opinion as to the basic cause of the problem. If the basic problem lies in unreasonable judgments by the courts, the answer may be sought in one direction. If the problem lies in unreasonable or unclear provisions of the law, the direction may be somewhat different. If the problem lies in the insurance industry's failure to adjust properly to conditions in different jurisdictions, a third direction is indicated. If the problem lies in the quality of work of the auditing profession, still another direction is indicated. If there are several contributory causes, several remedial courses of action may be appropriate.

6.89 Our inquiry into public expectations and expectation gaps has been limited as it relates to insurance questions and thus does not provide a basis for firm conclusions on these questions. It merely confirms that a problem exists. The problems of escalation of liability and of insurance cost and inadequate coverage, however, affects other professionals and other business activities as well as auditors. It may be that a solution will have to be sought in the broader context, or it may be that the auditor's case is so urgent that some special measures, such as limited liability, are justified on their own. In either event, legislators are likely to want assurance, before granting relief, that the auditing profession has its house in order and is meeting reasonable public expectations. This fact adds force to the recommendations made in this Report. Moreover, every recommendation implemented that reduces the expectation gap will also reduce exposure to professional liability. In turn, it may be hoped that this will have a favourable effect on the market for indemnity insurance.

SUMMARY

6.90 This chapter comments on the professional behaviour of auditors. These comments are addressed to all accountants in public practice and do not speak to accountants otherwise employed, even though they too may be regarded as professionals.

6.91 The accounting profession—using the term "profession" in its broadest sense—is not a monolithic institution. There are three major bodies of accountants and each has societies at both the provincial and national level. The Commission believes that the public expects auditors to display common standards and skills across the country, considering that so many public companies are national in scope. Because some self-regulatory functions of the auditing profession, such as professional discipline, stem from provincial legislation, it is not easy for the profession to enforce absolutely common standards across the country. The Commission believes, however, that this should be the goal and recommends an interprovincial committee to study the need for greater country-wide consistency in self-regulation and ways to improve public awareness of the profession's self-regulation. It also believes that professional discipline should be directed to audit firms as well as individual auditors. It is essential that the public have reason to believe that there is substance to self-regulation and that it works for the public and not just for the profession.

6.92 The Commission has been made aware of threats to the professionalism of auditors. In part, these stem from the somewhat weak position in which the auditor is placed because the audit appointment is subject to management influence. Some threats also stem from the fact that fees for audit services are established in a market setting and the market is currently very competitive. The Commission has recommended in Chapter 4 that the auditor's

position be strengthened through better communication with audit committees and through better accounting standards. The Commission's recommendations in Chapter 5 for specific additional disclosure should also reduce the pressure on the auditor by ensuring that such significant financial information is provided as a matter of course.

6.93 Apart from this, the Commission believes that the answer to threats to professionalism must lie principally in responsible and ethical behaviour by individual auditors and audit firms. Suggestions or comments are made concerning the maintenance of financial independence, maintenance of auditor objectivity when consulting services have been rendered to an audit client, and the protocol to be observed when clients seek accounting opinions from an accountant other than their auditor.

6.94 The Commission has also considered auditing standards and standard setting, which is a national function conducted by the CICA. The public has an interest in seeing that auditing standards meet its expectations to the extent feasible, and that the standards call for clear communication through the audit report. We recommend that a body with lay representation be set up to provide a public perspective on what the auditing profession should be attempting to accomplish, including consideration of the cost/benefit justification for individual auditing standards.

6.95 The Commission has received little evidence of dissatisfaction with the way auditors perform their information-gathering and verification activities. Although this means that auditor performance in the field is not a significant factor in any expectation gap, the Commission believes that it is not in itself grounds for complacency. The profession is faced with many challenges. For example, its members must keep up-to-date with rapid changes in the business activities of their clients and the manner they are carried on. They must maintain their technological competence over their careers. And the profession as a whole must maintain continuing concern for the quality of entrants to the profession and their education.

6.96 Finally, the Commission has reviewed the problem the profession faces of apparently increasing professional liability and the danger that insurance available will be inadequate to cover it. Once again, this is not a major factor in any expectation gap. The Commission, therefore, has not made the exhaustive study necessary to come to firm conclusions on appropriate remedies for the problem. It is agreed, however, that the profession needs to study how it can contribute to a solution that will be responsive to the requirements of both the public and the profession. In the meantime, any steps taken to reduce the expectation gap should alleviate both the liability and insurance problems.

References

1. This was the position taken by the CICA Long-Range Strategic Planning Committee in *Meeting The Challenge of Change* (Toronto: CICA, 1986).

2. Ibid., pp. 26-27.

3. *The Report of The Professional Organizations Committee* (Toronto: Ministry of the Attorney General, 1980), pp. 34, 136. See also Michael J. Trebilcock, Carolyn J. Tuohy, and Alan D. Wolfson, *Professional Regulation: A Staff Study of Accounting, Architecture, Engineering and Law in Ontario* prepared for the Professional Organizations Committee (Toronto: Ministry of the Attorney General, 1979), pp. 97, 336, 340.

4. National Commission on Fraudulent Financial Reporting, *Report* (n.p.: The Commission, 1987), p.55.

5. See The Commission on Auditors' Responsibilities, *Report, Conclusions, and Recommendations* (New York: AICPA, 1978), p. 109. For a more thorough study see two articles by Kent St. Pierre and James A. Anderson: "An Analysis of Audit Failures Based on Documented Legal Cases," *Journal of Accounting, Auditing & Finance*, Spring 1982, pp. 229-47; and "An Analysis of the Factors Associated with Lawsuits Against Public Accountants," *The Accounting Review*, April 1984, pp. 242-63.

6. Commission on Auditors' Responsibilities, *Report*, p. 121.

7. The Adams Committee, "The Report of the Special Committee to Examine the Role of the Auditor," *CAmagazine*, April 1978, par. G15(b).

8. Ibid., par. G13.

9. Audits & Surveys, Inc., *Public Perceptions of Management Advisory Services Performed by CPA Firms for Audit Clients*, a research report prepared for Public Oversight Board, SEC Practice Section of the Division for CPA Firms, AICPA (New York: Public Oversight Board, 1986).

10. See Adams Committee, *Report*, par. G15(a).

11. Commission on Auditors' Responsibilities, *Report*, pp. 137-38.

12. Commission on Fraudulent Financial Reporting, *Report*, pp. 59-62.

13. CICA Special Committee on Standard-Setting, *Report to CICA Board of Governors* (n.p.: 1980), pp. 138-40.

14. See studies cited in reference no. 5 above.

15. Some examples, all drawn from *CAmagazine*, are: Giles R. Meikle, "Let's Abandon Accounting Education!," May 1986, pp. 24-27; Joel H. Amernic, "Challenges and Opportunities in Accounting Education," March 1984, pp. 84-87; R.J. Anderson, "CA Education by Computer: A Programmed Approach," pp. 32-35; L.S. Rosen, "Restoring the Importance of Accounting Education," September 1982, pp. 32-36; Gordon H. Cowperthwaite and Robert J. Gayton,"Accounting Education: Brave New Proposals," September 1981, pp. 34-40; and L.S. Rosen, "Accounting Education: A Grim Report Card," June 1978, pp. 30-35. See also *CICA Symposium on Education and the Professional Accountant* (Toronto: CICA, November 1979) and Thomas M. Beechy, *University Accounting Programs in Canada: Inventory and Analysis* (Toronto: The Canadian Academic Accounting Association, November 1980).

7

Fraud; Illegal Acts; Change of Auditor

7.1   This chapter contains four major sections.

- In the first, we consider (1) how the possibility of fraud should affect the planning and performance of audits, (2) the significance of fraud for financial statements, and (3) the auditor's responsibility to report frauds discovered to the audit committee or board of directors.

- In the second, we consider how financial reporting and the auditor's responsibilities are affected by illegal activities engaged in by a client.

- In the third, we consider what further action the auditor might or should take when fraudulent or other illegal activities by a client are discovered.

- In the fourth, we discuss the auditor's responsibility to disclose to shareholders or other parties external to the company any matters that the auditor believes should be known in relation to his or her resignation or dismissal from the engagement. This discussion might equally well have been included in Chapter 6, which deals with the auditor's professional responsibilities. We have chosen to present it in this chapter, however, because of its particular significance in the context of fraud or other illegal acts by an auditor's client.

FRAUD

Reasons for this Discussion

7.2   We have not received many representations from the general public or from the financial com-

munity, excluding auditing firms themselves, on the subject of fraud. One might ask, therefore, why we have chosen to address this subject in a separate chapter. The principal reason is that we believe a significant expectation gap may exist in this area.

- If we go back far enough, we find that major auditing textbooks used to state that the detection of fraud was a major objective, if not the chief objective, of an audit. A mystique developed—if employee fraud was suspected, a business called in the auditors. As for fraudulent financial statements, what was an auditor for if not to prevent them? In this, tradition dies hard. As will be noted shortly, the evidence we have received concerning the auditor's responsibility with respect to fraud is somewhat inconsistent. Most members of the public realize that an audit does not guarantee the discovery of fraud even if it is material. However, there is a strong feeling that the auditor does have a responsibility for its discovery.

- Fraud can be a major source of financial loss to investors. Moreover, a number of the most celebrated episodes in which audit failure has been suggested have also involved allegations of fraudulent activity.

- Submissions to us from several public accounting firms indicated their belief that the public held unrealistic expectations concerning the detection of fraud by auditors.

7.3   We are influenced, too, by the fact that the auditor's responsibility for fraud is a very live issue internationally, especially in the United States and the United Kingdom. There is a strong feeling in some influential circles in those countries that auditors should take more active responsibility for the detection of fraud, thereby possibly assisting in its prevention as well. Recently, professional committees in both the United States and the United Kingdom have made proposals (now adopted in the U.S.) to redefine the auditor's responsibility to search for fraud and to increase the probability that audit procedures will detect material fraud.[1]

The Meaning of Fraud

7.4 The *CICA Handbook* provides the following definition of "fraud."

> *"Fraud" refers to acts committed with an intent to deceive involving either misappropriation of assets or misrepresentations of financial information either to conceal misappropriations of assets or for other purposes...*[2]

This definition is similar in substance, although not in wording, to an American definition of "irregularities."[3] An English definition also provides a similar definition of "irregularities," but then goes on to say that fraud is *one type* of irregularity which involves the use of criminal deception to obtain an unjust or illegal advantage.[4]

7.5 Niceties of definition need not concern us. What we are concerned with in this chapter are actions that are intended to deceive the recipients of financial information in order to gain an advantage. It may be that these should be referred to as "irregularities" rather than "fraud" to avoid any suggestion that there necessarily has to be a court finding that the actions are criminal. However, for convenience we shall continue to use the term "fraud" as defined in the *Handbook*. We note, however, that the term does not include simple theft of assets by employees or others. To be described as fraud, a misappropriation of assets must be accompanied by some attempt to deceive through falsification of the accounts or the financial statements.

Types of Fraud

7.6 There are various types or classifications of fraud. A fraud may be directed against the company,

as when an employee misappropriates assets and falsifies the accounting records to cover up. Alternatively, a fraud may be directed against outside parties, as when financial statements are misstated to induce others to invest in or lend money to an enterprise. In the first case, the company is the victim of fraud. In the second case, it is the perpetrator. Both are of concern to the auditor. The former type may be committed by an employee at any level in the organization. The latter is more likely to be committed by, or under the direction of, senior management.

7.7 Every misrepresentation of financial information is not necessarily fraud as we have described it. Misrepresentation may occur even though judgment is exercised honestly. It may also result from negligence. Misrepresentation from either of these causes is not fraud. There must be the intention to deceive or, at least, a reckless disregard of the truth, to constitute fraud. Since intentions are hard to prove, this means that there may well be times when it is difficult to say whether a misrepresentation is fraudulent. It may also be difficult, in some cases, to say whether financial information is really misrepresented.

Public Expectations

7.8 The Decima survey showed the following results. A strong majority, 86 percent of the respondents, did not believe that an unqualified audit opinion provided a guarantee that no fraud had occurred. Opinion was almost equally divided on the question whether an auditor had a duty to actively search for fraud or merely to react to fraud that he or she happened to come across. However, those who believed the auditor should actively search for fraud held that opinion quite strongly. Seventy percent of that group felt that an active search should be conducted even if it meant a doubling of the cost of the audit.[5] It seems likely that most respondents were thinking of fraud by employees against the company in their answers to this question, although the question made no distinction between employee and management fraud.

7.9 The evidence we gathered concerning the opinions of members of the financial community was as follows. Most believed that employee fraud is not normally material and that it is the responsibility of management to institute internal controls to prevent fraud or detect it when it has occurred. On the other hand, most believed that auditors have a responsibility to detect material fraud, particularly at the management level, although recognizing that it may be difficult to do so.

7.10 Taken altogether, the evidence seems to us to indicate that, if an expectation gap exists, it may lie largely in possible public misunderstanding of the degree of assurance that material fraud will be discovered by present audit procedures and not in disagreement over what the objectives of the audit should be. Nonetheless, there is probably some difference between the views of public and of much of the profession as to the auditor's degree of responsibility to actively search out fraud.

Critique of Existing *Handbook* Standards Related to Fraud

7.11 An environment in which the risk of fraud is high may be indicated by various "red flags" ranging from the general to the specific. Many of these relate to the way in which a business is managed. First, the corporation may display a weak ethical climate. For example, a single person who has a poor reputation in the business community may dominate operating and financial decisions. Second, financial pressures may exist. When a debt or stock offering is planned or concern about solvency exists, there is some motivation to make the financial situation appear better than it really is. Equally, management pressures to attain quantitative financial goals, particularly if that attainment is linked to bonuses or other types of management compensation, should trigger increased audit vigilance. Third, management style may contribute to the potential for fraud. Examples include a decentralized organization without proper provision for monitoring or reporting, constant crisis conditions in operating departments, or chronic understaffing of financial and accounting functions. Fourth, an ineffective internal control system necessarily increases the opportunities for and risks of fraud.

7.12 Current auditing standards with respect to fraud are set out in Section 5300 of the *Handbook*.[6] The substance of the *Handbook* advice may be summarized as follows:

- The auditor's objective is to express an opinion on the fairness of the presentation of information in the financial statements.

- The auditor must recognize that the financial statements may be misstated as a result of fraud or error.

- Therefore, the auditor seeks "reasonable assurance" through the application of audit procedures that fraud and error that is material to the financial statements has not occurred, or if either has occurred it has been corrected or properly accounted for.

- There is no separate or additional responsibility to detect fraud or error. To say that another way, there is no obligation to design audit procedures to detect fraud or error that is *not* material to the financial statements.

- Audit procedures cannot provide a guarantee that fraud or error is detected because they are conducted on a test basis and because internal controls contain inherent limitations. Audit procedures merely provide "reasonable assurance."

- The degree of assurance provided that material fraud will be detected is lower than the assurance that material error will be detected. The reason, in essence, is that attempts will usually be made to cover up the existence of fraud. For example, collusion between personnel within the enterprise and outside parties may succeed in falsifying the evidence on which auditors rely. In the absence of suspicion of fraud, the auditor is not likely to question such evidence.

7.13 The *Handbook* also notes that specific circumstances encountered in the examination may alert the auditor to the possibility of fraud or error. If there is suspicion of fraud or error, the auditor must perform procedures to dispel suspicion and, if unable to do so, would normally communicate with management.[7] Some additional guidance is given to appropriate action by the auditor if a member of management is involved in fraud, or the auditor encounters circumstances that suggest that management lacks good faith.[8]

7.14 Although the *Handbook* guidance is useful, we have three reservations concerning it. First, by dealing with the assessment of risk of fraud and error together, the guidance tends to downplay the need for special consideration of the risk of fraud in view of the lower level of assurance that fraud will be discovered by normal audit procedures. Second, the guidance, including that specifically directed to management fraud, sounds too much as though the auditor *reacts* to circumstances that arouse suspicions rather than planning a program to specifically look for indicators of fraud. Finally, we think the guidance would be more helpful if it discussed even more fully (1) the indicators suggesting risk of fraud, (2) what the auditor should do if the risk appears significant, and (3) the kinds of procedures that should be performed to confirm or allay suspicion of fraud.

7.15 In addition, the idea that an audit provides a lower level of assurance with respect to absence of fraud than it does to absence of error probably has not occurred to most members of the public. Even if it has, we are reasonably certain that the public would expect the auditor to do everything that is economically possible to minimize the difference in assurance. We believe that it is in this area that efforts to narrow the expectation gap should be concentrated. We deal separately below with fraud in which the company is the victim (frequently described as "employee fraud") and fraud committed by the company (frequently described as "management fraud").

Employee Fraud

7.16 *Audit procedures with respect to employee fraud.* We wish to stress that the primary responsibility for prevention and detection of employee fraud lies with management and not with the auditor. The most effective defence is a well-designed internal control system. Such a system includes the employment of competent personnel, arrangement of duties so that the work of one employee substantiates the work of another, the efficient recording of all transactions, appropriate authorization of transactions, and limitations on physical access to assets. The responsibility for the design and functioning of such a system rests with management. In fulfilling that responsibility, of course, management should balance the cost of the controls against the risks, taking into account recoveries available from fidelity bonds if fraud is discovered.

7.17 The auditor's primary objective, on the other hand, is to express an opinion on the fair presentation of financial statements. In view of that objective, it should be acknowledged that the auditor must be concerned about the possibility of undiscovered employee fraud that is material. Since the primary responsibility for discovery of employee fraud rests with a well-devised system of internal controls, it follows that the auditor should evaluate and test the functioning of the controls that are intended to reduce that vulnerability. If the auditor finds the controls defective, then an extension of audit procedures is called for. Conceivably, there might be occasions when the risk of material employee fraud is high and audit procedures after the event cannot provide reasonable assurance that such fraud has not occurred. In such a case, a qualification of the audit report would be called for accompanied, if necessary, by a comment on the inadequacy of the accounting records.

RECOMMENDATION

R-32 The CICA Auditing Standards Committee should modify auditing standards to take greater account of the possibility of material undiscovered employee fraud. The auditor normally tests the functioning of internal controls only to the extent it is proposed to rely upon them in planning audit tests. In the auditor's initial review of internal controls, however, specific consideration should be given to the vulnerability of the enterprise to material employee fraud, and to the controls against such fraud. These controls should be tested even though some other parts of the internal control system are not tested. The need for extension of audit procedures should be considered if the controls against material employee fraud appear to be weak.

7.18 *Significance to the financial statements of employee fraud.* When the auditor discovers employee fraud or is informed by management that fraud has been discovered, the first step must be to ascertain the extent of the fraud. The auditor must then consider its consequences for the financial statements. We believe that if a fraud loss is material in amount, there would need to be an indication under present accounting standards of the fact that this unusual item has affected income reported for the year. We suggest, however, that the Accounting and Auditing Standards Committees consider whether there is any need to provide additional guidance with respect to the disclosure of employee fraud.

7.19 *Reporting employee fraud to the audit committee.* If our recommendations in Chapter 4 are followed, the audit committee and auditor will discuss the financial statements before they are submitted to the full board for approval. At that time, if not before, the auditor should discuss the fraud with the audit committee and make sure the committee fully understands its ramifications. This leaves open the question of frauds that are not material to the financial statements. In some types of business, immaterial employee frauds occur regularly. The audit committee is often kept abreast of such frauds through summary reports prepared by management. We think the audit committee ordinarily need not be separately informed about such frauds by the auditor, except by specific request. However, there may be occasions when certain immaterial frauds cast light on the company's internal control system, and on the risk of loss through fraud to which the company is exposed. In such cases, the auditor should ensure that the audit committee is informed.

7.20 In general, we think the auditor should have an obligation to call material weaknesses in internal controls of which the auditor is aware to the attention of the audit committee. Such weaknesses are not only of concern to the auditor and management. The audit committee, too, cannot fulfil its responsibilities if the auditors have not ensured that it is fully aware of such discoveries. Of course, from the company's point of view internal controls should be instituted only to the extent that their benefit in reducing the possibility of fraud exceeds their cost. Especially in a smaller business, this may mean that internal controls will be few and simple. On similar grounds, the auditor would not be expected to repeatedly warn the audit committee about the absence of controls that might be required in a foolproof system, but that have been judged by management and the audit committee to be uneconomic. However, a prudent auditor will err on the side of caution in deciding when and how often to warn the audit committee of

situations in which material loss could occur, even if its likelihood is small.

7.21 At present, the *Handbook* is inadequate in its recommendations for reporting fraud and internal control weaknesses. It calls for a material fraud to be brought to the attention of management only, and it calls for possible fraud by members of management to be brought to the attention of a level of management above that thought to be implicated in the fraud.[9] With respect to control weaknesses, the *Handbook* suggests, but does not require, reporting internal control weaknesses to management.[10]

RECOMMENDATION

R-33 The CICA Auditing Standards Committee should recommend that the auditor ensure that the audit committee (or board of directors if there is no audit committee) is adequately informed about material employee frauds that have occurred, and significant weaknesses in internal controls of which the auditor is aware, particularly those that are important to fraud prevention.

Management Fraud

7.22 Management bears the primary responsibility for preparing financial reports and is legally and morally obligated not to produce misleading financial information for the purpose of gaining an improper advantage. However, since management is usually in a position to override internal controls against fraud, and since management is responsible for the preparation of the financial statements, the auditor is the first line of defence, along with the directors, against management fraud. In cases where the directors participate in fraudulent financial reporting, the auditor may well be the sole line of defence.

7.23 *Audit procedures with respect to management fraud.* We believe the profession will narrow any existing or prospective expectation gap if it faces up to the logical consequences of these observations. Accounting literature states that the auditor is justified in assuming the honesty of management in the absence of suspicious circumstances. That is perfectly reasonable. However, the auditor should also know that management fraud does occur. That being so, it is not enough for the auditor to wait for suspicions to be aroused—sometimes rather belatedly. Rather, the auditor should give explicit consideration at the planning stage of the audit, and throughout the engagement, to the risk that management is not, in fact, to be relied upon. In addition, when it is concluded that the existence of such a risk is indicated by the circumstances, the auditor must plan extended procedures to substitute for the former reliance upon the assumption of honesty.

7.24   In brief, we think the separate guidance with respect to audit procedures specifically directed to the possibility of fraud, especially management fraud, should take the following general form:

- At the planning stage of the audit, the risk of fraud should be specifically evaluated by a senior experienced auditor. The auditor should look for danger signals or "red flags." A representative list of these is set out in an exhibit to this chapter. The danger signals listed range in character from those relating to general environmental risks to those that are specific to the company being audited. If the engagement is new to the auditor, he or she will be well advised to start with some presumption of risk since experience shows that audit difficulties are encountered more frequently in engagements where the client is unfamiliar to the auditor.

- When the risk of fraud appears to be higher than usual, the auditor should respond with measures such as assigning more experienced staff to the engagement and providing more extensive supervision. It may well be necessary, also, to change the nature, extent, and timing of the verification procedures that normally would be performed.

- Throughout the audit engagement, the auditor should continue to be alert to the possibility of fraud. More red flags may appear, such as large unusual transactions just at the year-end. If those red flags appear, the auditor must again respond with new or extended procedures.

RECOMMENDATION

R-34 The CICA Auditing Standards Committee should extend its guidance to audit procedures related to the discovery of management fraud. Since normal audit procedures provide a lower level of assurance with respect to the discovery of management fraud than they do with respect to the discovery of simple errors, the auditor should extend his or her work to give specific consideration to the possibility that such fraud may have occurred. If that consideration raises any question in the auditor's mind about the validity of the traditional assumption of management honesty, additional audit procedures should be devised to provide additional assurance.

7.25   While our recommendation is for more organized effort by the auditor to search for both employee and management fraud, we wish to state one caution. Although such efforts should increase the likelihood that fraud will be discovered, we still believe that the audit will provide no more than reasonable assurance on this point. As the Treadway Commission, referring to the inherent limitation of the audit process, said:

> The auditor cannot and should not be held responsible for detecting all material frauds, particularly those involving careful concealment through forgery or collusion by members of management or management and third parties. Auditors nonetheless should be responsible for actively considering the potential for fraudulent financial reporting in a given audit engagement and for designing specific audit tests to recognize these risks.[11]

Accordingly, we think the profession would be wise to avoid the use of the word "detect" in its guidance on this subject, because it could lead to public misunderstanding. An auditor is not a detective, in the sense of being a person whose job it is to investigate crime, and a failure to detect a material fraud is not necessarily evidence of negligence, although sometimes it may be.

7.26 *Financial statements and management fraud.* Financial statements may be made instruments of management fraud by recording fictitious assets or omitting or understating liabilities. Financial statements may also be misleading as a result of improper valuations and estimates or a failure to adhere to GAAP. If done with an intention to deceive, these actions by management are also fraudulent, although there is not always a sharp line of division between mere optimism and fraudulent deception. Since the auditor's duty is to report upon the financial statements, it is self-evident that the auditor must plan the audit program to catch fraudulent financial reporting and require appropriate correction of the financial statements.

7.27 *Reporting management fraud to the audit committee.* If management persists in maintaining its position with respect to financial statements that the auditor considers misleading or deceptive, the auditor's disagreement with management will automatically come before the audit committee. If, however, management accepts the changes required by the auditor before the draft statements are submitted to the audit committee, the disagreement will not be apparent in the accompanying draft audit report. In paragraph 4.13 we recommended that the audit committee should request to be informed about any serious difference of opinion between management and the auditor, whether or not the difference has been resolved. We consider such action essential if the auditor has a belief that the accounting initially proposed by management was drawn up with fraudulent intent. The *Handbook* guidance we advocate in Recommendation R-2 in paragraph 4.28 should cover this point.

7.28 As well as seeing that attempted management fraud is fully disclosed to the audit committee and accounted for properly, the auditor must consider its effect on his or her position. Unless action is taken so that the fraud or attempted fraud is unlikely to recur, the auditor will be subject to greater than normal risk in continuing with the engagement. Normally, top management or the board will have taken steps to control any risk of further fraud. If such action is not forthcoming, the auditor must consider whether he or she should resign the appointment. Similarly, if serious internal control weaknesses are allowed to go uncorrected and this could permit material employee fraud, the auditor must consider the risk to his or her position.

ILLEGAL ACTS

7.29 Management fraud is one form of illegal activity by a company; hence, there is some connection between the subjects of fraud and illegal acts generally. Our particular concern in this part of the chapter is with (1) the question whether the auditor has, or should assume, some responsibility with respect to the discovery of illegal acts other than fraud and (2) the implications of the possibility of illegal activity by a company to its financial reporting.

Audit Procedures with respect to Illegal Acts

7.30 Many laws and regulations affect almost every business. Laws relating to employee safety, product hazards, environmental protection, and competitive practices represent some examples. The auditor is unlikely to learn of violations of such laws in the normal course of an audit examination unless they have financial consequences. As well, since the auditor is not an expert in law, he or she is not equipped to seek out breaches of the law. Therefore, it ought to be clear to begin with that an audit cannot be relied upon to discover all or most infractions of the law, even if the infractions are quite serious. The most that can practically be expected is that the auditor be alert to the possibility of illegal acts and inquire carefully into any indications suggesting their existence. Such inquiries should include seeking the advice of the company's legal counsel if there is any doubt whether a certain activity is illegal.

7.31 The auditor may need guidance also with respect to the nature of audit evidence concerning illegal acts. It is quite likely that any receipts and payments connected with illegal acts will be poorly documented. The auditor is thus faced with the question whether the audit evidence is sufficient to enable expression of an unqualified audit opinion. For example, there may be evidence that a particular payment was authorized, but the documentation expected in a normal transaction, such as suppliers' invoices or evidence of receipt of service, is absent.

7.32 In our opinion, any important case in which normal audit evidence is lacking because of the illicit nature of the transaction should be reported to the audit committee, even though management has provided a good explanation. Upon occasion, the transaction may appear so important that the auditor must bring it directly to the attention of the full board of directors. The auditor must then decide what effect this lack of normal audit evidence will have on the audit report. Even though the documentation of the transaction does not, by itself, provide good evidence, the auditor may well have received an explanation that appears believable, especially when reinforced by audit committee or board approval. It would be helpful if auditing standards provided guidance to the auditor for such cases, although no auditing standard can impart the acute sense of danger that is critical in such circumstances.

RECOMMENDATION

R-35 The CICA Auditing Standards Committee should provide additional guidance to the implications for the auditor's report of illegal actions that have had or may have material financial consequences.

Financial Statements and Illegal Activity

7.33 When the auditor suspects or concludes that a client company has engaged in illegal activities, he or she must consider the accounting and reporting consequences. There are two aspects to this. The first concerns the possible effect of discovery of illegal acts upon the financial position of a company. A possible loss through fines, penalties, or damage awards is covered in the accounting literature on contingencies. But there is also the possibility of indirect effects if the business of the company might be seriously disrupted by the discovery of illegal acts (for example, if the result would be that the company lost the ability to operate in a certain territory or was forced to incur a substantial increase in operating costs). The question of the need for and manner of disclosure of these risks is one of the subjects that should be included in the study of risk disclosure that we recommended in Chapter 5.

RECOMMENDATION

R-36 The CICA Accounting Standards Committee should provide additional guidance to the implications for financial statement disclosure of illegal actions that have had or may have material financial consequences.

Reporting Illegal Activities to the Audit Committee

7.34 There should be little doubt about the auditor's reporting responsibility within the company when he or she becomes aware of illegal activities carried on by it. The directors are entitled to know whether or not the company's business is being carried on in an ethical manner and in compliance with the law and the company's code of conduct, if one exists. Accordingly, we believe the auditor should have an obligation to see that the audit committee has been fully informed of any serious infraction of the law committed in carrying on the company's operations of which the auditor becomes aware. This reporting responsibility of the auditor is similar to that with respect to the responsibility for reporting fraud.

RECOMMENDATION

R-37 The CICA Auditing Standards Committee should state specifically that the auditor should ensure that the audit committee (or board of directors if there is no audit committee) is fully informed about serious infractions of the law committed in carrying on the business of the company of which the auditor is aware.

FRAUD AND ILLEGAL ACTS: OTHER QUESTIONS

7.35 Probably few will dispute that the audit committee should be fully informed about material fraud or illegal acts, as we have indicated above. Whether the auditor should have any responsibility to make any public report with respect to such situations (beyond the responsibility to see that the financial statements make appropriate disclosure) is much more debatable. If any such obligation were imposed upon auditors, some thought would be required to make it workable. For example, there would be the question of how certain the auditor would have to be concerning the illegality of a particular action.

7.36 One question asked in the Decima survey of public opinion throws some light on public expectations on this issue. When asked what the auditor should do when a problem, such as senior management fraud, has a serious effect on the financial condition of a client, 44 percent of the respondents recommended going to the board of directors, and a further 15 percent recommended a demand for corrective action by management. However, approximately one quarter suggested reporting to the government or to the police.[12] When asked further what the auditor should do if not satisfied with the resulting action, the percentage advocating recourse to the government or police almost doubled. Since these questions referred strictly to fraud, which is a recognized concern of the auditor, the answers are not directly applicable to the auditor's responsibility with respect to illegal acts in general, but they are suggestive.

7.37 We have already referred to the possible financial reporting problems that the auditor must grapple with when he or she becomes aware that a client company has engaged in possibly illegal activities. Because the auditor's primary responsibility is to report on fair presentation of the financial statements, these issues cannot be avoided. Our concern here, however, is with the question whether the auditor should have a "public duty" to report illegal acts, actual or suspected, to public authorities.

7.38 A number of reasons are customarily given for not placing an obligation upon the auditor to report illegal acts performed by a client to persons outside the company:

• The auditor is not a lawyer and is not competent to judge whether or not actions are illegal.

• The auditor has an obligation under professional ethics to maintain complete confidentiality with respect to a client's affairs except when specific disclosures are required by law. If the auditor cannot be trusted to do so, management will have

an incentive to withhold as much information as possible from the auditor. Such a result would seriously impair the effectiveness of audits.

• There is no general legal obligation for anyone to report illegal acts committed by others to the authorities.[13]

• Most important of all, the responsibility for the conduct of a company lies with its directors and management, not with the auditor. If there should be any responsibility for reporting illegal acts to the authorities, it should rest upon those responsible parties.

7.39 We find these arguments persuasive so far as they go. We have one concern, however. There may be occasions when those responsible for the direction of a company are inclined to cover up its illegal activities and, indeed, may be the persons responsible for them. It seems likely to us that a significant segment of the public would expect the auditor to take some action in such a case, especially if the illegal activity is continuing. If this is so, and the auditor recognizes no such obligation, an expectation gap exists.

7.40 Significant questions of public policy are involved in this issue, and we would not presume to suggest final answers to these questions without a great deal of study that would go well beyond our mandate. We can, however, suggest the following general principles that seem to us to be appropriate.

• It is, and should remain, the responsibility of the directors of a company to set ethical standards for its conduct and see that the laws are observed.

• An auditor's primary responsibility remains that of reporting on the fair presentation of the client's financial statements. To fulfil that responsibility effectively, the auditor must normally retain in confidence information gained about the client's affairs. That duty of confidentiality should not be set aside lightly.

• Nevertheless, the auditor has a professional responsibility not to knowingly lend his or her name or services to any unlawful activity.[14] This means that an auditor should resign an engagement if he or she becomes aware of serious illegal activity by a client and is not satisfied that the directors and management can be trusted to rectify the situation.

- If the auditor of a public company resigns or is dismissed, the general public should be entitled to know of any major disagreements between the auditor and the company relating to financial reporting for a reasonable period prior to the resignation.

- In some limited circumstances, the public should also be entitled to know of reasons for the auditor's resignation or dismissal that are not related to specific disagreements with the company concerning financial reporting. The auditor should not be asked to decide when these other reasons should be publicly disclosed, in breach of the normal duty of confidentiality. Rather, the law should be amended so that the auditor is required to report these other reasons to a designated public agency, and that agency should be responsible for the public disclosure decision.

- Any communication made by the auditor in connection with his or her resignation or dismissal should have qualified privilege.

7.41 Our key suggestion is that where an auditor's reasons for resignation or dismissal are not directly related to specific disagreements with a client concerning financial reporting matters, these reasons should be communicated in confidence to an appropriate public agency. This public agency should have the power and the responsibility to make further investigation if deemed necessary and to decide whether disclosure of these reasons is in the public interest. In the next section of this chapter we comment on the present mechanisms for disclosure of this nature and possible changes that should be made in them.

PUBLIC NOTICE UPON AN AUDITOR'S RESIGNATION OR REPLACEMENT

7.42 At present, some reporting requirements exist that apply both when the auditor of a public com-

pany resigns and when the company decides to replace an incumbent auditor. National Policy Statement No. 31 of the Canadian Securities Administrators requires certain disclosure, highlights of which may be summarized as follows:

- Within 30 days of a proposal being made to replace an incumbent auditor, or of receipt of notification from the auditor of resignation or intention not to stand for reappointment, a company must notify the holders of voting securities to that effect. This notice must also be sent to securities administrators in provinces where the company is a reporting issuer.

- The notice must contain a description of the nature of any qualifications in the auditor's opinion on the audited financial statements for the two fiscal years preceding the date of notice, and any similar reservations contained in any auditor's comments on interim financial information for any subsequent period up to the date of the notice.

- The notice must also contain a description of any "reportable disagreements" and the effect of the decisions that caused the disagreements, if reasonably determinable or quantifiable. A reportable disagreement is a disagreement between the auditor and the company at the decision-making level that occurred in connection with the audits of the two most recent fiscal years and any subsequent period up to the date of notice. The disagreements would relate to any matter of audit scope or procedure or any matter of accounting principles or practices or financial statement disclosure. The test of the disagreement is whether it caused the auditor to refer to the matter in audit reports or comments on unaudited interim information in the periods just referred to, or would have caused the auditor to make such references if his or her term of office had been completed.

- When reportable disagreements exist in the view of the reporting issuer or outgoing auditor, the company's notice must be released to the public information media. The reporting issuer must request the auditor to provide a letter within 15 days, addressed to the securities commissions, stating agreement or disagreement with the information contained in the notice. The auditor's letter is to accompany the notice to all parties entitled to receive it.

7.43   This policy is useful so far as it goes. Its effectiveness obviously depends upon the alertness of securities commissions to what is going on, and their willingness to intervene when desirable in the public interest. The policy also contains some weaknesses.

- The 30-day notification period may be too long in some circumstances. If the reason for the auditor's resignation were some actions adverse to the public interest (for example, fraud upon the public) any delay in notification could be damaging.

- The expressed concept of a reportable disagreement (to be disclosed in the public notice) is too weak. Suppose an auditor disagrees with a client's proposed financial statements on the grounds they are misleading, and the client changes them to avoid an audit qualification. Since the financial statements, once published, would contain an unqualified audit report, the disagreement, which might have been extremely heated, would not be a reportable disagreement. The United States requirements that are equivalent to National Policy Statement No. 31 do classify such disagreements as reportable.[15]

- It is also arguable that the policy is too narrow in its scope. Suppose, for whatever reason, an auditor concludes that the management of a company is untrustworthy, even though management has always hitherto agreed to changes in its financial disclosure that have been required by the auditor. Under the policy there would be nothing with which the auditor could disagree in the notice furnished by the company. As a result, the public would have no inkling of the cause of the auditor's resignation.

7.44   We, therefore, believe that some changes should be made in the existing requirements for public notification upon a change in auditor. These changes should respect management's need for confidentiality in its relationship with its auditor, but nevertheless permit a limited modification of that right in cases where the shareholders' and public's

interests require. We believe the securities regulator should play a more positive role in receiving auditors' explanations as to reasons for their resignation or dismissal and determining the extent to which the public interest requires publication of those reasons. The normal rule that the company provides information and the auditor attests to it seems to us not to be relevant in this situation. We suggest changes be considered along the following lines:

- When an auditor decides to resign or not to stand for reappointment, or a company determines to ask for an auditor's resignation or not to recommend reappointment, the party taking the decision should notify the appropriate securities commission(s) with a copy to the other party. That notification should be made immediately after the decision is taken and, in any event, not more than 5 days thereafter.

- When the auditor has taken the initiative in resigning or declining to seek reappointment, that notice should include a statement by the auditor of all the significant reasons for that decision, segregated between reportable disagreements and other reasons.

- When the initiative is taken by the company, the auditor should be required to inform the securities commission(s) of any reason that he or she considers of immediate importance to the public interest and believes to have been a factor in the client's decision to change auditors. That reply by the auditor should be made as soon as possible and, in any event, in not more than 10 days after learning of the client's decision. If there are no such reasons, the auditor should so state. The auditor should make a supplementary statement if new information comes to light after the 10-day period that he or she deems should be reported.

- The auditor should not be liable for claims for damages as a result of statements made in these notifications to the securities commissions, provided they are made in good faith.

- An appropriate securities commission (e.g. the securities commission in the province where a majority of the company's shareholders reside) should assume the responsibility of deciding whether it is important that shareholders and the public receive early notice of the auditor's resignation or dismissal and the nature and extent of the information to be disclosed. To help in that decision, the securities commission may, of course, exercise its investigative powers to obtain further information from the company, the auditor, or other parties.

- When the securities commission decides to take no action on the early notification, the present procedure should be followed for giving public notice of a change of auditor within 30 days, accompanied by a description of reportable disagreements. In this way, shareholders and others will be assured of learning of all disagreements directly related to the company's financial reporting.

- As suggested in paragraph 7.43, the definition of reportable disagreement should be strengthened.

7.45 These suggestions, no doubt, require further study. Our main objective is to see that the public interest is protected in those unusual cases when an auditor resigns or is dismissed in circumstances where important information known to the auditor might not otherwise be communicated to the shareholders and the public.

RECOMMENDATIONS

R-38 Changes should be made to securities legislation or regulations with the objectives of (1) improving the timeliness of notification of auditor changes, (2) improving the ability of an auditor to make adequate disclosure of the reasons for the change in auditor, and (3) enabling proper and timely public disclosure of the reasons when, in the discretion of the securities commissions, the shareholders' and public's interests demand it.

R-39 National Policy Statement No. 31 of the Canadian Securities Administrators, providing for disclosure upon resignation or replacement of an auditor, should be strengthened. The definition of a "reportable disagreement" should be revised so as to ensure disclosure of disagreements between an auditor and management

that would have led to an audit qualification or comment had management not altered the financial information that was published.

Private Companies

7.46 These suggestions apply only to public companies since the securities laws do not apply to private companies. In addition, not all private companies have auditors. Nevertheless, there could be occasions when an auditor of a private company receives information concerning serious illegal activity on the part of the client that ought to be disclosed in the interest of minimizing further damage to the public. We suggest that the appropriate governmental authorities consider whether some legislative changes along the lines we have suggested for securities legislation be enacted to facilitate such disclosure.

Successor Auditors

7.47 At present, professional codes of conduct and many corporations statutes require that an auditor, when approached to take over an appointment held by another, should inquire from the latter whether there are any reasons why the audit appointment should not be accepted. The value of this communication is reduced, however, by the fact that any statement made by the auditor being replaced is limited by the professional duty of confidentiality, unless a release is obtained from the client. We suggest that this rule should be amended to be consistent with the profession's prohibition against an auditor being associated with unlawful activity. We suggest that the auditor being replaced or resigning an appointment should be obligated to respond to a possible successor's inquiry if he or she considers that suspected fraud or other illegal activity by the client was an important factor in the decision to resign or in the client's decision to appoint a different auditor.

7.48 If this change in codes of conduct is made, it will become more important that a proposed successor auditor communicate with the predecessor before accepting the appointment. If the successor fails to do so, he or she may, unknowingly, assume the risk attached to association with an untrustworthy client.

RECOMMENDATION

R-40 Provincial institutes of chartered accountants should amend their codes of conduct so that an auditor resigning or being replaced is obliged to inform a possible successor auditor if suspected fraud or other illegal activity by the client was an important factor in the resignation or in the client's decision to appoint a different auditor.

SUMMARY

7.49 The questions of the consequences of fraud for financial reporting and for the auditor's responsibility with respect to fraud have been matters of concern internationally for several years. The public may well have greater expectations with respect to the auditor's ability to discover fraud than is warranted by present audit procedures. Questions also exist concerning the auditor's obligation to report fraud that is discovered, including the level of reporting within the company and the need for reporting to public authorities. In all of this, it is to be recognized that undiscovered frauds that cause loss to members of the public will damage the public's image of the profession, regardless of how correctly the profession has performed. This means that there must be a strong sense of danger by auditors in relation to fraud. Their approach to fraud, even more than the approach to audit matters generally, must be strongly informed by a recognition that the purpose of the audit is to protect the public, not the auditors.

7.50 The auditor's objective is to report upon the fair presentation of the financial statements. It follows that the auditor has an obligation to search for fraud and error that might cause material misstatements. Fraud is more difficult to discover than error because of the efforts that will be made to conceal it. Accordingly, the Commission believes the auditor should give special attention to the risk of material fraud.

7.51 The auditor should pay special attention in the review of internal control to those controls that provide protection against material employee fraud and should test their operation during all engagements. Auditing standards should be amended to state the

above more directly and to give guidance to indicators of heightened risk of fraud and to appropriate additional audit procedures in the presence of that risk.

7.52 When the effect of employee fraud is material, the auditor must see that suitable disclosure of that effect is made in the financial statements. The auditor must also see that the audit committee is fully informed about material employee fraud that has been discovered and about any major weaknesses in internal control.

7.53 Management fraud involving falsification of the asset and liability position, or the choice of accounting policies or valuations and estimates made with a deliberate intention to deceive, is of particular concern to the auditor. The audit program should include (1) consideration at the planning stage of each engagement whether there are any special indicators of a higher-than-normal risk of fraud; (2) when such are identified, the use of more experienced staff and appropriate adaptation of the planned audit program; and (3) continued alertness throughout the engagement to any further conditions arousing suspicion.

7.54 The auditor, of course, must see that financial statements that are fraudulent are corrected. In addition, whether or not the statements are corrected, the auditor must see that the audit committee is fully informed about the attempted fraud.

7.55 Fraud is only one type of illegal act. There are many other types, most of which leave no trace in the accounts. It would be impractical, therefore, to lay an obligation upon the auditor to discover illegal acts committed by, or on behalf of, a company even though they may be significant. On the other hand, the auditor should be alert to indications of illegal acts that come to light in the course of the audit examination. When the auditor becomes aware of illegal activities, he or she must consider their possible significance for disclosure in the financial statements and for the audit report. The auditor must also ensure that the audit committee is fully informed.

7.56 At present, under a policy of the Canadian Securities Administrators, public disclosure of a change in the auditor of a public company must be made.

That disclosure is required to include a description of "reportable disagreements" between the auditor and the management of the company in the two preceding fiscal years and the period since then up to the date of the notice. The Commission has concerns that these requirements do not cover all the occasions when some public disclosure should be made, nor do they always require disclosure of all the information that should be made public.

7.57 The Commission suggests improvements to present requirements along the following lines. There should be much earlier notification to the securities commissions of a decision by an auditor to resign or a decision by a company not to reappoint its auditor. An auditor should be obliged to inform the commissions of the significant reasons for his or her resignation or, when the auditor has been dismissed, of those reasons which, in his or her opinion, might be of immediate importance to the public interest. Upon receipt of such information from an auditor, the appropriate securities commission should consider whether the information should lead to any early

public disclosure or other action in the interests of the public. Present requirements should be continued for the disclosure within 30 days of "reportable disagreements" relating to financial reporting, assuming that these have not already been disclosed. However, the definition of reportable disagreement should be broadened to ensure that all recent major disagreements between the auditor and management of the company relating to audit scope or financial reporting are disclosed, whether or not they led to a reservation in the auditor's opinion or comments on any of the company's financial disclosure.

7.58 The Commission also suggests consideration whether a need exists for disclosure of changes of auditors of private companies that is parallel to that for public companies. In any event, the Commission suggests that the profession's rules of conduct should be relaxed to require that an incumbent auditor reply fully to a possible successor's inquiry if the incumbent believes that fraud or suspected illegal activity may be an important factor in the change of auditors.

References

1. Cited in references 3 and 4 below.
2. *CICA Handbook*, Section 5300, "Audit Evidence" (Toronto: CICA), par. 40(b).
3. AICPA Auditing Standards Board, *The Auditor's Responsibility to Detect and Report Errors and Irregularities*, Proposed Statement on Auditing Standards (New York: AICPA, 1986).
4. Auditing Practices Committee, *The Auditor's Responsibility for Detecting and Reporting Fraud and Other Illegal Acts*, Draft Auditing Guideline (London: Institute of Chartered Accountants in England and Wales, 1987).
5. Decima Research Limited, Executive Summary of *Public Opinion Survey* (1986), see Appendix B, pp. 150, 151.
6. *CICA Handbook*, "Audit Evidence."
7. Ibid., pars. 46, 47.
8. Ibid., pars. 50-55.
9. *CICA Handbook*, "Audit Evidence," par. 54.

10. Ibid., Section 5210, "Auditor's Objective Regarding Internal Control," pars. 07-08.
11. National Commission on Fraudulent Financial Reporting, *Report* (n.p.: The Commission, 1987), p. 51.
12. Decima, *Survey*, Appendix B, p. 151.
13. However, a person reporting illegal acts to the authorities will generally have a legal defence against a claim for damages in defamation or similar actions. This defence is based upon the courts' recognition of a social or moral duty to report such acts.
14. This wording is used in Rule 203 of the Rules of Professional Conduct of the Institute of Chartered Accountants of Ontario.
15. In Form 8-K filings with the Securities and Exchange Commission, a description of all disagreements is to be given, including those disagreements that were resolved to the satisfaction of the reporting accountant. See Securities and Exchange Commission Accounting Series Releases 165 and 247, or Codification of Financial Reporting Releases, Section 603.02.

EXHIBIT

DANGER SIGNALS TO THE AUDITOR

The following list contains a brief description of a number of conditions that should heighten an auditor's sensitivity to the possibility of fraud. The list is representative rather than exhaustive. None of these conditions, by itself, is a strong indicator that fraud is likely. Indeed, some will be found in almost every audit engagement. Rather, it is the existence of a number of these danger signals in one engagement that should arouse the auditor to the need for extra care in planning and carrying out the audit. A review of these and other danger signals should be made at least annually at the time of the development of the audit plan for the ensuing year.

Corporate Environment

Weak corporate ethical climate

Absence of enforcement of formal code of conduct

Absence of strong Board of Directors or Audit Committee

Poor management reputation in the business community

Management operating and financial decisions dominated by a single person

Aggressive management attitude in financial reporting

Financial Pressures

Business or industry decline (revenue or market share)

Inadequate or inconsistent profitability relative to industry

Financial difficulties

Low equity to debt ratio, especially if the result of a recent acquisition

Forthcoming debt or stock offering

Bonuses (or management profit-sharing arrangements) based on short-term financial results

Overemphasis of quantified targets that are linked to management compensation

Management places undue emphasis on meeting earnings projections (to support market price of stock)

Unrealistic budget pressures

Desire for personal gain on the part of individual executives (through increased compensation, to achieve promotion, or to cover bad performance)

Management Style

Constant crisis conditions in operating areas (disorganized work areas, frequent/excessive back orders, shortages, delays)

Ineffective responsibility reporting system

Turnover in key financial positions

Understaffed accounting and financial functions (constant crisis conditions)

Organization decentralized without adequate monitoring

Changed control, especially if a high price was paid

Internal Control

Poor internal control

Ineffective internal audit function

Company does not correct material weaknesses that are possible to correct

Lack of control over computer process (weak control over movement of assets, too many processing errors, delays in providing results and reports)

Inadequate policies and processes for security of assets (not limiting access to authorized employees, not investigating employees before hiring, not bonding employees)

Audit Environment Difficulties

Unusual or complex transactions (particularly close to year-end)

Related party transactions

Significant misstatements in prior period's financial statement

Significant difficult-to-audit figures in the accounts

Accounting records seriously inadequate

Problems related to reliability of accounting estimates (personnel lack knowledge, careless/inexperienced supervisors, poor history)

Frequent disputes about aggressive application of accounting principles

Management-imposed limitation on audit scope

Information provided to auditors unwillingly or after unreasonable delay (records or files not produced promptly when requested, evasive responses to audit inquiries)

In the case of a financial institution, poor relationship of client with the regulator and an unwillingness to engage in frank three-way or four-way communication involving management, the audit committee or board, the regulator, and the auditor

Unrealistic time deadlines for audit completion

New client, no prior audit history or none available from predecessor

Audit Findings

Transactions not recorded in accordance with management's general or specific authorization

Transactions not supported by proper documentation

Discrepancies between control and subsidiary accounts not investigated and corrected on a timely basis

Differences disclosed from confirmations

Fewer responses to confirmations than expected

Unusual documentary evidence (handwritten alterations or handwritten documents that are normally typed)

Missing vouchers or documents

Evidence of falsified documents

Conflicting evidence on important matters

Discovery of important matters that were previously known to client personnel but not voluntarily disclosed to the auditor

Unsatisfactory explanations

Unexplained items on reconciliations or in suspense accounts

Anomalies noted in analytical review of accounts that cannot be explained

Inadequate segregation or unusual investment of funds received as a fiduciary

Evidence of unduly lavish lifestyle by officers and employees

8

Regulated Financial Institutions

8.1 This chapter discusses recommendations contained in previous chapters specifically as they relate to regulated financial institutions. Unless stated otherwise, the reader may assume that all previous recommendations apply in principle to regulated financial institutions. Our focus here is on those recommendations that need to be modified to fit the circumstances of this specific industry, together with new recommendations covering the relationships between auditors, audit committees, and regulators.

8.2 The Commission has given special consideration to regulated financial institutions for a number of reasons.

- The existence of a regulator introduces another party who both relies upon and has responsibilities for the financial disclosure provided and must interact with the other parties, including auditors, who bear financial reporting responsibility.

- Regulated financial institutions are the most broadly exposed of all enterprises to the public. Any failure of a financial institution, therefore, is likely to have a severe impact on public perceptions of audits and auditors. This is all the more true because 95 percent or more (depending on the institution) of monies at risk may be public monies, not shareholder monies.

- This degree of leverage, especially in today's volatile, vulnerable, and rapidly changing financial environment, suggests the need for conservatism in accounting presentation and the greatest rigour in auditing procedures.

- Accounting problems in financial institutions tend to be differentiated from those of other enterprises. Asset and liability valuations (with associated recognition of gain and loss) tend to be much more important to results reported than they are for other enterprises. In addition, until relatively recently CICA accounting standards provided little or no guidance to the special accounting problems of most types of financial institutions.

- Financial institutions, as part of their normal business, often undertake risks in markets that are much more volatile than those in which an ordinary company deals. In addition, a financial institution needs comprehensive and up-to-date information about the economic situation in all industries and locations in which the institution is at risk as a result of its investment and credit activities. Accordingly, strong internal control systems and successful management of risk are vital to financial institutions and central to public expectations.

- Because financial institutions are regulated in the public interest, the public tends to have confidence in every institution in the system. Correspondingly, if confidence is shaken in one institution as a result of its financial disclosure or for other reasons, confidence may well be shaken in the system as a whole. Consequently, the financial disclosure of financial institutions can involve much more sensitive issues than that of non-financial institutions.

- A high percentage of the comments we have received that are critical of auditors have related to their work on and knowledge about financial institutions. Since the evidence-gathering phase of our study, further failures of financial institutions have occurred. Since such failures are so much in the public's eye, the profession's reputation will largely stand or fall on its ability to meet public expectations with respect to audits in this industry. Criticisms of the profession's performance in this area must be taken very seriously.

8.3   There are several types of financial institutions, including chartered banks, trust and loan companies, insurance companies dealing in both general and life insurance, credit unions, investment companies, and investment brokers and dealers. The characteristic that marks an enterprise as a financial institution is the fact that its business entails receiving and holding funds from the public in amounts that are usually far in excess of the capital invested in the enterprise by shareholders and bondholders. Because of this large public stake in financial institutions, as well as their importance to the functioning of the capital markets and the economy generally, some scheme for oversight and regulation of their affairs will almost invariably be established by government. In Canada, both federal and provincial governments regulate financial institutions within their jurisdictions.

8.4   Some types of financial institutions, including notably the chartered banks and loan and trust companies, accept deposits from the public repayable upon demand or on short-term notice. These institutions are peculiarly sensitive to a loss of public confidence because such a loss can lead to rapid withdrawals of funds on deposit and severe liquidity problems, even when the institution is otherwise basically sound. Other types of financial institutions are less subject to this problem. For example, a serious cash drain upon an insurance company caused by policyholder loans and cancellation of policies is rather unlikely. Our comments in this chapter are, therefore, particularly directed to the deposit-taking institutions, although some will be relevant to other types of financial institutions as well.

IMPORTANCE OF PUBLIC CONFIDENCE TO DEPOSIT-TAKING INSTITUTIONS

8.5   A principal difference between deposit-taking institutions and other commercial entities is the importance of public confidence to the ability to carry on business. The importance of confidence results from two main factors:

• Depositors' funds are frequently callable on demand; assets are generally not as liquid. A significant call on deposits (a "deposit run") generally cannot be met by liquidation of assets over the short term by even the most stable of financial institutions. In some cases liquidity problems can be resolved over time through careful asset/liability management and obtaining a combination of new short and long-term funding. Delicacy is required. If new funding cannot be attracted because of lack of confidence in the institution, illiquidity may force it to close its doors, even though the realizable value of its assets in the longer term is greater than the amount of its debts.

• Financial institution assets are frequently many times greater than shareholders' capital; a ratio of assets to shareholders' capital of 20:1 is not uncommon. In such a situation a decline in asset value of only 5 percent effectively eliminates shareholders' equity. If the value decline cannot be reversed, it will usually be just a matter of time until the institution faces a liquidity crisis. If the result is a forced liquidation, this will usually be accompanied by a further substantial decline in realizable asset values. The shareholders' equity having been exhausted, that decline will be at the expense of general creditors, depositors, insurers, and/or the government.

PUBLIC EXPECTATIONS

8.6   One important question in the Decima survey concerned financial institutions. The respondents were close to unanimous that auditors of financial institutions should have a legal right and obligation to report serious matters to the regulator if management of the institution does not do so.[1] Written submissions to us that commented on financial institutions came largely from auditing firms, regulators, and financial industry associations. There was a fair measure of agreement that the audit environment in a regulated industry is different from that in a non-regulated industry. It was agreed that the auditor should exhibit a very high standard of care in view of the ripple effect of failure of a regulated financial institution. There was also concern that the relationship between auditors and regulators was not sufficiently clear. Our conclusion is that the public has no special expectation with respect to financial institutions other than that auditors should cooperate with regulators so that the financial health of such institutions remains undoubted. An expectation gap may well exist, therefore, since auditors themselves are uncertain about the extent of their responsibility to the regulator, and perhaps vice versa.

NEED FOR COOPERATION BETWEEN PARTIES RESPONSIBLE

8.7 As is true of other companies, the directors of financial institutions have responsibility for financial reporting to shareholders (and/or policyholders in the case of insurance companies). Management customarily will prepare the financial statements and may have additional reporting responsibilities to the regulatory authority under the governing legislation.[2] Auditors have the customary responsibility to attest to the fair presentation of the financial statements and may also have legislated obligations to attest to information presented by management to the regulator or to report certain audit findings directly to the regulator.[3] There are two aspects of this that distinguish the position of a regulated financial institution from that of the normal company. The first is the presence of the regulator as a very interested party with some measure of control over the institution's financial reporting. The second is the fact, already referred to, that until recently the CICA has paid relatively little attention to the accounting problems of most financial institutions.

8.8 The principal role of government-appointed regulatory bodies is to monitor the financial health and liquidity of financial institutions and, when deemed necessary, to take or force corrective measures in the event of financial difficulties. Regulators rely on financial reports from the institution to help them perform this role. Accordingly, they are often given the power to prescribe the basis of accounting and form of reporting by a financial institution, or else financial reporting requirements are set out in

the governing legislation. Regulators also place some reliance upon the shareholders' auditors. The fact that the annual financial statements are audited provides a significant level of assurance to the regulator. Also, the auditor may have additional obligations to the regulator as described in the previous paragraph.

8.9 The auditor's primary responsibility, on the other hand, is to report on the fair presentation of annual financial statements presented to shareholders. In performing this function, auditors could be said to place some implicit reliance upon the regulator, since any evidence of regulator concern usually prompts additional audit effort. The auditor's task is also directly affected when the regulator or the governing legislation has prescribed the basis or form of the annual financial statements. In a few cases, prescribed accounting bases are clearly contrary to what would be called for by generally accepted accounting principles in unregulated industries. The principal example, namely, the provision for loan losses by the Canadian chartered banks based on five-year average loss ratios, has been abandoned effective only in 1988. When prescribed accounting differs materially from GAAP, the auditor words the audit opinion to the effect that the financial statements are fairly presented "in accordance with prescribed accounting principles" instead of "in accordance with GAAP." It seems highly probable that the significance of this is not perceived by the general public.

8.10 Submissions from regulators have strongly suggested that auditors are not meeting regulators' expectations. Specifically, regulators have expressed dissatisfaction with their inability to use valuations reported under current accounting principles for measurement of an institution's financial safety. They also believe that auditors are reluctant to report concerns to regulators. On the other hand, auditors and industry representatives stress that communication between regulators and auditors has been unsatisfactory in the past. The problem is perceived to result from both inadequate formal reporting guidelines and insufficient ongoing contact between the profession and regulators, as well as between regulators and boards of directors or audit committees.

8.11 The lack of communication was discussed at length by Mr. Justice Estey and Coopers & Lybrand in their respective reports. To correct the problem, Mr. Justice Estey recommended a legislated solution:

> It is recommended that s.242 of the Bank Act be amended to provide that the auditors be expressly required to report annually to the federal regulatory body as to the adequacy of the internal controls and inspections, the extent of the auditors' review of the bank's loan portfolio, any change in the bank's accounting policy, other matters specifically required by the Bank Act, and generally as to any matters which materially affect the bank's financial position. The auditors should be required to include in such annual report a statement that there are no other matters as described in the Act which require their comment or, where no matters need be reported upon, the auditors shall so state in writing.

> It is recommended that the Bank Act be amended to require that the regulator inform the shareholders' auditors, the Chief Executive Officer, and the board of directors of:

> a. the fact that the bank has been placed on a "watch list"; and

> b. the rating of the bank at the annual inspection, and any changes thereto on an on-going basis.[4]

Coopers & Lybrand, on the other hand, recommended that expectations guidelines be developed by the regulator and that existing disclosure provisions already in the Bank Act be employed more frequently by the regulator. Some specific recommendations were:

> • We recommend, therefore, that the OIGB [Office of the Inspector General of Banks] issue guidelines which set out its expectations in respect of reports from the shareholders' auditors and, prior to the issuance of such guidelines, discuss them with its Advisory Committee of Bank Auditors so as to ensure the practicality of its expectations being met.[5]

> • We recommend that should there be any question by either the OIGB or the shareholders' auditors as to the accounting principles to be applied, they should so notify each other and

> resolve the matter as soon as practicable. Where there is some doubt as to the effect of the application of alternative principles, the OIGB should ensure that an extension of the shareholders' auditors work is requested in accordance with Section 242(2) so as to make such a determination.[6]

> • Specifically, we recommend that the OIGB establish guidelines on internal control reporting over areas at risk. These guidelines would have the following components...

> (c) A requirement for the shareholders' auditors to review the management assertions and test the work of the internal auditors, and to report to the OIGB on their findings.[7]

> • Based on our review of the current OIGB inspection process...we recommend...

> (f) the preparation of written reports covering the results of the inspection and matters requiring further action, which reports would then be distributed to the bank's audit committee and management, the shareholders' auditors and the other concerned divisions within the OIGB.[8]

While the solutions proposed in the two reports are different, their message is the same: communication between auditors and regulators must be improved if either party is to succeed in its mandate.

8.12 One factor that has probably impeded free communication between the auditor and the regulator is the requirement in professional codes of conduct that the auditor maintain confidentiality concerning a client's affairs. Any breach of this requirement not only exposes the auditor to discipline proceedings but also is likely to cause conflict with the management of the client institution. In these circumstances, an auditor is likely to be reluctant to disclose matters to the regulator beyond those disclosures specifically required by law. Conversely, regulators may well be uncertain with respect to how far it is proper for them to disclose information gathered in the course of their work to outside parties, even parties as intimately concerned with an institution's affairs as its auditors. Both the auditor and regulator may also be doubtful concerning the extent to which each may communicate information to the other without the knowledge or participation of management or the directors of the financial institution itself. Taken altogether, we suspect these factors have, in the past, created substantial practical barriers to free communication between auditors and regulators.

8.13 While the preceding paragraphs have been directed to communication between regulators and auditors, the issue of better communication is much broader than that. Many submissions to the Commission and both the Estey and Coopers & Lybrand reports stressed the need for enhanced communication involving management and audit committees or directors as well as auditors and regulators.[9] The public expects all parties will perform their several responsibilities well. If they are to fulfil these responsibilities and limit their liability, communication barriers between them are unacceptable.

8.14 The question then is: How may these barriers to communication best be overcome? Authorities in the United Kingdom have given considerable thought to this in recent years, and legislation has been passed that lays the groundwork for change with respect to certain types of financial institutions.[10] The thrust of this legislation and of supplementary guidance promulgated or proposed by the accounting profession is as follows:

- The regulatory body (which varies depending upon the type of financial institution) is empowered to obtain information from the institution and to require that it be attested to by the auditor (or occasionally another "reporting accountant").

- The information to be furnished by the institution and reported on by the auditor includes assurance concerning the effective functioning of the institution's accounting records and systems of control, as well as financial data needed to help the regulatory agency monitor the institution's financial health.

- There will be, or may be, regular or ad hoc trilateral meetings between representatives of the regulatory authority, the institution, and the auditor to discuss the planning and execution of work by the institution and the auditor to fulfil the reporting requirements referred to. At such meetings, the auditor is entitled to discuss the affairs of the institution based on knowledge gained in the course of the audit examination.

- Any one of the parties may arrange a trilateral meeting at any time if important matters affecting the institution come to its attention.

- The regulatory authority is empowered to disclose confidential information to an auditor if it helps the authority discharge its responsibility or is considered in the interests of depositors and shareholders. The authority should disclose anything that it considers important to the auditor's report.

- Auditors should take the initiative in triggering a report to the regulatory authority if it is deemed necessary to protect the interests of the depositors. However, auditors are not expected to continually monitor the client's affairs so as to be able to make such a report. The occasion only arises when an auditor, in the normal course of his or her duties, acquires knowledge of some adverse occurrence or change in circumstances of the institution that has given rise to a material loss or a probability of material loss.

- The auditor normally would request the institution to report such adverse events to the regulator. Only if the institution did not make the required report promptly would the auditor feel compelled to communicate directly with the regulator.

- In extremely exceptional circumstances the auditor might communicate with the regulator without advance notice to the institution. Those circumstances include situations in which speed of communication is of the essence, such as when imminent collapse of the institution is apprehended, and cases in which some occurrence has caused the auditor to lose confidence in the integrity or competence of management and the directors.

- The auditor is entitled to convey information to the regulatory authority in good faith, notwithstanding any duty of confidentiality.

8.15 Essential aspects of the above are: (1) the institution retains primary responsibility for providing information to the regulator, (2) the way is cleared for full communication between auditor, regulator, and representatives of the institution, (3) the auditor has a clear responsibility to the regulator as well as to the institution, and (4) the auditor is protected from liability that might otherwise be caused by communication with the regulator so long as it is in good faith. It seems to us these four principles are appropriate. We would only add a strong recommendation that the audit committee of the institution should be included as a party to the communication process in view of its special responsibilities for the effectiveness of the institution's accounting and financial reporting and for monitoring communication with, and performance of, the auditor.

8.16 We believe that recent failures of financial institutions have already stimulated a trend to enhanced communication between auditors, regulators, management, and audit committees. This trend should continue without waiting for new laws or rules. For best results, however, we think the right and requirement to communicate should be formalized in the various laws and regulations governing financial institutions. At present, some but not all Canadian laws governing financial institutions contain provisions along these lines, but such legislative provisions vary in their content and some may not be sufficiently directive to accomplish all that they should. We support, as does the CICA, the enactment of provisions to enable and require satisfactory communication between regulators and other parties bearing responsibility for the financial reporting of financial institutions.[11]

8.17 We also believe that regulators of various types of financial institutions should publish an explanation or listing of their expectations concerning matters that should be communicated by auditors, management, audit committees, and directors to assist them in the performance of their regulatory responsibilities.

RECOMMENDATIONS

R-41 The CICA, together with representatives of provincial institutes of chartered accountants and regulators, should initiate a task force to study and recommend a model set of legal pro-

visions to govern communications between auditors, regulators, management, and audit committees or directors of financial institutions. When completed, the CICA and the provincial institutes should actively support efforts to have the proposed provisions incorporated in appropriate legislation. The same task force should suggest a sample list of matters that a regulator might publish as matters to be communicated under present legislation.

R-42 To facilitate the communication process, changes should also be made to certain laws so that all financial institutions are required to have audit committees made up of outside directors.

8.18 Changes in legislation inevitably take time. Pending achievement of these changes we think it would be helpful to act immediately to amend the confidentiality requirements in provincial codes of professional conduct. We recommend changes so that an auditor of a regulated financial institution has an obligation to communicate information gained from the audit of a financial institution to a legally appointed regulator in certain situations. These would be occasions when material losses to the institution have occurred or are apprehended and the auditor has been unable to persuade management and the directors to inform the regulator.

8.19 If such a change is made in the codes of professional conduct, an auditor of a financial institution should make it a condition of acceptance of an engagement that he or she be entitled to make such disclosure to the regulator (with substantially simultaneous notice to the directors), and such condition should be set out in the engagement letter. We do not suggest that the auditor should unilaterally demand a right to communicate with the regulator without the knowledge of the directors. If any such right or obligation is considered desirable, it should be imposed by law and be accompanied by qualified privilege with respect to the communication with the regulator. At the same time, we would expect boards and audit committees to encourage active and easy communication between auditors and regulators.

RECOMMENDATION

R-43 Pending changes in the law, the provincial institutes of chartered accountants should immediately amend their codes of conduct to enable the auditor of a financial institution to communicate matters of great moment to the regulator (with notice to the directors) if the institution itself fails to do so.

ACCOUNTING STANDARDS FOR REGULATED FINANCIAL INSTITUTIONS

8.20 We have pointed out that until recently the CICA has not been active in setting standards to govern the bases of accounting and financial reporting by financial institutions. In part, this lack of activity is explained by the fact that specific provisions in governing legislation and regulations and instructions from regulators have preempted the field. The extent of such direction, however, has varied from one type of financial institution to another. There are always instructions concerning the manner of presentation of financial statements, but there is considerable variation in the extent of guidance given to the bases of valuation of assets and liabilities. Traditionally, very detailed guidance has been given to such valuation bases for insurance companies. Some other types of financial institutions are much less controlled in this respect, with the result that their accounting methods have developed rather informally with considerable scope for differences from one company to another.

8.21 This rather confused picture with respect to the accounting of financial institutions gives auditors a problem. By what standards can they judge whether the financial statements of a financial institution are fairly presented? At one time it was customary for the auditor simply to state that the financial statements were (or were not) fairly presented, without reference to any standard of fairness. Presumably the auditor relied largely on methods of accounting and statement presentation that were common in the industry and on the auditor's own judgment. However, auditing standards now require the auditor to indicate the basis for judging fair presentation, and this is normally expected to be GAAP. The auditor is thus faced with a decision whether the accounting methods or statement presentation and disclosure of a financial institution can be considered to be consistent with GAAP.

8.22 This decision involves more than gathering evidence that the accounting methods are commonly used within that particular industry. It also involves a judgment whether those methods, even if commonly used, meet the overriding aims of accounting theory, especially the provision of a satisfactory measure of income year by year. For many years it was clear in many cases that they did not, often because the accounting methods were conservatively biased or because they were designed to smooth out fluctuations in reported income over a period of years. Such individual accounting methods were adopted largely on the basis of instructions by the regulator, or at least with the consent of the regulator. This was the reason for audit reports stating that financial statements were fairly presented in accordance with prescribed accounting principles.

8.23 The accounting profession has generally taken the position that the accounting of financial institutions ought to be modified to conform with GAAP— by which is meant that accounting methods should be designed to provide a relatively unbiased measure of annual income and of financial position so long as the institution can be assumed to be a going concern. Over the years, progress has been made in cooperation with regulators in achieving this objective. It is now customary for the auditors of investment companies, investment brokers and dealers, general insurance companies, trust and loan companies, and credit unions to report that their financial statements are in accordance with GAAP. One problem in reaching this state of affairs has been the fact that the business of some financial institutions is so specialized that considerable study can be required in order to decide which accounting methods would be appropriate to meet the overall objectives of GAAP.

8.24 An outstanding example is provided by the life insurance industry. To meet the objectives of GAAP, it has been necessary to develop accounting methods for life insurance companies that represent an adaptation of traditional practices based on actuarial valuations and consequently are quite different from those found in other industries. The study necessary to design these methods was completed only in 1987 and has resulted in the first section of the *CICA Handbook* devoted to the accounting of a specific industry. At the time of writing, the *Handbook* recommendations have not yet been accepted by the regulator. The need for a reasonable level of acceptance by regulators and the affected industry only serves to underline the difficulty in establishing appropriate standards for important but specialized industries.

8.25   Important questions are implicit in the above description of the historical development of accounting methods and financial reporting in financial institutions. First, should or should not financial institutions adopt the overriding objectives of unbiased presentation of income and financial position? For example, is there an argument that there should be a deliberate conservative bias in their financial reporting so that the public receives early warning of potential financial difficulty? Or is some smoothing of gain or loss recognition with respect to the assets of financial institutions, such as investment portfolios and loans, justified by the desire to portray long-run earnings better and avoid the shock to public confidence that might be caused by recognition of large but occasional losses?

8.26   The answer to these questions may be a matter of degree rather than black and white. Some accounting methods that are part of GAAP for ordinary commercial enterprises do contain a conservative bias, principally to increase the "hardness" of the figures of assets and liabilities reported. Also, some perfectly accepted accounting methods, such as depreciation accounting, could be argued to contain some income-smoothing element. Hence the key question might better be phrased: "How far can the accounting methods of a financial institution depart from the goal of even-handed measurement of financial position and results of operations without being considered outside GAAP?"

8.27   A further question is: Does the regulator need audited financial reports on a basis different from GAAP in order to effectively fulfil the responsibility to protect public monies entrusted to a financial institution? In the insurance industry, for example, regulators traditionally required financial statements

filed with them that took conservative positions with respect to the types of assets "admitted" to be reported in balance sheets and to the valuation of policy reserves on annuity and life insurance business. The result was a conservatively biased, but unrealistic, computation of the capital in the business, which served as a form of control against a company becoming overextended.

8.28   As to this, the question may be more whether the regulator's responsibilities could be fulfilled in a different way. For example, if the proposition is that an institution's right to accept deposits or write new business should be tied to the amount of the capital invested, a conservative bias can be implemented in two ways. Either unduly conservative accounting methods can be adopted so as to understate the actual capital investment. Or the amount of capital required can be raised in proportion to deposits accepted or business written. If the former approach is adopted, there is nothing that should require the capital shown on the financial statements to be identical to the amount calculated for regulatory purposes. However, it should be clear in this case that the regulator *is* using artificial values and is not, in effect, disagreeing with the values in the published financial statements. If there were any indication that the regulator thought the published figures were not sufficiently conservative, management and the auditor would be at risk in the event of a subsequent failure of the financial institution.

8.29   Further study clearly is needed. However, we think the present situation, although considerably improved over a few years ago, is unsatisfactory. At present the introduction to the accounting recommendations in the *Handbook* states that recommendations are intended to apply to all profit-oriented enterprises except for banks. We believe it should be an objective of the accounting profession and the federal Superintendent of Financial Institutions to arrive at mutually agreed changes in financial reporting for banks so that their financial statements can be described as being in accordance with GAAP. If a regulator wishes to receive deliberately biased figures in the interest of providing an early warning of potential problems, that should be his or her prerogative. However, unduly biased figures are not appropriate for shareholders, whose interests and concerns are different from those of a regulator.

8.30 We would not stop there, however. We have already noted that there is little guidance in the *Handbook* to the special accounting problems of financial institutions. We understand that in practice there can be significant variation between companies in their accounting methods in particular areas, even though their accounting as a whole is described as being in accordance with GAAP. Examination of the accounting practices of several types of financial institutions should be high on the list of priorities in the general program we recommended in Chapter 4 for the reduction of alternatives and for improved guidance in special situations. It is important to ensure that regulatory authorities agree with any guidance proposed as a result of this examination.

8.31 We do not underestimate the obstacles in such a program. Both federal and provincial legislation exists to govern most types of financial institutions, with individual companies being governed by one authority or the other depending upon their jurisdiction of incorporation and where they operate. Consequently, to the extent that accounting is affected by laws and regulations, it may be necessary to deal with a large number of authorities to attain country-wide consistency. The need to deal with provincial authorities means that provincial institutes of chartered accountants must be involved; the CICA cannot act entirely on its own.

8.32 It would obviously be in the broad public interest if the authorities could coordinate their accounting requirements so far as possible. Up to the present, the usual approach has been that a provincial institute will take the lead in any discussion with provincial authorities and will involve the CICA in dealing with matters of accounting and auditing standards. On the other hand, the CICA alone deals with the federal government. Under this approach, the obvious danger is that there will be differences between the legislative and regulatory proposals of the federal and provincial governments or between individual provinces.

8.33 If it were possible politically, it would obviously be more efficient to have joint discussions involving both federal and provincial authorities and representatives of the CICA and provincial institutes whenever a particular type of financial institution is regulated by both levels of government. However, in

the current climate of concern for financial institutions, the present approach can achieve a reasonable measure of consistency as each jurisdiction monitors legislative and regulatory proposals made elsewhere and seeks to adopt their best features.

RECOMMENDATION

R-44 The CICA Accounting Standards Committee should continue its present efforts to define bank accounting standards that are both satisfactory to the industry and the federal Superintendent of Financial Institutions and can be considered in accordance with GAAP. The Accounting Standards Committee should also continue to give high priority to providing guidance with respect to the special accounting problems of other types of financial institutions. This would be an important part of the program recommended to eliminate holes in the coverage of accounting standards and reduce the number of alternative accounting practices that are not justified by differences in circumstances. The CICA should seek the cooperation of industry representatives and both federal and provincial regulators in this task and should continue to work with provincial institutes of chartered accountants to that end. If sufficient cooperation of all interested parties is not forthcoming, the CICA may have to consider more heroic measures to protect auditors and the public generally.

8.34 Notwithstanding our belief that the published financial statements of financial institutions should be consistent with GAAP, expanded and refined as necessary to fit their special situations, we have recognized that some regulators may find it useful for their supervisory purposes to ask for financial statements prepared on one or more prescribed accounting bases that differ from GAAP and that are unrealistic in some respects (as described in paragraphs 8.27 to 8.29). We do not suggest that the regulator should not have that right. We do suggest that any such financial statements be provided as special purpose reports addressed to the regulator only and, to avoid confusion, should not be given general distribution. However, if the regulator requests information that does not consist of figures measured on a different basis from GAAP, but simply represents supplementary or more detailed disclosure, management should carefully consider whether that disclosure ought to be made in the published financial statements as well.

RECOMMENDATION

R-45 A regulator of any type of financial institution for which GAAP have been established should be urged to treat any financial statement requested on an artificial or unrealistic basis of accounting as a special-purpose report and not as a substitute for statements prepared in accordance with GAAP.

8.35 The fact that the financial reporting of most types of financial institutions is now considered to be consistent with GAAP does not mean that all accounting issues peculiar to a particular type of institution have been resolved. We give special consideration in succeeding paragraphs to the following subjects: (1) risk disclosure in financial institutions, (2) disclosure related to liquidity, and (3) valuation of assets and liabilities.

Risk Disclosure

8.36 In Chapter 5, the Commission recommended a study of risks and uncertainties with a view to improved disclosure to the public in financial statements or elsewhere. Financial institutions are exposed to, or may assume, a wide variety of risks and may well need special consideration. For example, consider the following risks to which many financial institutions are directly exposed:[12]

- Unbalanced position risk. A deposit-taking institution owes money to depositors and has rights to receive money from loans and investments. If these rights and obligations are approximately equal and offsetting, the institution has effectively hedged its risk. If, however, the positions are not in balance, risk has been assumed. For example, if an institution has borrowed on a short-term basis and lent on a long-term basis at fixed interest, it is exposed to the risk that interest rates on the short-

term borrowings may rise while the interest return on the long-term amounts receivable is fixed. Similarly, if money borrowed in one currency is converted into a loan in another currency, the institution is at risk from a change in the exchange rate between the two currencies. Difficulties arise in quantifying exposure to interest and currency fluctuations, given the diversity and interrelationship of the lines of business that an institution may be involved in and the complexity and number of financial instruments used to control the risk.

- Market risk. This risk can be considered a form of unbalanced position risk since the existence of an unbalanced position implies that the market value of assets may change at a different rate, or in a different direction, from that of liabilities. However, some types of financial institutions do not consciously invest so as to hedge all their liability positions, and also may invest some of their capital base (which represents a margin of protection for depositors and creditors) in risky assets. It is, perhaps, more obvious to the layman to think of this exposure as a market risk rather than an unbalanced position risk. Market risk is particularly significant when an institution actively trades in securities, currencies, and commodities or in derivative instruments such as options and futures contracts.

- Credit risk. Credit risk exists for all assets involving a cash claim on a third party. It is the risk that loan and investment principal and related interest and fee income earned will not be collectible in full. Risk may be compounded by loan concentration in various industries (e.g. oil and gas, real estate, mining) and the long-term effect of economic cycles (global and regional).

- Liquidity risk. This is the risk that liquid asset reserves will be insufficient to meet demands for funds. In a deposit-taking institution this risk becomes critical as public confidence wanes and the likelihood of a deposit run increases. Further comment will be found in paragraphs 8.39 to 8.44.

- Settlement risk. An institution bears this risk when it acts as an intermediary between two other parties in arranging or settling transactions between them. For example, if the institution pays funds to one party before receiving payment from the other, the institution is at risk that the latter may default. There is also a risk attributable to delays or errors in the system for clearing transactions.

- Country and cross-border risk. These are the risks associated with investments in and loans to entities in foreign jurisdictions. Risks include the possibility that foreign governments will be unable to meet their debt commitments, or that enactment of adverse laws in the foreign country, such as exchange controls or expropriations, may prevent the intended working out of investment and loan transactions.

8.37 Disclosure of risks can be complicated in financial institutions for several reasons. As can be inferred from the above list, the sheer volume of information to be organized and condensed is immense. Information disclosed must be highly summarized but still meaningful. Striking an appropriate balance will be no mean feat. In addition, many of the relatively new financial instruments result in transferring of risk from one type to another. For example, a foreign currency swap of an exposed position might eliminate the risk of an unbalanced position while increasing credit and settlement risk. Categorization and quantification of risk will be difficult but must be undertaken if investors, depositors, and regulators are to obtain a sufficient understanding of the risks facing an institution, and of the way in which risk is managed and controlled by it.

8.38 There is wide disparity in the amount of information and method of disclosure of risks and uncertainties by financial institutions in Canada. There is a need for some action to promote some degree of uniformity in disclosure through the setting of standards.

RECOMMENDATION

R-46 The CICA Task Force on Financial Institutions, in conjunction with regulators and representatives of financial institutions, should initiate a separate study similar to that proposed in Recommendation R-12 in Chapter 5, to determine the best manner of disclosing risks and uncertainties.

Disclosure Related to Liquidity

8.39 In recent years a great deal of attention has been given to improved disclosure of net liquid financial resources available to an entity (both financial institutions and ordinary trading enterprises) and to changes in such resources period by period. There are two aspects to disclosure associated with liquidity. The first aspect is concerned with the liquidity position at a single point of time, the reporting date. The second aspect is the change in liquidity over the period up to the reporting date. Both are important. A good indication of the realizability of assets and the likely demand for liquidation of liabilities within a relatively short time frame is essential to an assessment of liquidity risk at the reporting date. An explanation of the change in liquidity over the most recent reporting period is helpful in providing a basis for prediction of possible future liquidity problems, which, in turn, is a factor in assessment of an entity's going-concern status.

8.40 In an ordinary trading enterprise, a good indication of liquidity at the reporting date is provided simply by the description and classification of assets and liabilities in the balance sheet. Accounts receivable, inventories, trade liabilities, and so on that are classified as "current" are usually realized or paid in the short term. Their individual amounts in relation to the gross revenue for a period provide an approximate indication of how short the period of realization or payment is for such assets and liabilities. In addition, disclosure of maturity dates of longer-term debt is specifically required providing an indication of future changes in the existing liquid position.

8.41 For the trading enterprise, changes in net liquid resources over a period are explained in a statement of "changes in financial position." This statement classifies those changes broadly between those that result from operations (often described as "cash flow from operations"), those resulting from investment and disinvestment activities, and those resulting from financing activities (i.e. debt or equity raised or retired). The main indicator of possible liquidity problems is usually the cash flow from operations, apart from occasional needs to meet maturing debt. In 1985 the CICA released *Handbook* recommendations to improve the presentation of the statement of changes in financial position.[13]

8.42 Unfortunately, in the case of financial institutions, especially deposit-taking institutions, financial statements as currently designed do not succeed in conveying meaningful information about liquidity. For example, the classification of assets and liabilities as current or non-current does not fit the situation of a financial institution. The major part of the liabilities of such an institution, although nominally payable on demand or in the short term, form aggregates which normally (but not assuredly) have the same properties as longer-term funds. On the other hand, the major part of their assets are realizable on short notice only in theory. In practice, a considerable period of time would be required if a substantial liquidation had to be made in an orderly fashion. Because of the short-term or demand characteristics of deposits and the difficulty in achieving orderly realization of assets, the liquidity risk of financial institutions is, in theory, very high. In practice, however, pressures on liquidity are quite moderate most of the time. It is only in special circumstances that the liquidity risk becomes acute. Unfortunately, it is very difficult, if not impossible, to be confident of foreseeing those circumstances.

8.43 No cure to this problem is to be found in the statement of changes of financial position as presently designed. The cash flow from operations, although quite informative in the case of trading companies, is largely irrelevant to a financial institution. Cash flow from operations, whether large or small in relation to shareholders' equity, is always just a trickle compared to the massive cash movements generated daily by depositors and borrowers. (The profitability of operations is, of course, important, since it contributes to building up the capital base of the institution and inspiring confidence in it. The profit and loss statement, however, should provide adequate information on this.) Moreover, the overall size of movements in deposits and borrowing overwhelms trends in subcategories within them, as well as the significance of other parts of the present statement of changes in financial position.

8.44 For all these reasons, a sufficiently descriptive disclosure of the liquidity position of a financial institution is difficult, and any forecast of changes in liquidity is necessarily extremely speculative. Nonetheless, liquidity is a vital element in the financial position and well-being of a financial institution.

If it were possible to improve disclosure pertinent to the liquidity position of such an institution, it would be most desirable to do so and we recommend study to this end.

RECOMMENDATION

R-47 The CICA Task Force on Financial Institutions, in conjunction with regulators and representatives of financial institutions, should study the best manner of presentation of information bearing on liquidity in the financial statements or annual reports of such institutions.

Asset and Liability Valuation in Financial Institutions

8.45 The capital invested in a financial institution provides a margin of safety for depositors, policyholders, and creditors of all sorts against losses on assets. Accordingly, regulators typically require that financial institutions maintain capital so that it never falls below a given percentage or a given fraction of the amount of liabilities. Capital consists of the original funds contributed to the institution together with earnings retained within it. The amount of the latter is affected by the valuation of assets and liabilities. That is to say, a high valuation of assets or a low valuation of liabilities increases the amount of reported capital; a writedown of assets or increase in the valuation of liabilities decreases reported capital and, in the extreme, can wipe it out.

8.46 Even though the accounting of most types of financial institutions is now considered to be consistent with GAAP, it cannot be assumed that bases for valuation of assets and liabilities are uniform within each type of institution. In fact, very little guidance is given to the valuation of assets and liabilities of financial institutions in the *Handbook*. The valuation of loans receivable provides a significant example. It is generally accepted that allowances for loan loss should be made if there is significant doubt concerning loan collectibility. However, no authoritative guidance exists concerning the basis for assessing collectibility or assessing degree of significant doubt.

8.47 Such assessment can be a very complex task involving, among other things, valuation of the collateral underlying specific loans and formation of judgments concerning future economic conditions and the likelihood of recovery of values. Neither is there authoritative guidance concerning the basis for writedown of a loan if it is concluded that such should be made. There has been a tradition that the writedown should be to the figure of the amount estimated to be recoverable upon the loan principal. That figure can be quite different from the current realizable value of the loan or its collateral, particularly if the recovery on the loan is not likely to take place in the near future.

8.48 To the extent that valuations made depend upon management judgment, there may be a need for disclosure of the basis of judgment. For example, if an estimate of loan collectibility is to be the basis of valuation, how can the reader form an idea of the quality of management judgment concerning collectibility? In paragraph 5.42 we recommended that the Accounting Standards Committee give consideration to this general problem. The problem is particularly acute in financial institutions since the valuation of assets and liabilities is so important to judgments concerning the solvency of the enterprise. At the same time, disclosure may well be very difficult because of the vast number of individual valuation judgments made and the consequent need for meaningful summarization.

8.49 In any event, the problem needs to be studied. There is an urgency about this for three reasons: first, existing guidance is significantly inadequate; second, the present and foreseeable environment is one of considerable risk for financial institutions; and, finally, audit performance in relation to financial institutions, more than in respect of any other sector, will have a major effect on the public's perception of whether its expectations are being met.

RECOMMENDATION

R-48 The CICA Task Force on Financial Institutions, in conjunction with regulators and representatives of financial institutions, should study asset and liability valuation problems in financial institutions and furnish recommendations. Guidance should be provided with respect to

the valuation of major categories of assets, actuarial liabilities, and loss provisions required for off-balance-sheet assets and liabilities, to the extent guidance is not already available.

THE AUDITOR AND REGULATED FINANCIAL INSTITUTIONS

8.50 We have some additional comments about the special responsibilities of the auditor of a financial institution. These comments concern: (1) the auditor's duties with respect to internal control in a financial institution, (2) the auditor's responsibility with respect to management estimates, and (3) what the auditor should do when he or she has a serious difference of opinion with management over estimates or the presentation of the financial statements.

Internal Controls and the Auditor's Responsibility

8.51 Under present auditing standards, an auditor studies and evaluates those internal controls of a client upon which reliance is placed in planning audit procedures. In most audit engagements the auditor relies upon some internal controls, but not all. The decisions whether or not to rely upon internal controls in a given area and as to the degree of reliance are governed by economic considerations. The question is: What is the most effective way to attain a sufficient degree of audit assurance? The general tendency is that the larger the enterprise and the number of its transactions, the greater will be the reliance upon internal controls. However, complete reliance will never be placed by the auditor solely upon the internal control systems.

8.52 Financial institutions typically fall into the category of a high-volume business. They are major users of computers and they often receive and disburse large sums of money by means of electronic communications. In addition, financial institutions often enter into many types of off-balance-sheet commitments that could involve significant risk. It is important to have strong internal controls to ensure that all transactions are properly recorded. In the normal course, the auditor of a financial institution will place considerable reliance on its internal controls. Typically, also, reliance will be placed upon the internal auditors of the institution who are likely to have a well-developed function, including the important responsibility to see that the internal control systems work well.

8.53 Regulators of financial institutions also rely, indirectly, upon the strength of their internal controls. Regulators have a responsibility to monitor the health of the institutions regulated by them, and they need reliable information for that purpose. Thus, regulators and auditors have a common need for reassurance about the strength of internal controls. Since the auditor must have some knowledge of those internal controls, the question naturally arises whether it would be convenient and economic for the auditor to extend his or her work so as to be in a position to offer some assessment of the control structure to the regulator, independent of management's assurances. Sentiment seems to be developing that auditors should be asked to undertake some such responsibility to the regulators of financial institutions. In the United Kingdom, new legislation with respect to financial institutions envisages that auditors will report to regulators on the internal control systems, and details of the manner of reporting are being worked out. The submission to us of the Canadian Bankers' Association suggested that this additional responsibility should be taken on by auditors of deposit-taking institutions here. This suggestion is also made in the excerpts from both the Estey and Coopers & Lybrand reports quoted in paragraph 8.11 above.

8.54 In the United Kingdom, the proposed reporting responsibilities are based on several principles that appear to us to be appropriate. First, the responsibility for maintaining appropriate control systems clearly rests with the management of the institution. Second, the regulator has a responsibility to see that the institutions supervised maintain adequate accounting and other records as well as adequate controls to enable the directors and managements of the institutions to carry on business in a prudent manner. Third, the regulator should set out in some detail the criteria it considers should be met by adequate accounting and control systems. Fourth, auditors should be asked to report on a regular basis their opinion whether the records and control systems of the institutions have been established and

maintained during the period reviewed so as to meet the regulator's criteria. In larger institutions, it is visualized that the auditor's examinations required to cover all the systems would be spread over a period of years.

8.55 There are two matters to be considered in connection with this proposal for extending the auditor's duties. The first is that of cost. Inevitably there would be some extra cost, possibly significant in relation to the present level of audit fees. We think it is important to ensure that costs associated with an auditor's review of the internal control and risk management structure are not unduly burdensome. This may affect the planning of work undertaken by the auditor. For example, a complete review of a large institution may need to be planned in a phased program extending over several years as is the intention in the United Kingdom. Consideration of cost will also affect decisions as to the degree of assurance that can be conveyed to the regulator and the appropriate language for expressing that degree of assurance. However, our ultimate conclusion is that there almost certainly is some point at which the cost of additional auditor assurance within the framework of regulation of financial institutions is justified on a cost/benefit test, given the billions of dollars of public money at risk in financial institutions.

8.56 A further objection to the assignment of this increased responsibility to the auditor is the difficulty in conveying assurance in clear terms on a system of internal control. No control structure can ever be foolproof, and it is often a matter of judgment whether specific controls are worth their cost in the context of risk probabilities. Accordingly, it is hard to report in simple terms whether the control structure, as a whole, is satisfactory. We agree that this is a problem. To deal with the problem, it seems necessary to sharpen the specification of what the auditor is reporting. The proposal in the United Kingdom is that the regulator should set out criteria in some detail to define those features that ought to be found in a well-designed internal control structure. The auditor is then able to express an opinion whether these individual criteria appear to be met in the system's design and functioning. It is thereby made much clearer what the audit opinion covers. We believe that this is the approach that should be taken in Canada as well.

RECOMMENDATION

R-49 The CICA should look favourably upon a request that the auditor report to the regulator on the design and functioning of internal control systems of financial institutions, provided satisfactory guidance is developed concerning the specific types of assurance that would be rendered in such a report. To this end, the CICA, in conjunction with regulators, auditors, and representatives of the various types of financial institutions, should develop criteria for effective and prudent systems of record-keeping, control, and internal audit for each type of institution.

The Auditor's Responsibility with Respect to Estimates

8.57 We have emphasized in Chapter 5 that the auditor has a responsibility to arrive at an independent opinion about the reasonableness of the many estimates that management must make for the purpose of preparing financial statements. That duty is no different in the audit of a financial institution. It may be urged that the auditor lacks the knowledge and experience to question many of management's judgments. Our answer to this is that the auditor must equip himself or herself with the requisite skills to make those judgments. The whole purpose of the audit is to bring the skill of an impartial outsider to bear upon the problem of fair financial disclosure. A tough approach by the auditor in the examination of the statements of financial institutions could have a salutary effect over time on the willingness of managements to risk running the institutions in a way that will expose them to confidence-threatening disclosure.

8.58 Mr. Justice Estey recommended that, "...the Bank Act be amended to require that the auditor who is in active charge of the audit of the bank should have at least five years experience in the performance at a senior level of bank audits or audits of other deposit-taking financial institutions."[14] The Coopers & Lybrand report suggested that, "Consideration be given to amending the Act to require that one of the partners of each of the firms who is to be responsible

for the conduct of the audit has reasonably extensive experience in the audits of banks or similar deposit-taking financial institutions."[15] Both reports recommend a legislated approach to ensuring auditor knowledge of the business. We do not believe that setting minimum experience requirements by law will ensure adequate business knowledge in such a rapidly evolving industry. We believe that the level of knowledge and experience required of a financial institution auditor must and can be monitored by the profession itself, primarily by the firms responsible. We are sure the courts will not overlook this issue in assessing professional responsibility when financial institutions suffer major losses.

8.59 Currently, large auditing firms have well-developed in-house quality control programs. These programs should be expanded to include a review of the quality of audits of financial institutions if these are not currently included. Practice review standards may need to be strengthened at the provincial level. Concurrently, the CICA could expand its industry studies publishing program to include accounting and auditing guides for financial institutions. A similar program has been conducted by the AICPA in the United States.

RECOMMENDATION

R-50 The *CICA Handbook* should include a section dealing with the knowledge of the business required by auditors of companies in specialized industries. Particular emphasis should be given to the special requirements and characteristics of regulated financial institutions. The importance of an auditor's previous experience and commitment to ongoing professional development in the field should be stressed.

Qualifications of Audit Reports in Deposit-taking Financial Institutions

8.60 A number of submissions to the Commission mentioned the pressure that can be placed upon an auditor to issue an unqualified report on a deposit-taking financial institution, even when he or she has significant misgivings about the fairness of the financial statements. The perception is that a qualification of the financial statements of such an institution will destroy public confidence in it, and this will shortly lead to its collapse. Moreover, the collapse of one major institution could well erode public confidence sufficiently to trigger a string of further collapses. It is understandable that an auditor faced with such a situation will consider the position very seriously, and so he or she should.

8.61   We wish to state unequivocally that we do not believe the contemplation of these serious consequences can be allowed to deter an auditor from qualifying the audit report when professional standards indicate that it is proper to do so. We believe this to be so even if the regulator, or the government itself, were to request the auditor to refrain from qualifying. The primary role of the auditor is still that of attesting to the fairness of financial statements, regardless of how difficult a negative conclusion may be. If auditors were to fail in this duty, the public would be deprived of a protection it thought it had, and in some respects would be worse off than if no auditor at all had been appointed. Indeed, it is essential that the auditor not give management the impression of being open to being influenced by the consequences of otherwise proper disclosure and presentation. Such an impression could only contribute to a failure by management to deal promptly and forthrightly with developing problems.

8.62   Having said this, we must concede that efforts need to be made to mitigate the potentially disastrous effect of full and proper disclosure and/or of an audit qualification. We think the enhanced communication between the regulator, management, audit committee, and auditor, as recommended earlier, is the answer to this problem. It is the regulator's responsibility to monitor the financial health of a financial institution and initiate corrective action when management is apparently unable to cope with its financial problems. If an auditor were to qualify an audit report without prior notice to the appropriate regulatory body, the practical result could be preemption of the regulator's ability to take the most appropriate action—to save the institution if that were considered in the public interest, or to take other action. It seems clear to us, therefore, that an auditor should be required to notify the regulator, as well as management and the directors, when qualification of the audit report or potentially confidence-shaking disclosure is a

serious possibility. The recommendations we have made in paragraphs 8.16 to 8.19 are intended to enable this.

SUMMARY

8.63   In this chapter we discuss the special case of financial institutions, with particular emphasis on deposit-taking institutions. The very large public stake in such institutions makes it imperative that the auditor's responsibilities be clearly spelled out and that audit performance be of the highest quality.

8.64   Because of their public significance, financial institutions are almost invariably monitored by regulators appointed by the government. The public clearly expects that auditors should communicate to regulators information acquired that is relevant to the regulator's responsibility. We agree that such communication is most desirable. We also believe that the regulator should give the auditor any information relevant to the auditor's responsibility to report on fair presentation of the financial statements. We think further that both auditors and regulators should be in communication with the directors of a financial institution, normally through the audit committee. It appears to us that such communication is best fostered by legislation, and we recommend changes in present laws to accomplish this. Pending legislated changes there could be merit in modification of the profession's code of conduct to require communication with the regulator in cases of great urgency. Also, each of the parties would be well advised not to wait for legislation to find ways to ensure effective regular communication with all other parties concerned. For example, auditors should seek from management and/or the audit committee or directors the authority to communicate on a regular basis with the regulator.

8.65   To some extent the development of accounting standards for regulated financial institutions has fallen between two stools. Until recently, the CICA has given little attention to the accounting of financial institutions, in part because of the overriding control of accounting by the regulator and in legislation. On the other hand, although regulators have provided guidance to the accounting that varies in detail from one type of financial institution to another, some aspects have been left inadequately defined.

8.66 We believe that cooperative efforts of the CICA, regulators, and financial institutions themselves are required to improve the accounting. Efforts should be made to develop accounting standards for chartered banks that can be considered reasonably consistent with the theory that underlies GAAP for other industries. The special nature of banks, of course, is likely to mean that some standards will be peculiar to them, but it should nevertheless be clear that these are compatible with GAAP. Consideration also needs to be given to the question of how best to disclose risks for the several types of financial institutions and how to provide information that helps an understanding of their present and prospective liquidity. Finally, more guidance is required with respect to the valuation of assets and liabilities of financial institutions.

8.67 The audit of a financial institution, especially a deposit-taking institution, is difficult. Its accounting can require more judgment in the valuation of assets and liabilities than does the normal audit engagement. Also, the consequences of a qualification of the audit report are very serious for a financial institution, and therefore there may be great pressure on the auditor not to qualify. We wish to stress that an auditor's basic responsibilities are not changed by these difficulties. The auditor must acquire and retain the skills to be able to monitor management's accounting judgments. Having done so, the auditor must be prepared to qualify the audit report when qualification is called for. The only difference that should exist from the responsibilities in a normal audit engagement is the need to communicate with the regulator, and in particular to give warning when an audit qualification appears probable.

8.68 For the reasons mentioned in the preceding paragraph, there is an urgent need to deal with the several special issues related to financial institutions. The CICA, individual firms, the regulators, and the financial institutions should separately and collectively activate themselves on an urgent basis. If any one party cannot get the effective cooperation of the others, it should press on with those parts of the more general issues that it can deal with on its own.

References

1.   Decima Research Limited, Executive Summary of *Public Opinion Survey* (1986), see Appendix B, p. 151.

2.   See, for example, the Bank Act, Part I of the *Banks and Bank Law Revision Act, 1980*, Statutes of Canada 1980-81-82-83, Chapter 40, Sections 219-230.

3.   Ibid., Section 242.

4.   The Honourable Willard Z. Estey, *Report of The Inquiry into the Collapse of the CCB and Northland Bank* (Ottawa: Minister of Supply and Services Canada, 1986), Recommendations 23 and 24, pp. 299, 300.

5.   Coopers & Lybrand, *A Study to Assess the Current Mandate and Operations of the Office of the Inspector General of Banks*, Submitted to The Honourable Barbara McDougall, Minister of State (Finance), (n.p., 1986), Recommendation 6.2.3.2(a), p. 72.

6.   Ibid., Recommendation 6.2.3.6, pp. 72-73.

7.   Ibid., Recommendation 4.6.5(c), pp. 45-46.

8.   Ibid., Recommendation 4.7.5.5(f), p. 49.

9.   See Estey, *Report*, Recommendation 17, p. 292 and Coopers & Lybrand, *Study*, pp. 58-9.

10. See Building Societies Act, 1986; Financial Services Act, 1986; Banking Act, 1987. See also the guidance issued by the Auditing Practices Committee, "Interim Guidance on Ad Hoc Reporting," *Accountancy*, August 1987, pp. 134-36.

11. The CICA has made several submissions to the Minister of State (Finance) on the subject of Financial Sector Reform, including a letter dated December 3, 1986 commenting on recommendations made by Mr. Justice Estey, and two briefs, the first, dated October 30, 1987, dealing with proposals for financial institutions legislation, and the second, dated February 23, 1988, commenting on the government's discussion draft on Trust and Loan Companies Legislation. A number of the recommendations this Commission proposes in this chapter, including our recommendation to facilitate communication between auditors, regulators, management, and audit committees, have been made independently in these CICA submissions.

12. This description is largely based upon *Recent Innovations in International Banking* (n.p.: Bank for International Settlements, 1986), Chapter 10.

13. *CICA Handbook*, Section 1540, "Statement of Changes in Financial Position," (Toronto: CICA).

14. Estey, *Report*, Recommendation 22, p. 298.

15. Coopers & Lybrand, *Study*, Recommendation 6.1.1.6, p. 66.

9

Summary of Conclusions

9.1   In this chapter we sum up the conclusions we have reached. Their essence can be stated in a few brief sentences. We have found some expectation gaps. At present, the number of people who think that their expectations from audits are not fulfilled in significant respects is small, but that number is probably increasing. That trend, if unchecked, could threaten the basis of the auditing profession since the value of an audit rests upon trust in the auditor. We say this in part because those who have expressed the most concern about both the present and the future include regulators who rely heavily on audited financial information, members of the business community who are involved as preparers of financial statements, and some of the most knowledgeable and thoughtful members of the auditing profession itself. Moreover, since the Commission was established, further reports of public companies in financial difficulty have intensified questions about the adequacy of audited financial statements.

9.2   We have not found an immediate or pressing problem of lack of respect for auditors or, on the whole, a concern about the value of audits. Nonetheless, prudence suggests this apparently satisfactory state of affairs should be seen as vulnerable to disruption. The present measure of trust in the profession is consistent with the attitudes of Canadians towards their institutions. But such a trust is best treated as fragile and in need of continuous and solid nourishment. A few instances of losses to the public that are attributed to perceived audit failures could easily shatter the trust and create a situation that would be difficult to deal with for both government and the profession.

9.3   The profession's vulnerability to a rapid loss in public esteem is magnified by a substantial measure of public ignorance concerning the responsibilities entrusted to auditors within our legal system and the limitations on what an audit can reasonably be expected to achieve. The public will judge auditors and audited information by results. If the public believes financial disclosure to be unsatisfactory in a particular case, it will not easily accept arcane explanations of professional responsibility as an excuse for a failure to communicate relevant financial information clearly. Neither will the public accept what it takes to be turf barriers between various parties (including regulators) who share in the responsibility for the financial reporting. Each party will be held to account for the deficient financial disclosure and will not be excused because some other party failed to perform his or her duty. Auditors, however, are particularly at risk. They are seen as the party whose job it is to protect the public from failures or misfeasance on the part of other parties. Moreover, in any suit for damages from alleged deficient financial information, auditors are likely to be seen as having "deep pockets" and therefore become the prime target for attack.

9.4   Our Commission has two aims in this Report. The first, and more important, is to recommend actions the auditing profession can take that will help it come closer to meeting public expectations in all significant respects. It is apparent to us that in any relationship, such as that existing between auditors and users of financial and other information, mutual satisfaction depends upon fairly close correspondence between what is expected (reasonably or unreasonably) and what is actually delivered. If that close correspondence is not achieved, the relationship will be unstable and subject to change in a manner that may not please any of the interested parties.

9.5   Our second aim is to suggest ways that the profession can lessen public misunderstanding and thereby reduce expectation gaps attributable to such misunderstanding. We lay much more stress on the previous aim than upon this one. We have considerable doubts as to the profession's ability to educate the public. More than that, however, we believe that public expectations are for the most part reasonable and achievable, notwithstanding the public's lack of knowledge about the practical problems involved.

9.6   We believe that it is urgent that members of the profession take steps, individually and collectively, to check the growth of the expectation gaps we have identified and reduce or eliminate them to the extent possible. Our Report is intended to outline the most important of those steps needed now. But these may not be sufficient for long. Public expectations are bound to change along with dynamic change in business conditions. Moreover, we do not believe any practical program can eliminate expectation gaps entirely. There is all the more reason, then, to maintain constant vigilance so as to keep to a minimum the strain on public trust in the profession.

CHALLENGES TO BE FACED

9.7   The auditing profession faces several fundamental difficulties in its efforts to meet public expectations.

- The first is that the public assigns a heavy responsibility to the auditor for financial information, yet the auditor does not control its production. This follows from the basic concept of accountability—that the party responsible for performance must account for the performance. It is not the auditor's role to tell the story. Rather, it is the auditor's role—and a vital one—to provide independent assurance that management's reporting of facts is accurate, its judgments in estimates and valuations are fair, and important information is not omitted. To fulfil this role effectively, the auditor must have the cooperation of management. How-

ever, if management is to bear the responsibility for reporting on its stewardship, the auditor not only cannot, but should not, be put in an autocratic position. It is legitimate to establish a generally accepted framework of standards for stewardship reporting. But, to give the auditor control beyond that derived from the recognized standards is to take away the accountability responsibility from the party to whom it belongs.

- The second difficulty is related to the first. The basic division of responsibility means that financial statements are prepared by companies in accordance with accounting standards and are evaluated by auditors in accordance with auditing standards. Moreover, the independent auditor not only does not prepare the statements but also must choose between providing a clean or qualified opinion, a qualified opinion being regarded by the public, including regulators, as an unacceptable black mark. Frequently, this is not a very strong position for the auditor, for one of two reasons. One is that when the accounting standards are not clear and fairly precise in their application, the auditor will often not have a strong or compelling argument to require adherence to a particular interpretation of the standards. The other reason is that the act of qualifying a public financial statement can be so damaging to the company that the auditor may have difficulty in finding a sufficiently strong basis to justify such extreme action.

- The third difficulty relates to the arrangements by which the auditor is remunerated. In a normal commercial relationship, the person who receives a service is the one who pays for it and therefore is in a position to negotiate the price and terms of service. Contracts for audit services, however, follow a different pattern. As a practical matter, the person who selects and pays the auditor is the preparer of the financial statements, not the people who are the primary users of the statements. There can be conflicts between the goals of the preparer and the users. In terms of public expectations, these ought always to be resolved in favour of the third-party users of the statements. Yet, if auditors are to be cost-effective and successful, this must be accomplished without sacrificing the goodwill and cooperation of preparers.

• Finally, there are the inherent difficulties of financial reporting. Business activity is complex and takes place in an ever-changing environment. It is no simple task to maintain satisfactory standards that will ensure the reporting of results of such activity in an understandable and sufficiently complete manner. At present, financial reporting largely relies upon the record of hard transactions between an enterprise and outside parties and on cost figures established by those transactions. It has not, to date, proved possible to replace or supplement this approach by comprehensive current-value information.

• Similarly, it is necessary to go outside the accounting systems for other information that may, upon occasion, be important, such as information about risks and uncertainties, or valuations that might be significant when there are doubts concerning the solvency of the enterprise. The essence of the financial reporting problem is that, to attain generally acceptable standards, it is necessary (1) to establish a framework of concepts and assumptions that inevitably puts some boundaries on what is reported, and (2) to accept some compromises to make the standards workable. The resulting standards are almost certain to be less than completely ideal in many of the situations that can be encountered in the real world.

9.8   There are no easy solutions to these structural problems. There are no changes to the assignment of responsibility for financial reporting or to the arrangements for appointment of auditors that are feasible in practice and sound in principle. This means that we must look to other ways to fortify the independence of the auditor and relieve the commercial strains on his or her professionalism. The profession must learn to live with the present structure of relationships with management, users, and other interested parties. It should seek to manage the relationships better, and it should strive for a constantly improved system of accounting and auditing standards that will strengthen, rather than weaken, the auditor's ability to maintain independence and professionalism.

9.9   We did feel that the rigid division of function whereby management has sole responsibility for furnishing financial information and the auditor is

restricted to reporting on the fair presentation of that information could, in principle, be capable of some relaxation. In the end, however, we concluded that it would be more effective to improve the present body of accounting and auditing standards than to place some new reporting responsibility on the auditor, the boundaries of which would be hard to define. As to accounting standards with their present reliance on transactions and historical costs, a detailed assessment would be beyond our mandate. We have, however, some suggestions for individual extensions or modifications that appear desirable from the standpoint of meeting public expectations.

PRINCIPAL OBJECTIVES

9.10   Having concluded that the present financial reporting structure is not open to basic change, we have attempted to frame a strategy for meeting public expectations within that structure. We consider that three major objectives must be achieved in order to reduce the public expectation gap and hold it to manageable proportions.

• The first objective is to strengthen and maintain the professional integrity of auditors, the principal ingredient of which is independence. We have commented on the pressures on auditor independence created by the unusual structure of the relationship with their clients. In recent years, economic forces have added to that pressure. Serious concerns have been expressed to us on this score by senior members of the profession in Canada, the United States, and the United Kingdom.

• A second and closely related objective is to strengthen the professionalism of auditors generally in their conduct and performance. We see professionalism as the basis for the value added by the audit function, and hence as an essential requirement for meeting public expectations. In the ultimate, it is the foundation of a free and independent public accounting profession. If professionalism should fade as a practical matter, and commercial animus were to prevail in actual decisions made in individual audit situations, there would be a serious danger that public accounting could become indistinguishable from any other commercial enterprise. This would invite government intervention to regulate the public interest component in the auditor's work, at the expense of the freedom and independence of the profession. Although we have a large number of specific recommendations in this area, we wish to stress that the achievement of a mature professionalism must come principally from auditors' own efforts.

• A third objective is to address public expectations directly by extending and improving standards for financial disclosure. Achievement of this objective will carry incidental benefits by way of enhancing the auditor's position and reducing the risk of liability for inadequate disclosure.

9.11   To these positive objectives we add one defensive objective—namely, to lessen public misunderstanding through improved communication. We have already stated that we doubt that the profession can educate the public. Nevertheless, we believe some limited but worthwhile measures can be taken.

9.12   Achievement of these objectives requires the setting of specific goals and actions to attain those goals. Our recommendations for action are summarized below in the context of the broad objectives and specific goals. In making these recommendations we have followed certain working principles. The recommendations should be effective in meeting their goals. They should not carry disadvantages that outweigh their advantages. Finally, they must take into account the reality of what cannot be changed.

STRENGTHENING THE INDEPENDENCE OF THE AUDITOR

9.13   We believe the independence of the auditor can be strengthened if three goals are achieved.

• The first goal follows logically from our conclusion that changes to the present legal structure of responsibility for financial reporting would not be workable. This being so, it is important to the public interest that each party bearing financial reporting responsibilities fulfil its role with max-

imum effectiveness. Our first goal, therefore, is to improve the management of the relationships between the responsible parties as a vital element in fulfilling public expectations. We believe that such effective management will materially strengthen the independence of the auditor, since the other responsible parties will need and should value the assistance of the auditor's impartial opinion and advice in performing their own roles.

• The second goal is to strengthen accounting standards. Given the division of responsibility for financial reporting, the auditor cannot control the quality of financial disclosure. The best that he or she can do is to influence it within the limits established under accounting standards. Since the auditor will always be deemed to have some responsibility when there is a perceived shortcoming in the quality of financial disclosure, these standards, in conjunction with the way in which the auditor manages relationships with other responsible parties, are central to the auditor's ability to meet public expectations. Indeed, we see accounting standards as essential bulwarks for the auditor's independence. Although business is far too complex to permit development of a specific accounting rule to cover every imaginable situation, well-reasoned, well-articulated, and timely standards should substantially reduce the scope for legitimate disagreement.

• The third goal is to strengthen the profession's code of conduct and its enforcement in those aspects that relate to the auditor's independence.

Management of the Relationships between Parties Responsible for Financial Reporting

9.14   Our view is that each party involved in financial reporting has its own role to play and its own problems in doing so, but the handling of the relationships between them is a problem they have in common. This means that no one party is entitled to ignore its own responsibility simply on the assumption that some other party is to be relied upon. We believe the public and the courts will expect each party to assume full responsibility for its own role. To discharge that responsibility fully, each party will be expected to satisfy itself that any reliance placed on other parties is justified.

9.15   Strengthening the communication among parties responsible for financial reporting should be a significant help to the performance of the auditor's responsibility. Establishing easy and active communication between directors and auditors is particularly important. Directors have responsibility for the final approval of the audited financial statements, but they lack the detailed knowledge of the company's activities necessary to ensure that the disclosure is the best possible. For this detailed knowledge they rely in the first instance upon management personnel. However, they should also not only welcome the independent viewpoint of the auditor but recognize they have an obligation to obtain it. For their part, auditors are able to perform their monitoring and evaluation role much better if they are able to communicate easily with those who have the ultimate responsibility for the financial report. An effective audit committee has proved itself a valuable channel of communication between the auditor and the board. We believe it will become even more important in the future, and that the courts are likely to recognize this to an increasing degree when called upon to assess the performance and related responsibilities of auditors, audit committees, and directors in general.

9.16   We urge that auditors be aggressive in using this means of communication. Accordingly, we recommend that guidance be provided in the *CICA Handbook* concerning matters that auditors ought to raise with audit committees and how to conduct relations with them (Recommendation R-2). To facilitate this better liaison and performance, we recommend changes in the law as necessary to require that boards of public companies appoint audit committees composed entirely of outside directors (R-1). We also recommend that the law recognize the key role of audit committees by requiring that boards of directors make public the responsibilities assigned to their audit committees, that audit committees report annually to the shareholders on the performance of their mandate, and, specifically, that audit committees review interim financial statements as well as annual financial statements before publication (R-3).

9.17   We further recommend that auditors see that audit committees are fully informed about frauds that have, or could have had, a material effect on the financial statements and any significant weaknesses in internal controls, particularly those that are important to fraud prevention. Similarly, the auditor should see that the audit committee is fully informed about any significant infractions of the law committed in carrying on the business of the company of which the auditor is aware (R-33, 37).

9.18   A regulator of a financial institution is another party with a significant interest in its financial reporting. We believe that regulators are entitled to full disclosure of information in the possession of the management, directors, and auditors of a financial institution that is pertinent to the regulators' responsibilities. We also believe that regulators have a positive reciprocal obligation to disclose information to auditors and directors that may be important to the institution's financial statements. We recommend that all financial institutions be required to have audit committees composed of outside directors (R-42). We suggest that model legal provisions be developed to facilitate communication between auditors, regulators, and directors of financial institutions (R-41). In addition, we recommend that, to cover the situation where legal obligations to communicate are absent or deficient, the provincial institutes of chartered accountants relax professional confidentiality requirements to enable the auditor to communicate matters of great moment to the regulator (with notice to the directors) if the institution itself fails to do so (R-43).

9.19   Finally, it must be recognized that there will be times when it proves impossible to achieve a strong relationship between the parties responsible for a company's financial reporting. There will even be occasions, fortunately rare, when an auditor feels compelled to resign because of loss of confidence in the trustworthiness of the managers and/or directors of a client, or for other reasons. It seems likely that on some, but not necessarily all, of these occasions the shareholders and public have a right to know why the auditor has resigned or has been replaced.

9.20   We think the auditor's existing responsibilities in connection with public notification of resignation or replacement should be modified. The present policy of the Canadian Securities Administrators requires public notification by the company of changes in auditors, accompanied by a description of "reportable disagreements" between the company and the auditor. A reportable disagreement, in essence, is a disagreement that led to a reservation of the auditor's opinion on financial disclosure of the company, or would have led to such reservation had the auditor completed the engagement. This policy should continue, but the definition of reportable disagreement should be strengthened (R-39).

9.21   A major amendment to the policy should also be made to cover the situation of auditor changes for reasons that are important—such as lack of trust by the auditor in the management of the client—but that do not fall under the definition of a reportable disagreement. We suggest that the present policy be expanded so that securities commissions would receive more timely notification from the auditor of the significant reasons he or she believes explain the auditor's resignation or dismissal. Upon receipt of this notification, the commissions should have the discretion to make further inquiries and require early public disclosure, or take such other action as may be decided is in the public interest (R-38).

9.22   We also recommend a change in the profession's codes of conduct for the protection of possible successor auditors of both public and private companies. We advocate a change in the codes so as to require an auditor who resigns or is displaced to disclose to a proposed successor auditor any knowledge of fraud or illegal activity by the company that the incumbent auditor believes was an important factor in the change of auditors (R-40). In general, we may note that securities regulators, like regulators of financial institutions, also have a significant responsibility for financial reporting of companies under their oversight. Better communication between them and auditors, and, where appropriate, audit committees, would be a desirable development.

Strengthening Accounting Standards

9.23   Although some criticisms of individual accounting standards have been expressed to us, we believe that, overall, the body of standards developed to date by the CICA is well regarded. At the same time, there is increasing dissatisfaction caused by holes in the coverage of accounting standards and by alternative methods of application which permit wide disparities in results reported in identical circumstances. In addition, there is marked dissatisfac-

tion with the speed of the standard-setting process and its apparent inability to date to deal satisfactorily with fast-emerging accounting problems.

9.24   We have several recommendations. We believe the CICA Accounting Standards Committee should mount a special effort to identify and deal, in order of priority and urgency, with issues not satisfactorily covered in present accounting standards (R-4). There should also be a program to identify and eliminate so far as possible those alternative accounting methods that cannot be justified by differences in circumstances (R-7). Both these recommendations have particular application to financial institutions. There is a need to arrive at suitable accounting standards for banks that are consistent with accepted accounting theory. There is also a need for reduction of the alternatives found in accounting for other financial institutions (R-44). If a regulator of a given type of financial institution desires financial statements that use artificial or unrealistically conservative valuations, we recommend that such statements be submitted as special-purpose reports and not be circulated in competition with financial statements prepared on the usual basis (R-45). We also see a need for a separate committee or task force to provide quick practical advice on new accounting issues (R-6).

9.25   Implementation of these recommendations will undoubtedly require an increase in the already substantial effort devoted to standard setting. We recommend a study how to expedite standard setting without sacrificing due process (R-5). We also suggest consideration of ways to increase output and obtain additional financial support for standard setting (R-9).

Auditor Independence and the Profession's Code of Conduct

9.26   In our view, the principal defence against pressures on the independence of auditors must lie in the integrity of individual auditors and audit firms. We have, however, some limited recommendations for actions by the provincial institutes to help ensure the auditor's independence. We suggest consideration of ways to limit overdependence upon a single client for revenue (R-28). We suggest a stronger warning in the profession's code of conduct that an auditor must not permit non-audit services performed for a client to affect the objectivity of the audit opinion (R-29). We also recommend that, when one firm is asked for an accounting opinion by the client of another firm, both firms should communicate fully with each other to establish the facts of the situation for which an opinion is requested and the bases of their separate opinions (R-30).

STRENGTHENING THE PROFESSIONALISM OF THE AUDITOR

9.27 Strengthening the auditor's independence is essential to meeting public expectations but is not enough by itself. The services offered must also meet the public's needs and be performed with professional skill and judgment. We have identified several goals that, if achieved, should strengthen auditor professionalism and thereby help meet public expectations.

- The first goal is to increase the profession's responsiveness to public concerns. We suggest several specific changes in auditing standards to that end.

- The second goal is to achieve renewed recognition of the vital role of professional judgment in performing an audit. Coupled with this is an emphasis on the requirement for a professional level of skill.

- The third goal is to improve the profession's self-regulation.

Increasing the Responsiveness of Auditing Standards to Public Needs

9.28 Auditing standards provide general criteria for satisfactory performance and specific guidance to auditing procedures. The CICA Auditing Standards Committee is composed largely of chartered accountants engaged in the practice of auditing. Since much of the work is highly technical, its members need to be familiar with what an auditor does. At the same time, the decisions of the committee concerning the scope of the auditor's work and the form of the audit report are of broad public interest. We believe the

public's views on these matters should be represented. We doubt, however, that direct lay representation on the Auditing Standards Committee would likely be effective in view of the largely technical nature of the committee's work. Our proposed answer is to form a small group of knowledgeable people drawn from business and government to advise the Auditing Standards Committee on such matters as public expectations for auditor performance, subjects that should be studied by the committee, and whether proposed auditing procedures are worth their cost (R-31).

9.29 We also recommend that auditing standards be modified and amplified in relation to the discovery of fraud. The auditor should give special attention to internal controls that guard against material employee fraud (R-32). Likewise, the auditor should give special attention to the possibility of fraud in view of the fact that attempts to cover up are likely to make discovery of management fraud by ordinary audit procedures less likely than discovery of error (R-34). Further, we recommend additional guidance with respect to the implications for the auditor's report and for financial disclosure of illegal acts by a client (R-35, 36).

9.30 Finally, recent events in Canada and other countries have suggested that the traditional audited financial statements of financial institutions have not provided the degree of warning of financial difficulty that the public feels entitled to expect. Financial institutions are in the business of investing and lending at risk. Careful monitoring and control of that risk is vital to their continued well-being. That monitoring and control cannot be exercised without well-thought-out systems of management information and internal control. We believe that the time has come when the auditors of financial institutions should be asked to make a more complete review of those systems. The purpose would be to assist management, the directors, and the regulator by providing an independent assessment whether the systems meet criteria indicative of effective and prudent systems of record-keeping, control, and internal audit (R-49).

The Need for Professional Judgment

9.31 It is natural that auditors seek rules for their guidance and protection and that regulators and companies sometimes overemphasize literal adherence to rules. Certainly rules and detailed guidance are essential, and we have made several recommendations for their improvement. It would be misleading, however, to suggest that rules can replace the need for professional judgment and the auditor's stand-back assessment, exercised within the framework of reasonable expectations of shareholders and third parties and of the underlying character of accounting principles and standards. Courts are traditionally unwilling to interpret rules in a narrow and literal sense when the results of doing so appear to be unfair or out of keeping with overriding standards and objectives. The same can be assumed to be the case with the expectations of the public at large.

9.32 The profession, audit firms, and individual auditors need to bear these realities constantly in mind if public expectations are to be met and liability exposure minimized. Perhaps the biggest single risk and source of danger for the profession in terms of both public expectations and liability exposure, apart from failures of independence and impartiality, is too literal an approach or cast of mind. Neither the courts nor the public have such a cast of mind, so a literal approach to accounting and auditing rules and their application can readily lead auditors to a false sense of security.

9.33 There is no ultimate answer to this other than a sense of danger, a sensitivity to what shareholders and other third parties are reasonably entitled to expect, and good professional judgment based on a mature understanding of the possibilities and limits of accounting and auditing. However, we recommend amplification of existing auditing standards to re-emphasize and explain more specifically these matters of judgment: (1) the auditor must be satisfied that the client's choices of significant accounting policies are justified in the circumstances (R-18), (2) the auditor must make an independent assessment of the reasonableness of management's estimates (R-19), and (3) the auditor must be satisfied that the financial statements, resulting after incorporation of all management's judgmental decisions, are not misleading in their overall effect (R-20).

9.34 The auditor, of course, must be competent in technical matters as well as having good judgment. We advocate that auditing standards stress the need

for the auditor to be knowledgeable about the client's business, especially when it is specialized in character (as are financial institutions, for example) (R-50).

Professional Self-Regulation

9.35 In the last analysis, maintenance of professional standards depends upon the behaviour of individual auditors and audit firms. They must maintain their competence and put service to the client ahead of their self-interest. We have also drawn attention to commercial practices that might not create problems in an ordinary business, but can do so for a profession operating within the structural arrangements we have described. To some extent auditors must control their commercial instincts. Or, perhaps more accurately, they must take full account of all factors important to their commercial well-being, including maintenance of reputation and avoidance of exposure to liability with consequent heavy insurance costs. They must be careful to accept and retain only clients with integrity. And, they must not price their services in such a way as to undermine their ability to attract qualified staff and perform work that meets professional standards on every engagement.

9.36 One of the principal functions of professional associations is to provide regulation to assist and encourage members to maintain professional standards. We have two observations to make about self-regulatory provisions in the auditing profession. First, we think that professional discipline procedures are somewhat outdated in that they are taken against individual members only and ignore a larger unit of responsibility—the audit firm. The vast majority of audit reports are signed in a firm name, not that of an individual practitioner. In these cases the public relies on the reputation of the firm and usually is unaware of the identity of the individuals who have worked on the engagement. It is only logical, then, that discipline procedures should be directed to the firm, as well as to individuals who may be at fault (R-27).

9.37 A second matter of some concern is the fact that self-regulatory procedures are largely the responsibility of provincial institutes, while the public expects uniform standards nation-wide. We believe the profession would be wise to create a mechanism for achieving common and high standards in codes of professional conduct, practice review procedures, and professional discipline, much as it has done in the field of educational admission standards (R-26).

EXTENDED AND IMPROVED FINANCIAL DISCLOSURE

9.38 A direct way to reduce any public disappointment with the output of auditors is to improve and expand audited financial information so as to more nearly approach public expectations. This suggests two specific goals:

- Expansion of accounting standards so as to lead to better disclosure, both inside and outside financial statements, in line with public expectations.

- Assumption of greater responsibility by the auditor for financial disclosure not contained within the financial statements but associated with them because of its inclusion in the same document. This latter goal suggests broader consideration of the potential role for the auditor in connection with financial disclosure in general, whether or not the disclosure is associated with audited information.

Expansion of Accounting Standards

9.39 The evidence submitted to us on public expectations suggests a number of significant extensions of existing accounting standards.

- Additional guidance should be given to the accounting and disclosure to be provided by a company that has failed or is in danger of failing. Guidance is particularly needed to answer what is proper disclosure in the latter situation (R-10). Related to this, we recommend a change in auditing standards. The auditor should be required to call special attention, in an extra paragraph of the audit report, to the financial statements' disclosure of concerns about the company's ability to continue as a going concern (R-11).

- We also recommend an in-depth study, followed by *Handbook* standards, of the disclosure that should be made of the risks and uncertainties to which a company is exposed (R-12). Commit-

ments by a business increase its potential risks and rewards. In view of the increase in the number of significant commitments undertaken by most businesses today, we recommend a comprehensive standard calling for more intensive disclosure of material commitments than is customary in today's practice (R-13). A separate study of risks and commitments in financial institutions is desirable because of their highly specialized nature (R-46).

- There is a risk that the increasing level of disclosure in financial statements could result in vital information being lost in routine, even if important, detail. We recommend consideration of ways to improve note disclosure so that matters of particular current importance will be highlighted (R-14).

- A number of representations were made to us concerning unsatisfactory asset valuations in current accounting. We are satisfied that clearer guidance is needed in accounting standards as to bases of writedowns of different types of assets in different circumstances (R-15). Such guidance is particularly needed for financial institutions (R-48). Consideration should also be given to the need for better disclosure of the bases of estimates and valuations generally (R-16).

- Study is also needed of the difficult problem of reporting information that is useful in assessing liquidity and liquidity trends in financial institutions (R-47).

- Finally, we believe present disclosure of accounting policies should be expanded to become a more comprehensive explanation of the basis for financial reporting, including explanation of management judgments required in the preparation of the financial statements (R-8, 23).

9.40 Many companies do provide considerable financial disclosure, in annual reports and elsewhere, over and above that in the audited financial statements. We did not discover a strong public demand for such financial information. We nevertheless believe that greater disclosure outside the financial statements could help public understanding of the significance of information inside the statements. We therefore recommend that the CICA assist and cooperate with securities commissions in developing standards for Management Discussion and Analysis to be presented in annual reports outside the audited financial statements (R-17).

Auditor Association with Financial Disclosure outside the Financial Statements

9.41   In view of the probable association of the auditor in the public mind with all financial disclosure in documents that contain audited financial statements, we recommend that auditors insist on the right to review any such information as a condition of accepting an engagement to report on the financial statements (R-21). Auditors may also be asked to take some responsibility for financial disclosure that is not provided in documents containing audited financial statements. Auditing standards should provide guidance to auditor review procedures and the form of reporting (if any) appropriate to the various types of information outside the financial statements (R-22).

PUBLIC MISUNDERSTANDING

9.42   Finally, our inquiries did disclose considerable confusion in the minds of some segments of the public concerning the work that an auditor actually performs and the extent of the auditor's responsibility for the financial information reported. A reduction of this confusion can only be beneficial in limiting expectation gaps. A specific goal, therefore, is to improve communication to the public of the extent of the auditor's responsibility, and that of other parties, for the financial information provided. We recommend two measures. First, a statement of management responsibility should be published in all documents that contain audited financial statements (R-24). Second, the standard audit report should be expanded to explain more fully the nature and extent of the auditor's work and the degree of assurance it provides (R-25). The audit committee's annual report to shareholders, which we have already mentioned, should also help reduce misunderstanding.

IMPLEMENTATION OF THIS REPORT

9.43   We have made a large number of recommendations in this Report, some major and some minor. The recommendations do not constitute an integrated package, in the sense that each recommendation is inextricably linked to all other recommendations. But they do constitute an integrated package in a much deeper and more important sense. They address real problems that go to the very fabric of the auditing profession. The expectation gaps we have identified are not susceptible to quick fixes by tinkering with the system or changing a technique here and there. Accordingly, each recommendation we have made, while technically separate from others, is part of an overall design to strengthen the fabric and, in this sense, is linked to every other recommendation. The Commission therefore considers every proposal important. There are no throwaways, and every recommendation is intended to be acceptable in principle, workable in practice, and to meet a cost-benefit test. Also, this Report is not intended to propose an ideal model or set out a long-term program for the future. It makes here-and-now recommendations to deal with issues that are with the profession now and to which the profession must respond with a sense, not of panic, but of urgency, putting the time that does exist to good use in well-considered strengthening of the fabric of the profession.

9.44   The Report discusses at various points the different roles and responsibilities for financial statements and disclosures of management (including chief executive officers), directors, audit committees, regulators of financial institutions, and auditors. The observations in the Report obviously carry no legal weight as such. Courts will make their determinations based on the facts in particular cases. Nonetheless, it would be surprising if courts examining the adequacy of the behaviour of these different parties in particular cases were not influenced by the concepts of reasonable behaviour that we have discussed as appropriate. From this perspective, it is not only the Institute and individual auditors and auditing firms that should reflect on the observations and suggestions made in the Report and formulate a program of action in response. Chief executive officers and other senior management, directors, audit committees, and regulators should each formulate their own implicit or explicit response programs. If they do not, they should not be surprised if they find themselves exposed to liability as a result of lawsuits brought in respect of alleged shortcomings in financial statements or other financial disclosure.

9.45 So far as the profession is concerned, implementation of our recommendations depends upon action by a number of individuals and institutions. Some recommendations, such as those dealing with changes in accounting and auditing standards, can be implemented by the CICA alone. Some require actions by provincial institutes of chartered accountants. A few require, or would be facilitated by, changes in laws, which means that the CICA and/or provincial institutes need to put forward recommendations for such changes. A significant number of recommendations also depend upon actions by, or changes in the behaviour of, individual auditors or the management of auditing firms.

9.46 A broad-ranging study such as this necessarily touches on many matters that deserve more intensive investigation than we have been able to provide. Our recommendations are intended to indicate directions in which the profession should move but, in some difficult areas, have had to be limited to a recommendation for further study. Even when we are confident of the action proposed in a recommendation, we fully expect that further careful consideration will be necessary to develop strategies for its implementation in workable form. In some cases, part of that consideration must be devoted to ensuring that additional responsibilities assumed by auditors are accompanied by legal protection with respect to the consequences of the appropriate use of judgment by the auditor. Thus, vigorous and sustained effort will be required to realize the full benefit of this study.

9.47 We have some concern that no one party will feel a sufficient incentive to push for implementation of this Report when so many must participate to achieve substantial success. We urge the Board of Governors to give careful thought to this problem of implementation. For example, it might be constructive to seek the cooperation of the provincial institutes in forming a committee of influential accountants, representative of the whole profession, which would be charged with examining each of our

recommendations and promoting appropriate action by those responsible.

EXPECTATIONS FROM IMPLEMENTATION OF THIS REPORT

9.48 If the hurdle of implementation is successfully cleared, we believe our work will be well rewarded. We see it contributing to a profession that meets all reasonable public expectations, has the ability and will to preserve its professional status in the face of commercial pressures, and continues to make an invaluable contribution to the integrity of financial disclosure and accountability that is so important in a modern society. These, we believe, are goals that deserve the profession's utmost efforts and dedication to achieve.

9.49 We expect that if the recommendations made are fully adopted and applied in daily audit practice by committed professionals of integrity, the result will be that the profession's ability to meet public expectations will be greatly strengthened. Moreover, the recommendations will simultaneously reduce the exposure of auditors to public liability. This should help to reduce the profession's concerns about insurance coverage and cost.

9.50 Lawsuits are unpleasant. Their outcome can be unfair and out of all proportion to real fault or reward. Nonetheless, the reality is that the threat of such lawsuits remains a potent means of establishing high standards of performance and ensuring that they are met. The most effective way for the several affected parties to respond to liability and insurance problems is to strengthen standards and performance and thus reduce risks and costs. This is not to say that legislated changes in the extent of liability exposure and in relation to insurance may not also be required. Whether and how such changes will be made cannot be predicted. One can surmise, however, that they are more likely to be won by a profession that is seen to be thoroughly dedicated to the maintenance of standards and the fulfilment of public needs.

CONCLUDING OBSERVATIONS

9.51   We have found a profession that is both strong and vulnerable at the same time. It is strong in part because of its competence, energy, and entrepreneurial drive and in part because, by and large, it has proven itself willing and able to address directly and in a reasonably timely manner the major issues that it faces. The principal evidence of its strength is that it has successfully adapted to the major changes of the past fifty years and has substantially enlarged its role by being responsive to the requirements of the marketplace and changing public needs. It is vulnerable because it is no different from any other significant human enterprise, in that the work of auditing carries special risks under special conditions. Indeed, if this were not so, the demand for, and importance of, auditing would be much less than it is. Like most human enterprises of significance, the source of its value and importance is also the source of its vulnerability.

9.52   There is a need at this particular juncture for the leaders of the profession to reflect upon and project a renewed vision of the profession. That vision should above all seek to preserve the continued independence of the profession, a goal that can only be achieved by deserving the public's trust. The vision should also encompass an outward-looking approach that always starts with a fair understanding of the reasonable expectations of the user, rather than the difficulties or problems of the auditor. Further, the vision should include taking the lead in innovation in financial information but in a manner that is jealous of the third-party credibility that audits provide. This means being assured that the kind of financial information to which the audit credibility is to be added is not only worthwhile but also is sufficiently capable of substantiation that an auditor's association with it means something. (For example, we have raised the question whether numerical forecasts can really meet such a test.)

9.53   No system, however well designed, can be a substitute for men and women of integrity and commitment. But it is equally important that the system in place reinforce the ability of individuals and firms to perform at their highest levels. The recommendations and observations in the Report should be recognized as at all times encompassing both elements: individual and firm responsibility, and system strength. Each recommendation and observation directed toward one element is premised on other recommendations or observations that are directed at the other. The fact that the system needs strengthening does not lessen the responsibility of individuals and firms. And the fact that the responsibility of individuals and firms is at all times central does not lessen the urgency of strengthening the system where that can be achieved. There is no magic. Constant hard work will be needed for as far ahead as one can see, both to strengthen the system and maintain individual integrity and commitment. This should not be surprising. This is what it is to be part of an important profession on which many rely in critical and often difficult situations. The need for commitment explains why the profession must remain free and independent. Equally, commitment is what is required to ensure that it does remain free and independent.

Appendix A

> The Report's formal Recommendations are reproduced below with paragraph numbers included for ease of reference. These Recommendations are broadly worded and are best understood in the context of the detailed discussion in the Report.

Listing of Recommendations

CHAPTER 4 — STRENGTHENING THE AUDIT ENVIRONMENT

Audit Committees

R-1 The CICA should enlist the support of provincial institutes and other interested bodies in seeking legislative amendments that would require all public companies to have audit committees composed entirely of outside directors. (4.28)

R-2 The CICA Auditing Standards Committee should provide guidance in the *CICA Handbook* to matters that should be raised by an auditor with an audit committee (or in the absence of an audit committee, with the board of directors) and to actions an auditor should take when not satisfied with the results of such communication. The guidance should stress the need for timeliness in communication. (4.28)

R-3 The CICA and provincial institutes of chartered accountants should press for changes in the law to require that (1) boards of directors draw up and publish to the shareholders a formal statement of responsibilities assigned to the audit committee, (2) audit committees report annually to the shareholders on the manner in which they have fulfilled their mandate, and that (3) audit committees review both interim financial statements and annual financial statements before publication. (4.28)

Accounting Standards

R-4 The CICA Accounting Standards Committee should make a comprehensive survey of the existing body of accounting theory, identify important issues for which accounting standards are unstated or unclear, determine priorities, and intensify its efforts to give guidance on those issues, all with a sense of real urgency. (4.35)

R-5 The CICA should move decisively so that the process for production of necessary standards is expedited without sacrificing due process. (4.39)

R-6 The CICA should sponsor a separate committee or task force to express considered opinions on new accounting issues that are likely to receive divergent or unsatisfactory accounting treatment in practice in the absence of some guidance. These opinions should be developed expeditiously and be given wide publicity so that members of the profession can give them due weight when dealing with the issues in question. (4.45)

R-7 The CICA Accounting Standards Committee should undertake a review of GAAP to identify situations in which alternative accounting methods are accepted under GAAP, and should make every effort to eliminate alternatives not justified by substantial differences in circumstances. When it is thought such justification exists, the criteria for selection of the appropriate policy should be stated clearly. (4.54)

R-8   If, in some individual area, support cannot be mustered for the elimination of alternatives not justified by substantial differences in circumstances, accounting standards should require disclosure that the choice of policies in this area is arbitrary. That disclosure should indicate the accounting result that would have been obtained by using the alternative. When disclosure of the result in quantitative terms would

be impractical or excessively costly, the indication may be in approximate or general terms (at a minimum stating whether the alternative is more or less conservative than that actually adopted). (See also Recommendation R-23 in Chapter 5.) (4.54)

R-9   The CICA should study how to increase the output of its standard-setting activities. As part of this study, it should consider the possibility of obtaining additional financial support from sources other than membership fees without jeopardizing the independence of the standard-setting function. (4.58)

CHAPTER 5 — FINANCIAL REPORTING: CONTENT, COMMUNICATION, AND AUDIT CONTRIBUTION

Extensions of Financial Disclosure

R-10   The CICA Accounting Standards Committee should study the question of financial reporting when an enterprise is in financial difficulty and issue explicit standards giving guidance to:

- The basis of reporting appropriate for a company that has failed.

- The disclosure that should be made by management in financial statements when an enterprise is a going concern at the reporting date but there is significant danger that it may not be able to continue as such throughout the foreseeable future. Since every enterprise carries some risk of failure, the standard should be as clear as possible concerning (1) how serious the risk of failure must be to require special disclosure of that risk, (2) whether or how gradations in the degree of risk should be indicated in the disclosure, (3) the length of the period ahead for which the risk of failure must be evaluated, and (4) whether or to what extent there is a need for indication of the extent of changes that might be required in the figures reported in the event of business failure. (5.19)

R-11   The CICA Auditing Standards Committee should hold to its present position that qualification of the audit report is not required if financial statements give adequate warning of a serious risk of business failure. It should, however, issue a new standard requiring the auditor to highlight the risk by calling special attention, in an additional paragraph in the audit report, to the financial statement disclosure. (5.19)

R-12   The CICA should initiate and complete as soon as possible a study of risks and uncertainties leading to conclusions as to how they may best be disclosed in financial statements or elsewhere (e.g. in Management's Discussion and Analysis in the annual report). Such a study should:

- Describe the nature of uncertainties and risks in some depth.

- Attempt a classification of different types of uncertainties and risks and provide guidelines for assessing their significance, particularly in terms of magnitude and probabilities.

- Consider how each category might best be disclosed and provide guidance on the form of disclosure.

- Indicate how and when gains and losses should be recognized in the financial statements (along the lines of present recommendations with respect to contingencies).

Handbook recommendations based upon this study should be issued as soon as possible after its completion. (5.28)

R-13 *CICA Handbook* recommendations with respect to disclosure of commitments should be amplified so that material commitments, when not capitalized as assets and liabilities in the balance sheet, will be disclosed in fuller detail than is customary in today's practice. (5.32)

R-14 The CICA Accounting Standards Committee should consider how financial disclosure in notes supplementing the financial statements might be arranged so as to highlight matters of particular importance—including disclosure of risks and doubts as to going-concern status—and provide guidance in a standard on disclosure. (5.34)

Valuations and Estimates

R-15 The CICA Accounting Standards Committee should give priority to defining more precisely the bases for writedowns of assets below cost-based figures, particularly in relation to the assets of specialized industries where the valuation placed on specific classes of assets is highly material to the reported net equity of the enterprise. (5.42)

R-16 The Committee should also consider whether there is a need for better guidance with respect to disclosure of the bases used in making accounting estimates and the possible range in the valuation figures that could have resulted within the exercise of reasonable judgment. (5.42)

Disclosure Outside Financial Statements

R-17 The CICA should look favourably on additional financial disclosure of a softer, more subjective nature in a Management Discussion and Analysis section of the annual report. The CICA should assist and cooperate with securities commissions in the development of standards for information in the MD & A. (5.46)

Exercise of Auditor's Judgment

R-18 The general principle that the auditor should be satisfied that the client's accounting policies are appropriate should be continued. The CICA Auditing Standards Committee should amplify that standard to emphasize that:

- When an accounting standard is stated in general terms and judgment is required as to the accounting policy to be adopted for implementation, the auditor should be satisfied that the accounting policy used is a fair and reasonable interpretation of the spirit of the standard.

- When new accounting policies are adopted in response to new types of transactions or new kinds of assets or obligations, the auditor should be satisfied that the accounting policies adopted properly reflect the economic substance of the transaction, asset, or liability in accordance with the broad theory governing present-day financial reporting and the established concept of conservatism in the face of uncertainty.

- When the selection of an accounting policy is arbitrary in certain named areas, the auditor is not expected to object to the selection of an established alternative, notwithstanding that the auditor may have a personal preference for one of the possible alternatives. (5.53)

R-19 The CICA Auditing Standards Committee should amplify auditing standards to emphasize the auditor's responsibility to come to an independent opinion on the reasonableness of management's estimates. (5.55)

R-20 The CICA Auditing Standards Committee should amplify auditing standards to stress the auditor's responsibility to be satisfied that the end result of the client's application of accounting principles, judgment estimates, and disclosure is not materially misleading. (5.59)

Additional Auditor Responsibilities

R-21 Auditing standards or provincial codes of conduct, whichever is the more appropriate, should be amended so that auditors will accept an engagement to report on financial statements for public distribution only on the condition that they have a right to (1) review and comment on financial disclosure outside the financial statements that is intended to be included in the document in which the audited statements are to be published, and (2) refuse consent to publication of the audit report in association with that disclosure if the latter is seriously objectionable. (5.63)

R-22 The CICA Auditing Standards Committee should provide more guidance to appropriate procedures to be undertaken by the auditor, and the appropriate form of communication of the auditor's involvement and findings, with respect to all types of financial disclosure outside the traditional financial statements. This includes both information with which the auditor is required to be involved by auditing standards, and information with which the auditor may be involved by special engagement with a client. (5.67)

Clarification of Financial Reporting Responsibilities

R-23 The CICA Accounting Standards Committee should amplify the present standard requiring disclosure of accounting policies, so as to emphasize:

- The underlying theory of accounting being followed.

- The judgments made in the selection of accounting policies and the effect, if significant, of choosing one alternative from two or more acceptable policies (see Recommendation R-8 in Chapter 4).

- The judgments and estimates made in the valuation of assets and liabilities and the implementation of accounting policies, together with the evidence supporting such judgments.

Detailed disclosure of actual judgments and estimates made by management could be usefully integrated with the disclosure. (5.73)

R-24 The CICA should support a legal requirement that management clearly acknowledge its basic responsibility for the information in the audited financial statements. The management statement should be outside the financial statements themselves, but should be published in close association with them. (5.77)

R-25 The CICA Auditing Standards Committee should adopt an expanded standard audit report to explain more fully the nature and extent of the auditor's work, and the degree of assurance it provides. To the extent possible, the same wording should be used in the Canadian standard audit report as that used in other major industrial countries. (5.83)

CHAPTER 6 — PROFESSIONALISM

Professional Self-Regulation

R-26 The provincial institutes of chartered accountants should seek effective practical mechanisms to promote country-wide uniformity in self-regulatory functions that are designed to ensure a high quality of service to the public. An incidental objective should be to find ways to increase public awareness of the profession's self-discipline procedures. Three subjects suggested for priority action are coordination or harmonization of (1) the profession's code of conduct, (2) the profession's practice review procedures, and (3) the profession's disciplinary procedures. (6.21)

R-27 Provincial institutes of chartered accountants should study how to effectively bring audit firms as well as individual members within the ambit of disciplinary proceedings. (6.23)

R-28 Provincial institutes of chartered accountants should consider how to limit potential threats to the auditor's independent judgment caused by the fact that a significant percentage of revenue comes from one client or associated group of clients. (6.42)

R-29 The profession's codes of conduct or interpretations of the codes should be amplified to speak to the potential consequences if non-audit services are performed for an audit client. It should be stressed that the auditor has a professional obligation in assessing audit evidence to avoid any bias or predisposition that could result from advice given to the client in a consulting capacity. Independent advice from third parties may be helpful on occasion to ensure compliance. (6.50)

R-30 The profession's codes of conduct should be amended to require an accountant from whom advice is sought by the client of an incumbent auditor to communicate with that auditor before expressing any form of opinion. In the course of that communication, the accountant requested to advise should confirm the pertinent facts of the situation with the incumbent auditor. The auditor and the accountant consulted should each have an obligation to discuss fully the factors that lead them to the position they have taken or propose to take. (6.60)

Public Input to Auditing Standards

R-31 The CICA standard-setting structure should be broadened to provide a practical channel for effective advice on auditing standards from knowledgeable members of the lay public. (6.74)

CHAPTER 7 — FRAUD; ILLEGAL ACTS; CHANGE OF AUDITOR

Employee Fraud

R-32 The CICA Auditing Standards Committee should modify auditing standards to take greater account of the possibility of material undiscovered employee fraud. The auditor normally tests the functioning of internal controls only to the extent it is proposed to rely upon them in planning audit tests. In the auditor's initial review of internal controls, however, specific consideration should be given to the vulnerability of the enterprise to material employee fraud, and to the controls against such fraud. These controls should be tested even though some other parts of the internal control system are not tested. The need for extension of audit procedures should be considered if the controls against material employee fraud appear to be weak. (7.17)

R-33 The CICA Auditing Standards Committee should recommend that the auditor ensure that the audit committee (or board of directors if there is no audit committee) is adequately informed about material employee frauds that have occurred, and significant weaknesses in internal controls of which the auditor is aware, particularly those that are important to fraud prevention. (7.21)

Management Fraud

R-34 The CICA Auditing Standards Committee should extend its guidance to audit procedures related to the discovery of management fraud. Since normal audit procedures provide a lower level of assurance with respect to the discovery of management fraud than they do with respect to the discovery of simple errors, the auditor should extend his or her work to give specific consideration to the possibility that such fraud may have occurred. If that consideration raises any question in the auditor's mind about the validity of the traditional assumption of management honesty, additional audit procedures should be devised to provide additional assurance. (7.24)

Illegal Acts

R-35 The CICA Auditing Standards Committee should provide additional guidance to the implications for the auditor's report of illegal actions that have had or may have material financial consequences. (7.32)

R-36 The CICA Accounting Standards Committee should provide additional guidance to the implications for financial statement disclosure of illegal actions that have had or may have material financial consequences. (7.33)

R-37 The CICA Auditing Standards Committee should state specifically that the auditor should ensure that the audit committee (or board of directors if there is no audit committee) is fully informed about serious infractions of the law committed in carrying on the business of the company of which the auditor is aware. (7.34)

Changes of Auditors

R-38 Changes should be made to securities legislation or regulations with the objectives of (1) improving the timeliness of notification of auditor changes, (2) improving the ability of an auditor to make adequate disclosure of the reasons for the change in auditor, and (3) enabling proper and timely public disclosure of the reasons when, in the discretion of the securities commissions, the shareholders' and public's interests demand it. (7.45)

R-39 National Policy Statement No. 31 of the Canadian Securities Administrators, providing for disclosure upon resignation or replacement of an auditor, should be strengthened. The definition of a "reportable disagreement" should be revised so as to ensure disclosure of disagreements between an auditor and management that would have led to an audit qualification or comment had management not altered the financial information that was published. (7.45)

R-40 Provincial institutes of chartered accountants should amend their codes of conduct so that an auditor resigning or being replaced is obliged to inform a possible successor auditor if suspected fraud or other illegal activity by the client was an important factor in the resignation or in the client's decision to appoint a different auditor. (7.48)

CHAPTER 8 — REGULATED FINANCIAL INSTITUTIONS

Communication with Regulators

R-41 The CICA, together with representatives of provincial institutes of chartered accountants and regulators, should initiate a task force to study and recommend a model set of legal provisions to govern communications between auditors, regulators, management, and audit committees or directors of financial institutions. When completed, the CICA and the provincial institutes should actively support efforts to have the proposed provisions incorporated in appropriate legislation. The same task force should suggest a sample list of matters that a regulator might publish as matters to be communicated under present legislation. (8.17)

R-42 To facilitate the communication process, changes should also be made to certain laws so that all financial institutions are required to have audit committees made up of outside directors. (8.17)

R-43 Pending changes in the law, the provincial institutes of chartered accountants should immediately amend their codes of conduct to enable the auditor of a financial institution to communicate matters of great moment to the regulator (with notice to the directors) if the institution itself fails to do so. (8.19)

Accounting Standards for Financial Institutions

R-44 The CICA Accounting Standards Committee should continue its present efforts to define bank accounting standards that are both satisfactory to the industry and the federal Superintendent of Financial Institutions and can be considered in accordance with GAAP. The Accounting Standards Committee should also continue to give high priority to providing guidance with respect to the special accounting problems of other types of financial institutions. This would be an important part of the program recommended to eliminate holes in the coverage of accounting standards and reduce the number of alternative accounting practices that are not justified by differences in circumstances. The CICA should seek the cooperation of industry representatives and both federal and provincial regulators in this task and should continue to work with provincial institutes of chartered accountants to that end. If sufficient cooperation of all interested parties is not forthcoming, the CICA may have to consider more heroic measures to protect auditors and the public generally. (8.33)

R-45 A regulator of any type of financial institution for which GAAP have been established should be urged to treat any financial statement requested on an artificial or unrealistic basis of accounting as a special-purpose report and not as a substitute for statements prepared in accordance with GAAP. (8.34)

R-46 The CICA Task Force on Financial Institutions, in conjunction with regulators and representatives of financial institutions, should initiate a separate study similar to that proposed in Recommendation R-12 in Chapter 5, to determine the best manner of disclosing risks and uncertainties. (8.38)

R-47 The CICA Task Force on Financial Institutions, in conjunction with regulators and representatives of financial institutions, should study the best manner of presentation of information bearing on liquidity in the financial statements or annual reports of such institutions. (8.44)

R-48 The CICA Task Force on Financial Institutions, in conjunction with regulators and representatives of financial institutions, should study asset and liability valuation problems in financial institutions and furnish recommendations. Guidance should be provided with respect to the valuation of major categories of assets, actuarial liabilities, and loss provisions required for off-balance-sheet assets and liabilities, to the extent guidance is not already available. (8.49)

Auditor Reporting on Internal Control

R-49 The CICA should look favourably upon a request that the auditor report to the regulator on the design and functioning of internal control systems of financial institutions, provided satisfactory guidance is developed concerning the specific types of assurance that would be rendered in such a report. To this end, the CICA, in conjunction with regulators, auditors, and representatives of the various types of financial institutions, should develop criteria for effective and prudent systems of record-keeping, control, and internal audit for each type of institution. (8.56)

Auditor's Knowledge of the Business

R-50 The *CICA Handbook* should include a section dealing with the knowledge of the business required by auditors of companies in specialized industries. Particular emphasis should be given to the special requirements and characteristics of regulated financial institutions. The importance of an auditor's previous experience and commitment to ongoing professional development in the field should be stressed. (8.59)

Appendix B

> This Executive Summary was prepared by Decima Research Limited and included in its report of a public opinion survey conducted by Decima for the Commission.

DECIMA

EXECUTIVE SUMMARY

Decima Research is pleased to present this Executive Summary of a public opinion survey conducted in July 1986 for the Commission to Study the Public's Expectations of Audits. Our complete report includes a more detailed analysis of the survey results and a full description of our sampling and data collection procedures.

Overview

The purpose of the public opinion survey is to provide the Commission with reliable information concerning the public's attitudes toward and understanding of audited financial statements, the audit process and the CA profession in general. In the course of the survey, we conducted telephone interviews with a random sample of 1,000 Canadian residents, 18 years of age and older. This sample group included 390 respondents who have either read audited financial statements or have invested in publicly traded shares. In order to broaden our understanding of the attitudes and perceptions of this "knowledgeable" group, we conducted telephone interviews with an additional sample of 150 individuals who met these criteria.

All interviews were conducted using a pre-designed questionnaire which was organized in a three-tier format. All respondents were asked to answer one group of basic questions. All "knowledgeable" respondents were asked to answer a group of questions which could only be answered meaningfully by individuals with some direct exposure to the financial disclosure system. Finally, "knowledgeable" respondents who have read audited financial statements and have expressed some familiarity with them were asked to answer a third group of questions relating specifically to such statements.

In analyzing the responses of the "knowledgeable" respondents, we were cognizant of the fact that this group was comprised of three basic subsets: those who invest but do not read audited financial statements; those who read audited financial statements but do not invest; and those who both read audited financial statements and invest. Those who invest but do not read audited financial statements (approximately 15% of the "knowledgeable" group) were not asked to respond to the third tier of questions, which, as noted above, related specifically to such statements. The remaining two subsets responded to the entire questionnaire. Our comparison of the responses of the entire "knowledgeable" group showed no significant differences among the subsets, and accordingly, the group has been treated as homogeneous for the purposes of analysis.

For the remainder of this Executive Summary, we refer to the views expressed by the "knowledgeable" group in response to the second and third tiers of questions as the views of the "reader/investor public." This is the "group" which will be most affected by and responsive to any changes in audited financial statements or the financial disclosure system. We refer to the views expressed by the entire sample population as the views of the "general public." This distinction is made because the views held by a majority of the general public in relation to auditors, audits and the financial disclosure system are based on broad perceptions rather than specific knowledge of the underlying subjects. Thus, the perceptions and attitudes of the general public may not be affected by changes in audited financial statements or the financial disclosure system in the same way or to the same extent as those of individuals with specific knowledge and understanding of these subjects. It should be noted, however, that even within the group of respondents classified as "knowledgeable," there are many individuals who indicate that they have limited exposure to and knowledge of audited financial statements.

The CA Profession

The survey results indicate that the CA profession enjoys a positive image in Canada. Eighty-six percent (86%) of the general public have a somewhat or very favourable impression of CAs, and 87% of the general public feel that CAs have maintained or improved their image in recent years. While the CA profession should be heartened by these findings, it must be recognized that 64% of the general public have never used the services of a CA and 67% have never read a set of audited financial statements. One possible implication of this lack of exposure is that changes to audited financial statements or the audit process will not have a significant effect on the overall image of the CA profession in Canada. Another possible implication, however, is that the views of the general public could change quite dramatically in response to adverse publicity concerning the profession, without regard to the particular facts and circumstances giving rise to such publicity.

Audit Process and Reporting

Questions relating to the audit process and the reporting of audit results were posed to "knowledgeable" respondents only, with one exception. The entire sample population was asked to describe what an auditor of a company does, by selecting a description from a limited list of alternatives. Forty-one percent (41%) of the general public believe that auditors report on the fairness of a company's financial statements. Twenty-four percent (24%) believe that auditors report on the efficiency, economy and effectiveness of the management process, and 25% believe that auditors guarantee the financial soundness of a company. The remaining 10% of the respondents state that they do not know what an auditor does. There is no significant difference between the responses of the "knowledgeable" group and those of the remaining portion of the sample population. This lack of consensus regarding the role of the auditor must be taken into consideration in interpreting the responses summarized below. For example, it may be of little comfort to the profession to know that a vast majority of the general and reader/investor publics are satisfied with the performance of auditors, if the profession concludes that the views of a substantial portion of both publics are based on a misperception of the role of the auditor.

The Audit Process — Eighty-nine percent (89%) of the reader/investor public believe that the performance of auditors in conducting audits has stayed the same or improved over the past few years. In response to a suggestion that price competition may have forced auditors to charge less than they should, 61% of the reader/investor public are of the view that such competition would either have no effect or a positive effect on the quality of audits performed. Thirty-five percent (35%) state that such competition would have a negative effect on the quality of audits.

There is also little consensus regarding what an auditor does in performing an audit. For example, when asked what percentage of a company's transactions auditors check during their audit, the answers of respondents are spread relatively evenly across four quartiles from 0 to 100%, with 37% of the reader/investor public believing that auditors check over 75% of transactions. There is also considerable disagreement concerning the role that judgement plays in the conduct of an audit. Approximately 45% of the reader/investor public are in moderate to strong agreement with the proposition that very little judgement is required in the conduct of an audit because auditors are required to follow generally accepted auditing standards. Approximately 31% of the reader/investor public moderately or strongly disagree with this proposition, and the remaining 24% are essentially neutral or express no opinion.

The effect of the auditor's relationship with management was also explored in the survey. Respondents were asked whether they believe that because auditors are paid by management, they "bend the rules" to make sure that the financial statements will have a "clean" or unqualified audit opinion. Forty-five percent (45%) of the reader/investor public disagree with this proposition. Twenty-four percent (24%) are neutral. Respondents were also asked whether they believe that there is a serious potential for auditors to

lose their objectivity when their auditing firm also undertakes other work, such as management consulting or tax advice, for the audit client. Fifty percent (50%) either moderately or strongly agree with this proposition.

Public opinion is almost evenly split regarding the auditor's responsibility for detecting fraud. Fifty-two percent (52%) of the reader/investor public believe that auditors should only react to fraud if they "come across it," while 47% believe that auditors should actively search for fraud. Of the 47% who believe that auditors should actively search for fraud, 70% would maintain that view even if an active search for fraud would double the audit fees. Public opinion concerning the auditor's duty to report fraud is discussed below.

Finally, respondents were asked if they believe it is "right and proper" for individuals or organizations to sue auditors if they feel that the auditors have failed in the performance of their duties. Fifty-two percent (52%) of the reader/investor public believe that it is "right and proper" for auditors to be sued in such circumstances, while 44% believe such lawsuits to be "wrong and improper." Of the 52% of the reader/investor public who are in favour of being able to sue auditors, 68% believe that there should be some monetary limit on the amount recoverable from auditors in these circumstances.

Reporting — Respondents were asked a series of questions concerning the method and form of reporting by auditors. Ninety-one percent (91%) of the reader/investor public indicate that they have some or a great deal of confidence in the audit report. There is a considerable divergence of opinion, however, as to what information is contained in the audit report. Eighteen percent (18%) of the reader/investor public describe the audit report as a factual presentation of assets or liabilities. Forty-eight percent (48%) describe the audit report as indicating the financial status or situation of a company. Thirty percent (30%) of the reader/investor public state in various ways that the audit report identifies the financial statements which have been examined and sets forth the auditor's opinion.

Respondents were also asked to identify the individuals or groups to whom auditors report. Up to two responses were accepted. On their initial response, 34% of the reader/investor public identify the board of directors, 27% identify management, 20% identify the shareholders and 13% identify the government. The remaining 6% identify the auditors. The ranking of these selections remain the same after combining the second responses with the first.

Several questions were posed to respondents to determine whether they view a "clean" or unqualified audit report as a guarantee of the financial soundness of a company. Ninety-three percent (93%) of the reader/investor public state that an unqualified audit report is not a guarantee that a company will not experience financial difficulties at some time in the future. The reader/investor public, however, are almost evenly split in their response to the proposition that an unqualified audit opinion means that there is no possibility that the company is presently experiencing serious financial problems. Thirty-nine percent (39%) indicate medium to strong agreement with this proposition, while

35% indicate medium to strong disagreement. Thus it would appear that a significant portion of the reader/investor public believe that an unqualified audit opinion is only issued in circumstances where a company is not presently experiencing financial problems.

Respondents were also asked to consider a hypothetical situation in which a company would otherwise receive an unqualified audit opinion, but there is some need to warn the reader about something in the financial statements. Forty-seven percent (47%) of the reader/investor public believe that a warning should be set out in the notes to the financial statements, while 49% are of the view that this warning should be contained in the audit report.

Sixty-six percent (66%) of the reader/investor public believe that a movement away from a standardized format for the audit report will make the message in the report more meaningful, and that people will then read it. On the other hand, 31% believe that a movement toward more flexibility in the audit report will make it more difficult to interpret, and that the message in the report "will be watered down."

Eighty-six percent (86%) of the reader/investor public believe that an unqualified audit opinion is not a guarantee that fraud does not exist. There does not appear to be any consensus, however, concerning the method of reporting frauds which have been detected by the auditor. Forty-four percent (44%) of the reader/investor public feel that auditors should report such frauds to the board of directors. Twenty-five percent (25%) believe that auditors should report such frauds to the government or to the police. The remaining respondents suggest that auditors should take some other action, such as demanding that management take corrective action, rendering a qualified opinion on the financial statements or resigning from the audit. Only 2% suggest the latter alternative.

Finally, 91% of the reader/investor public believe that the auditors of regulated financial institutions should have the "legal right and obligation" to report serious matters to the regulator if the company's management does not do so.

Audited Financial Statements

The only question posed to the entire sample population regarding financial statements was whether financial statements represent an exact account of a company's financial affairs or a reasonable approximation. Eighty-four percent (84%) of the general public believe that financial statements are a reasonable approximation rather than an exact account.

Eighty-eight percent (88%) of the reader/investor public state that they have some or a great deal of confidence in audited financial statements. Seventy-seven percent (77%) state that they place some or a lot of reliance on audited financial statements when making an investment decision. This percentage is even higher among investors in

publicly traded shares. While these responses indicate that audited financial statements are of value to the reader/investor public, the responses to another question in the survey suggest that there are many members of the public who do not distinguish between audited and unaudited financial statements. Twenty-seven percent (27%) of the reader/investor public state that in their view there is no difference between audited financial statements and unaudited financial statements, and a further 5% state that they do not know whether such a difference exists. Thus, a significant minority of the reader/investor public may derive little value from the audit function.

There is no clear consensus among the reader/investor public as to who actually prepares the financial statements to be audited. Twenty-nine percent (29%) state that the auditors prepare the financial statements, and a further 14% state that the financial statements are prepared by an accountant. This latter response is ambiguous, since the respondents may be referring to an accountant employed by the company, or to an accountant employed by the CA firm conducting the audit. Thirty-seven percent (37%) of the reader/investor public state that the financial statements are prepared by management, and 12% are of the view that financial statements are prepared by the board of directors.

Respondents were also asked to provide their views regarding the nature of the information conveyed by financial statements. Sixty-nine percent (69%) of the reader/investor public believe that financial statements generally show how much a company would be worth after paying all its debts. This might be interpreted to mean that a substantial majority of these people believe that financial statements provide a good indication of the value of a company. This would appear to be consistent with the opinion expressed by 78% of the reader/investor public that audited financial statements provide a very good indication of the state of health of a company.

The reader/investor public are generally content with the information presently disclosed in financial statements, with 72% responding that financial statements should not include any information other than what they now contain. When questioned more specifically on the adequacy of the disclosure of risks in the financial statements and the audit report, 65% state that such disclosure is either adequate or very adequate.

Approximately 45% of the reader/investor public moderately or strongly agree with the proposition that very little judgement is required in the preparation of financial statements because such statements are normally prepared on the basis of generally accepted accounting principles. Twenty-nine percent (29%) moderately or strongly disagree with this proposition and the remainder of the respondents are essentially neutral. When asked whether a company should be allowed to choose the most appropriate accounting method from a set of acceptable alternatives, 54% of the reader/investor public believe that the company should be allowed to make such a choice, while 45% believe that one accounting method should be required for all companies.

Summary

The CA profession is held in high regard by the Canadian general public. A majority of the general public, however, have never used the services of a CA or read a set of audited financial statements. The positive image of the profession is, therefore, based to a large extent on hearsay rather than personal experience, and may be vulnerable to adverse publicity, whether or not it is well-founded.

There are indications that even among the members of the general public who have had some exposure to auditors or audited financial statements, there is a substantial amount of confusion regarding the role of the auditor and the messages conveyed by the audit report and the financial statements. In some cases, this confusion may be alleviated through better communication to the readers of audited financial statements. In other cases, improved communication may not by itself cause members of the public to alter their opinions, and the CA profession may be required to re-examine its own views. The strategy ultimately adopted by the profession will need to be sufficiently innovative and flexible to accommodate future changes in public opinion, without over-reacting to temporary shifts in attitude.

August, 1986

Appendix C

This description of the CA profession in Canada was prepared by the CICA and included as Appendix I in its February 1986 submission to the Commission of Inquiry into the State of Affairs Surrounding the Cessation of Operations of the Canadian Commercial Bank and the Northland Bank ("Estey Inquiry").

The CA Profession in Canada

All 40,000 chartered accountants in Canada are members of the Canadian Institute of Chartered Accountants (CICA) which was originally formed in 1902 as the Dominion Association of Chartered Accountants. The CICA is the oldest and largest national body of professional accountants in Canada. Chartered accountants become members of the CICA through their membership in the provincial institutes upon completion of a uniform national final examination and professional training in public practice.

By virtue of a written agreement of affiliation with the CICA, members of The Institute of Chartered Accountants of Bermuda are also members of the CICA.

In accordance with the division of legislative powers in Canada, the practice of the professions, including education and examination, promulgation and enforcement of standards of practice, and discipline, is a provincial responsibility. Because of the national and international scope of business and finance and the desirability of uniform standards for the admission to and practice of the profession, the CICA has been given responsibility for certain functions in which a national interest has been identified. The CICA and provincial institutes each enjoy sovereignty in their respective jurisdictions with recognition that certain responsibilities are shared.

CICA responsibilities

- Accounting and auditing research in both the private and public sectors, including developing authoritative accounting and auditing standards.

- Liaison with the federal government and agencies and national organizations.

- Expression of the profession's viewpoint on national matters of concern.

- Publication of a professional journal and other publications.

- National communications and public relations.

- Representation of the Canadian profession internationally.

Provincial institute responsibilities

- The education, training, examination and admission of new members.

- The maintenance of appropriate standards of competence and conduct.

- Supervision and regulation of professional conduct and ethics, including the investigation of complaints and the disciplinary process.

- Liaison with provincial governments, agencies and organizations.

- Provincial public relations and community service programs.

Shared responsibilities

- Long-range planning for the profession as a whole.

- Continuing professional development programs and courses for CAs.

ENTRY INTO THE CA PROFESSION

Admission to the CA profession depends upon meeting the entry level education requirements, completing a prescribed program of practical experience and training instruction and passing the same rigorous final examinations that are uniformly administered across the country.

Level of education required

The minimum required level of education to enter the CA education program is a degree from a recognized university.

Although the undergraduate university degree may be completed in any program, there is also a prescribed requirement for instruction in areas such as financial accounting, management accounting, auditing, taxation, computer science, quantitative methods, finance, economics, law and management. Students who have not completed all of the required courses while enrolled in a recognized university degree program must complete them through further courses and examinations at a university level.

Provincial institutes also require the successful completion of post-university courses and examinations which cover subjects that further the student's knowledge of the profession's theory and practice. Concentration is therefore placed on areas of advanced auditing, professional practice, taxation, and advanced and specialized accounting. There are slight variations from province to province in this system.

Practical experience requirement

Experience in a CA firm is an essential part of a student's training. The minimum experience requirement is generally three years. In some provinces, there is a reduced two-year requirement for students with a high university educational standing. Only public accounting offices approved by the provincial institute may train CA students.

Uniform final examinations

Since 1939, all the provincial institutes have cooperated in setting annual Uniform Final Examinations (UFE) for Canadian CA candidates.

Each provincial institute retains the right to educate and examine its own CA students. The CICA there-

fore does not grant the CA designation, nor does it have any direct responsibility for establishing the syllabus for the UFE, setting questions or marking papers. Appointed provincial members form a committee, the Interprovincial Education Committee (IPEC), to make decisions relating to student education and the UFE. Interprovincial communication, cooperation and uniformity are thus achieved at the national level.

A significant benefit of having a national examination is that the CA designation granted by one province is recognized by all the others.

The Syllabus Subcommittee of IPEC ensures that the syllabus properly reflects both the knowledge and underlying professional skills required from the CA, both now and in the foreseeable future.

The Board of Examiners, also a subcommittee of IPEC, sets the specific questions for the annual examinations, and supervises the marking procedure. Care is taken in the marking process to preserve the candidate's anonymity, as well as to ensure consistency and fairness in the marks given.

REGULATION OF THE CHARTERED ACCOUNTANCY PROFESSION

Legislation enacted by the government of each province has granted to the provincial institutes of chartered accountants powers to prescribe standards and tests of competency that are a prerequisite to membership, the responsibility to promote the skill and proficiency of their members and the duty to regulate the discipline and professional conduct of members and students. The profession in Canada is, therefore, self governing and has adopted rules of professional conduct that are comprehensive in their scope, practical in their application and addressed to high standards.

The following is a brief illustrative summary of the way in which the provincial institutes of chartered accountants regulate the professional conduct of their members and maintain high standards of practice. The processes and procedures outlined in the following sections generally reflect those of the Province of Ontario but are typical of how the provincial institutes discharge their responsibilities in these areas.

Rules of professional conduct

While each provincial institute has the responsibility to establish and maintain its own rules of professional conduct or code of ethics, the underlying principles are common across the country and most of the rules are either similar or identical. The rules cover areas such as objectivity, relations with fellow members engaged in public accounting, organization and conduct of a professional practice, advertising and other standards of conduct affecting the public interest. Specifically, chartered accountants are required by the rules to comply with the Recommendations in the *CICA Handbook* when associated with or expressing an opinion on financial statements. A chartered accountant who fails to comply with this requirement may be subject to disciplinary action by the provincial institutes of which he or she is a member.

Professional conduct committee

A major responsibility of the provincial institutes' ethics groups concerns the protection of the public interest and the enforcement of ethical standards. The provincial institutes, as self regulating professional bodies, have a duty to investigate all written complaints received about their members and students, as well as any matters drawn to their attention in the public record which may indicate unprofessional conduct. The ethics staff at the provincial institutes provide administrative support to the professional conduct committees which review complaints and other matters brought to their attention and decide whether there are sufficient grounds to lay charges before a disciplinary committee (the staff does not have decision-making authority). The committees are comprised of volunteer members appointed by the provincial institutes' councils from a broad cross section of the membership.

Discipline committees

The provincial institutes' discipline committees also consists of a wide cross section of volunteer members appointed by the provincial councils. All hearings of charges are formal and are conducted in accordance with provincial legislation (for example, in Ontario, the Statutory Powers Procedures Act) and with any relevant provisions of the provincial institutes' bylaws.

A member/student who has been charged with professional misconduct has the right to be represented by legal counsel. The professional conduct committees are represented by separate legal counsel who present evidence in support of the charges. A provincial institute's general counsel is present at all times to advise its discipline committee on legal and procedural matters.

The discipline committee has the authority to summon witnesses and to require the production of relevant evidence. Witnesses are duly sworn and notified of their rights under Section 5 of the Canada Evidence Act. Standard legal procedure in respect of such matters as evidence and examination is followed to its conclusion prior to the committee's deliberations.

A discipline committee, in the absence of all parties, including its own counsel, then makes a decision. Courses of action open to the committee include:

A. A finding of not guilty

B. A finding of guilty and an order(s) that might include one or more sanctions such as the following:

   1. The member/student be reprimanded.

   2. The member/student be suspended from the institute.

   3. The student be struck off the register of students.

   4. The member be expelled from membership in the institute.

   5. The member/student be charged costs and/or a fine.

   6. The member's/student's name be publicized.

   7. Other orders that the committee may find appropriate in the circumstances, e.g., that the member satisfactorily complete a professional development course(s).

The secretary of the committee formally notifies the parties of the decision and any orders. If an order has been made, the secretary also outlines the appeal procedure for the benefit of the member charged.

Appeal procedures

To ensure its overall fairness, the provincial institutes' disciplinary systems provide for at least one level of appeal. Usually this appeal is to a subcommittee of the provincial institute council or to the entire council.

Any member or student found guilty of any charge by a provincial institute discipline committee or the professional conduct committee may appeal any of the discipline committee's findings or orders. The appeal body has all the powers conferred on a discipline committee and follows the same formal procedures. It can confirm, reject or amend the findings and orders of a discipline committee. Under certain circumstances and in some jurisdictions a member may appeal to the courts.

Advisory services

Provincial institutes' ethics staff and provincial institutes' professional conduct committees assist institute members with respect to the ethical dimensions of their day to day responsibilities as professionals. The scope of this assistance covers a wide range of topics including the objectivity of members, the confidentiality of information obtained by members during the course of their services, the acceptability or otherwise of proposed advertising by members and the professional behaviour of members to one another, their clients and the general public.

In addition, many provincial institutes have a practice advisory service where assistance is provided on standards of professional services and practice management.

Practice inspection

There is a system of mandatory practice inspection in all but one province. The precise method of operation varies depending on the provincial institute undertaking the inspection.

The main purpose of practice inspection is to ensure that all members in the practice of public accounting maintain an appropriate level of professional standards. The program is intended to be primarily educational—to help practitioners improve their professional standards where necessary. Essentially, through a review of a sample of current accounting and auditing engagement files, practice inspection identifies where a practising member may require assistance in maintaining an appropriate level of professional standards. The practice inspection program does not set new standards. Rather, the standards that a member is expected to maintain are those prescribed by the *CICA Handbook* and the *Handbook* of his or her provincial institute.

This method of assisting members in their conformity to accepted professional standards and of maintaining competence, when combined with a program of voluntary professional development, is felt to be effective in the protection of the public interest.

Generally, all members engaged in the practice of public accounting as it relates to the performance of auditing and accounting services are subject to inspection. This may involve the provision of information by the member through a questionnaire, followed by an examination of a sample of client files and a review of internal quality control practices. The emphasis is educational and focuses on the maintenance of appropriate professional standards including adherence to generally accepted auditing standards and documentation in working paper files.

Reports from inspectors, which contain the inspection findings along with any suggestions and recommendations, are dealt with by a practice inspection committee without the name of the member or office being identified. Where it is judged that improvements should be made, action may be taken ranging from another inspection within one year, to, in sufficiently serious cases, reporting the member to the professional conduct committee for its independent investigation.

Appendix D

The Auditor's Standard Report

CANADA

The auditor's unqualified report on the annual financial statements of a company normally takes the form suggested in the *CICA Handbook*, Section 5400, THE AUDITOR'S STANDARD REPORT, paragraph 21.

AUDITOR'S REPORT

To the Shareholders of ....

I have examined the balance sheet of .... as at .... , 19..... and the statements of income, retained earnings and changes in financial position for the year then ended. My examination was made in accordance with generally accepted auditing standards, and accordingly included such tests and other procedures as I considered necessary in the circumstances.

In my opinion, these financial statements present fairly the financial position of the company as at .... , 19..... and the results of its operations and the changes in its financial position for the year then ended in accordance with generally accepted accounting principles applied on a basis consistent with that of the preceding year.

City	(signed) ....
Date	CHARTERED ACCOUNTANT

UNITED STATES

The Auditing Standards Board of the American Institute of Certified Public Accountants recently approved revised wording for the auditor's report on the annual financial statements of a company. The new Statement on Auditing Standards will be effective for reports dated on or after January 1, 1989 with earlier application permissible.

Independent Auditor's Report

We have audited the accompanying balance sheets of X Company as of December 31, 19X2 and 19X1, and the related statements of income, retained earnings, and cash flows for the years then ended. These financial statements are the responsibility of the Company's management. Our responsibility is to express an opinion on these financial statements based on our audits.

We conducted our audits in accordance with generally accepted auditing standards. Those standards require that we plan and perform the audit to obtain reasonable assurance about whether the financial statements are free of material misstatement. An audit includes examining, on a test basis, evidence supporting the amounts and disclosures in the financial statements. An audit also includes assessing the accounting principles used and significant estimates made by management, as well as evaluating the overall financial statement presentation. We believe that our audits provide a reasonable basis for our opinion.

In our opinion, the financial statements referred to above present fairly, in all material respects, the financial position of X Company as of [at] December 31, 19X2 and 19X1, and the results of its operations and its cash flows for the years then ended in conformity with generally accepted accounting principles.

(Signature)
(Date)

Appendix E

Presentations to the Commission

The Commissioners are grateful for the assistance and advice of those listed in this appendix and equally grateful to many other persons and groups who assisted in a less formal way.

ACADEMIC

Joel H. Amernic, University of Toronto, Toronto
Robert H. Crandall, Queen's University, Kingston
Michael Gibbins, University of Alberta, Edmonton
Daniel L. McDonald, Simon Fraser University, Burnaby
The Canadian Academic Accounting Association

CA PROFESSION

Douglas F. Archer, Toronto; Kenneth M. Dye, Ottawa; Douglas W. Rogers, Edmonton
Arthur Andersen & Co., Chartered Accountants, Toronto
J. Wallace Beaton, Woodbridge
Roger H. Bedford, Vancouver
William W. Buchanan, Toronto
Richard S. Buski, Toronto
Warren Chippindale, Montreal
Clarkson Gordon, Chartered Accountants, Toronto
Coopers & Lybrand, Chartered Accountants, Toronto
G.W. Dawson, Victoria
Geoffrey L. Dean, Pembroke
Deloitte Haskins & Sells, Chartered Accountants, Toronto
William L. Groom, Vancouver
Kenneth S. Gunning, Vancouver
Frederick V. Harrison, Toronto
Laventhol & Horwath, Chartered Accountants, Toronto
Henry R. Lawrie, Calgary
Mallette Benoit Boulanger Rondeau & Associés, Chartered Accountants, Montreal
Graham R. McLellan, Mississauga
Roger J.A. Mutimer, Vancouver
Shervin M. Obahi, Vancouver

Glenn R. Ohlhauser, Vancouver
Peat Marwick, Chartered Accountants, Toronto
Price Waterhouse, Chartered Accountants, Toronto
Raymond, Chabot, Martin, Paré & Associés, Chartered Accountants, Montreal
Samson Bélair, Chartered Accountants, Montreal
Ross M. Skinner, Toronto
The Institute of Chartered Accountants of Alberta
The Institute of Chartered Accountants of Ontario
Thorne Ernst & Whinney, Chartered Accountants, Toronto
Touche Ross & Co., Chartered Accountants, Toronto
Keith Tse, Toronto
Zittrer, Siblin, Stein, Levine, Chartered Accountants, Montreal

GENERAL PUBLIC

J.R. Barnes, Toronto
Ted G. Davy, Calgary
Franz K. Drees, Toronto
Harold Geltman, Montreal
Basil V. Jesshope, Lakefield
John McCormick, Ottawa
Norman Moysa, North Vancouver
Sid Shelton, Mission

INTERNATIONAL

London

C.J. Farrow, Roger Lomax, Richard A. Symington (Bank of England)
Sarah Brown, Alistair Catto, Ann Wilks (Department of Trade and Industry)
Christopher G.A. Fletcher, Rachel Lomax (HM Treasury)

Tarn D. Phillips, Andrew J. Thrall (Securities and
  Investment Board)
Derek A. Boothman, Matthew L. Patient, Paul
  Rutteman, John Warne, Richard G. Wilkes (The
  Institute of Chartered Accountants in England and
  Wales)
Jeffrey Knight, David Porteous, Peter Stanley (The
  Stock Exchange)

New York

Camryn O. Carleton, Philip B. Chenok, Dan M. Guy,
  Thomas P. Kelley, Alan J. Winters (American
  Institute of Certified Public Accountants)
Douglas R. Carmichael (Baruch College)
Patricia McConnell, Lynn O'Neill, Lee J. Seidler (Bear
  Stearns & Co.)

MEDIA

Terence Corcoran, The Financial Times, Toronto
Charles Frank, Calgary Herald

PREPARERS OF FINANCIAL STATEMENTS

John W. Adams, London
Alcan Aluminium Limited, Montreal
Association of Canadian Venture Capital Companies
Bell Canada, Montreal
Canadian Institute of Public Real Estate Companies
Canadian Life and Health Insurance Association, Inc.
Purdy Crawford, Imasco Limited, Montreal
Sidney V. Cwinn, Erawan House (International)
  Limited, Ottawa
Financial Executives Institute Canada
Gilbert B. Johnson, Western Canada Lottery
  Corporation, Winnipeg
C.E. Ritchie, The Bank of Nova Scotia, Toronto
B.G. Smith, City of Halifax
The Mining Association of Canada
The Trust Companies Association of Canada Inc.

SECURITIES AND CORPORATE REGULATORS/ADMINISTRATORS

Stanley M. Beck and Paul G. Cherry, Ontario
  Securities Commission
Bureau de l'Inspecteur général des institutions
  financières, Québec

Consumer and Corporate Affairs, Alberta
Consumer and Corporate Affairs Canada
Roland Côté and Diane Joly, Commission des valeurs
  mobilières du Québec
Department of Consumer Affairs, Nova Scotia
Department of Justice, New Brunswick
Robert M. Hammond, Department of Insurance,
  Canada
Ministère de la Santé et des Services sociaux, Québec
Ministry of Consumer and Corporate Affairs, British
  Columbia
Ministry of Financial Institutions, Ontario
Office of the Superintendent of Brokers and Real
  Estate of British Columbia
W.T. Pidruchney, Alberta Securities Commission,
  Edmonton
The Manitoba Securities Commission
The National Association of Administrators of Co-
  operative and Credit Union Legislation
The Toronto Stock Exchange
Vancouver Stock Exchange

USERS OF FINANCIAL STATEMENTS

Canadian Insolvency Association
Luc Charron, RoyNat, Montreal
Peter Christie, Minet International Professional
  Indemnity Limited, Montreal
Pierre Comtois, General Trust of Canada, Montreal
A. Rendall Dick, The Law Society of Upper Canada,
  Toronto
Roy A. Frank, Toronto Dominion Bank, Toronto
William E. Hewitt, Imperial Oil Limited, Toronto
Imperial Trustees, Toronto
G.B. Maughan, Ogilvy, Renault, Montreal
Yvan Naud, Lévesque, Beaubien, Inc., Montreal
Alastair R. Paterson, Paterson MacDougall, Toronto
Napaul Poisson, Banque Nationale du Canada,
  Montreal
Lorne W. Rae, Vancouver
J. Michael G. Scott, McLeod Young Weir Limited,
  Toronto
The Canadian Bankers' Association
The Canadian Bar Association – Ontario, Business
  Law Section, Toronto
The Canadian Institute of Chartered Business
  Valuators
The Vancouver Society of Financial Analysts
Toronto Society of Financial Analysts
Keith A. Tracey, Minet International Professional
  Indemnity Limited, Montreal

Appendix F

Biographical Notes

William A. Macdonald, QC

A senior partner with the Toronto law firm McMillan, Binch, he has acted as a special adviser to business and government on tax reform and competition policy. An author and frequent speaker, he is a director, the chairman of the audit committee, and a member of the executive resources and contributions committees of Imperial Oil Limited; is a director and member of the executive and compensation committees of Marathon Realty Company Limited; is a director and member of the executive committee of National Trust Company, The National Victoria and Grey Trustco Limited, and Timminco Limited; and is a director of Honda of Canada Mfg., Inc.

J. Peter Gordon, B.Sc., LL.D (Hon), OC

Retired chairman and chief executive officer of Stelco Inc., he is a director of the Bank of Montreal, the Molson Companies, Bell Canada Enterprises Inc., Northern Telecom Limited, Inco Limited, Sun Life Assurance Company of Canada, and ENCOR Energy Corporation Inc.

Richard F. Haskayne, FCA

President, chief executive officer, and a director of Interprovincial Pipe Line Limited, he is also a director of Home Oil Company Limited, Scurry-Rainbow Oil Limited, Federated Pipe Lines Ltd., Home Energy Company Ltd., Sovereign Oil & Gas PLC, Fording Coal Limited, The Manufacturers Life Insurance Company, Royal LePage Limited, and the Canadian Imperial Bank of Commerce.

David L. Johnston, LL.B.

Principal, vice-chancellor and professor of law at McGill University, he is a director of Canada Trust Company Ltd., EMCO Ltd., and The Seagram Company Limited, and a public governor of The Montreal Exchange. He has served as a Commissioner of the Ontario Securities Commission and was a member of the CICA Special Committee to Examine the Role of the Auditor, 1978 (the Adams Committee).

Gilles Mercure, LL.L, MBA

Retired president and chief operating officer of the National Bank of Canada, he is chairman of the board of Cambior Inc. and Agrimont, Inc; a director of the National Bank of Canada, RoyNat Inc., Laurentienne Générale, The Personal Assurance Co. and Growth Investment Corp.; and a guest professor at École des Hautes Études Commerciales, Université de Montréal.

Michael H. Rayner, FCA

Throughout most of the period of study the Comptroller General of Canada and now a partner of Touche Ross & Co., he has been partner-in-charge of Price Waterhouse Associates, Management Consultants, Ottawa; and deputy and then acting Auditor General of Canada. He is a governor of the Canadian Comprehensive Auditing Foundation and the Canadian member of the International Federation of Accountants' Public Sector Committee.

Robert M. Rennie, FCA

Chairman of the Board of Governors of Touche Ross International, he was chairman of Touche Ross Canada for many years. He is a past chairman of the CICA Accounting and Auditing Research Committee, a founding member of the Canadian Comprehensive Auditing Foundation, and a member of the Panel of Senior Advisors to the Auditor General of Canada.

T. Robert Turnbull, FCA

Chairman of Thorne Ernst & Whinney in Canada and a member of the Ernst & Whinney International Executive Committee, he is a founding member of the Advisory Council of the Professional School of Accountancy of the University of Waterloo, a governor of the Canadian Comprehensive Auditing Foundation, and a member of the Panel of Senior Advisors to the Auditor General of Canada.

Index